How to Adopt Internationally

A Guide for Agency-Directed and Independent Adoptions

Revised and Updated Edition

by

Jean Nelson Erichsen
L.S.W., M.A., Human Development

Heino R. Erichsen
M.A., Human Development

Mesa House Publishing
A Division of Two Coyotes, Inc.
Fort Worth, Texas

362.734
nel

Cover and text design by Scott Anderson

Library of Congress Card Number: 2002115253

Copyright © 2003 by Mesa House Publishing

Editorial correspondence and requests for permission to reprint should be mailed to Mesa House Publishing, c/o Two Coyotes, Inc., 3228 College Avenue, Fort Worth, TX 76110. E-mail should be addressed to **editor@mesahouse.com**.

This publication is intended to provide accurate information in regard to the subject matter presented. It is sold with the understanding that the publisher is not engaged in rendering legal, financial, medical, or other professional services.

ISBN: 0-940352-15-X

Printed in the United States of America

ACKNOWLEDGMENTS

We would like to thank Jo-Anne Weaver, adoptive parent of a Chinese daughter, who put us in contact with Mesa House Publishing.

My publisher, Karee Galloway, has worked with me on several editions of this book over the years. Last year, she and her husband, Duane Bidwell, adopted a baby boy through our agency. This new book is our finest yet, thanks to the smiling presence of baby Ben, as well as Karee's diligence, flair, common sense, and a lot of other attributes too numerous to mention.

Several people and organizations have been kind enough to supply facts and figures included in the book. The Joint Council of International Children's Services, Amy Thurston of the National Adoption Information Clearinghouse, the staff at Adoptive Families of America, Peter Pfund, Assistant Legal Advisor for Private International Adoption Law at the U.S. Department of State, Mark Leno of the U.S. Department of Agriculture, and Lorraine Lewis of the U.S. Department of State.

A special thank you goes to Jerri Ann Jenista, M.D., who reviewed the medical section of this book.

TABLE OF CONTENTS

INTRODUCTION

When we wrote the first edition of *How to Adopt Internationally* more than 20 years ago, our legislators thought that transnational adoption was a social phenomenon that would vanish like a phase our idealistic culture was going though. On the contrary, statistics from the U.S. State Department cite that determined Americans adopt close to 20,000 foreign born orphans annually.

Looking back on our first international adoption experience way back in 1973, it seems like *deja vu*, with one important difference. We took the dearth of information both at home and abroad for granted. We'll find out when we get there, we reasoned.

Little did we know that the Information Age would change the way we view the world, including international adoption.

Today's prospective adoptive parents surf the World Wide Web for adoption agencies and make comparisons. They check out the U.S. State Department web site (**www.travel.state.gov/adopt.html**) that publishes adoption procedures country-by-country. They join Internet newsgroups and subscribe to e-mail list serves for emotional support and travel tips from recently returned adoptive parents. Their orphan referral might be emailed to them and an image of the orphan attached on gif or jpg files.

However, back when my German-American husband and I adopted twin babies from Colombia, we seemed to be the first parents adopting in South America. Aside from a quick home study and INS filing, we were unable to get much additional information about what would happen on our adoption trip. We had only a rough idea of how long it would take and how much it would cost.

And as for the twins, all we had were their names and gender — Rosana and Tatiana. Such beautiful Latin names for two little girls. We had no photographs, medical history, or social information. Just before we flew abroad, for some inexplicable reason, we received their birth certificates. Now we had birth dates. Still, it wasn't much to go on.

We were not too worried about how to take care of our new infants. At that point, we were seasoned parents. We had two sons, Jôrg and Art, who had already graduated high school and a baby boy named Kirk. We had started the process when Kirk was only six months old because we thought it would take a year or more to have a baby girl placed with us. Little did we know that we would soon have three babies!

When we finally laid eyes on our Spanish/Indian twins, we couldn't have been happier. But outside the orphanage, we bumbled along, shocked at the tiny beggar children and baffled by the adoption and visa procedures.

When we left the adoption agency in Bogotá, Colombia, with our new twin daughters in the spring of 1973, the director pressed photographs of eight older children in my husband's hand. We had no idea that we would soon become volunteers for adoption agencies trying to find homes for these "waiting children" who ranged in age from 3 to 6 years old. Back in the United States, prospective adoptive parents fell in love with the photos, and all eight children soon found homes. The new parents might have been slightly better prepared than we were in terms of the process of international adoption, but not all of them were able to contend with postplacement adjustment problems, such as the acting out of neglected, abused, institutionalized children or the acting out of biological children who don't want to share their parents with a newcomer. One of those adoptions disrupted within three months. The adoptive parents relinquished their rights to another family who raised the child. Disruptions continue to occur, although increased parent preparation, education and screening makes them a rarity in the adoption world.

Our involvement and knowledge of international adoption continued to grow. Soon we were volunteering for numerous adoption organizations. Adoption agencies referred couples to us for insight and information on international adoption. We spoke to other prospective parents at adoption seminars. Though it inspired and delighted us to see so many orphaned children from so many different countries find new homes with loving families, we also came across too many heartbreaking situations that could have been avoided.

Through an adoption support group, we met families who were trying to adopt through good-hearted but inexperienced missionaries or greedy, unlicensed, and unschooled facilitators. Time, money, and emotion were spent for naught. The missionaries helped with the adoption, but too often in the end, the child did not qualify for an immigrant orphan visa. The facilitators bribed and bulldozed their way through the adoption system. Unfortunately, the adopters had no recourse when things went wrong. Sometimes the child they longed for did not appear. And sometimes the facilitator vanished with the money.

We also met parents who had adopted children from Asia. Unlike us, they had adopted through established international adoption programs that had developed a procedure to follow. Korea, still recovering from war, had orphanages full of abandoned children. The orphans were brought under guardianships to the United States to approved couples. Unfortunately, most couples adopting from this Asian nation did not have any more information about heritage and culture than the Colombian adopters. They fell in love with a picture and had but a scant bit of social and medical history. Many fell into the same state of disappointment, expecting a quick adjustment, few language barriers and little pigment.

But for real Asian drama the Baby Lift orphans had every story beat. As Vietnam fell to the communists, panicked parents handed their children to American officials for quick transport to the United States. Unsure that they would survive themselves, parents were desperate to save their children. Yet, while children of the Baby Lift were being placed in adoptive American homes, some of their surviving parents were making their way toward freedom in Thailand and eventual immigration to the United States. Within a few years, they were holding a green card and a phone, hoping to find their children.

Custody suits — the only ones to ever result from an international adoption — followed.

The Baby Lift taught adoption authorities a lesson they never forgot. Refugee children are no longer placed for adoption unless there is documented proof that the child was legally relinquished, orphaned, or abandoned.

Still, it seems that every few years, the media plays on our heartstrings with images and stories of babies languishing in dismal orphanages across the world. And even in this age of information, not everyone knows that they cannot simply fly abroad to pick up an orphan that they have heard about. The parents are heartbroken and the orphan is stranded when the new family learns that they cannot bring the child home without an adoption decree and a U.S. orphan visa.

Such was the drama played out in Eastern Europe when televised scenes from Romania's orphanages were broadcast into U.S. living rooms. Good-hearted Americans quickly embarked on a rescue mission. With only the image of a white orphan in mind, they flew to Romania to visit orphanages, pick out a child, and find its parents in order to get them to sign a relinquishment. Sometimes they handed over their coats and jewelry to sweeten the deal. They flew home with their new children and became local celebrities. Unfortunately, not every adoption had a happy ending. Some adoptive parents who had little to go on beyond the vision of rescuing an orphan were not always able to cope with the reality of a needy, emotionally hurt child. Discussions of attachment disorders and reactive detachment disorders began to seep into the media and newsgroups, although this was not news to psychologists who have treated American families with the same problems for years.

The Romanian government eventually closed access to orphanages by individuals and set up a national Romanian Adoption Committee (RAC). The RAC has been in a state of flux ever since as they experiment with various social service systems. Hopefully, there will never be another situation like there was in Romania.

Despite the occasional stories of sadness and heartbreak, we saw the majority of families formed through international adoption — including our own — grow and flourish. Inspired, we began to form a plan for a new international adoption agency that could meet the needs of adoptive families as well as the unique needs of orphans. We founded Los Niños International Adoption Center in 1981. Our focus, then as now, is the preparation and education of adoptive parents. Today we are the proud parents and grandparents of a multiracial family. Regardless of whether our children and grandchildren are biological or adopted, they are our most precious treasures.

The number of homeless children has not diminished over the past 25 years. Unfortunately, the steps required to legally adopt and immigrate foreign orphans are still not common knowledge. Although individual details may change, the basic method to adopt abroad is fairly consistent.

Updates on rules and regulations are easy to access through sources and web sites we reference throughout the book.

By the year 2002, the agency we founded in 1981 had placed more than 2,500 foreign-born children in U.S. homes. And we are just one agency. The total result of international adoption is all around us — in loving families, neighborhoods, schools, and churches. We hope this latest edition of *How to Adopt Internationally* will continue to work the same miracles.

Jean Nelson Erichsen, LSW-MA
Heino Erichsen, MA

CHAPTER 1

Is International Adoption Right for You?

According to the National Adoption Information Clearinghouse, (**www.calib.com/naic**) currently there is no public or private attempt to collect comprehensive national data on adoption. Yet it's estimated that at any given time in the United States, approximately 500,000 couples or individuals seek to adopt a child. For many beginning to explore adoption, the process seems fraught with long waits and stringent requirements. While many older children, sibling groups, and special needs children are available for adoption, relatively few healthy, U.S.-born babies are available compared to the number of people looking to adopt. Because birth control and abortion are accessible to most U.S. citizens, fewer unplanned babies are born. In addition, most unmarried mothers are choosing to keep their babies.

Most adoption support groups advise couples looking to adopt a healthy, U.S.-born, Caucasian baby that the wait will be at least 12-36 months after approval of the home study, depending on the agency or attorney selected and the decision of the family to aggressively advertise or to wait for an agency referral. For those who don't fit an agency or birthmother's description of the ideal parents, the wait could be even longer. As a result, some couples turn to transracial adoption in the hope that the wait will be shorter and others turn to international adoption. Although thousands of Caucasian couples have adopted U.S.-born minority children, most have done so through private agencies or independent adoptions. Until recently, many states had laws and policies strongly favoring the placement of children (particularly African-American and Native-American children) with parents of the same race. Unfortunately, this policy resulted in continued foster care for children when same-race parents were not available. A federal law passed in 1996 forbids state public agencies from making same-race placements a priority over timely interracial placements. This law is helping more children leave foster care for permanent adoptive homes.

To better understand why some people choose international adoption over domestic adoption and to help you evaluate if international adoption might be right for you, it's

Figure 1-1: Types of Adoption

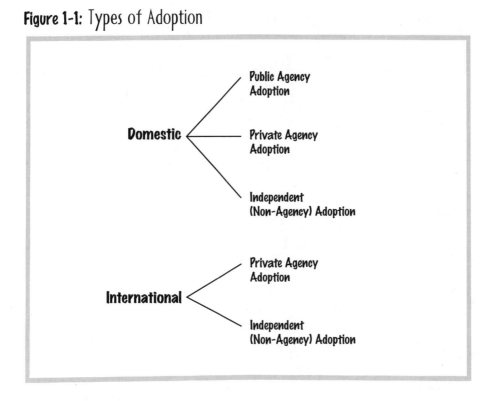

best to first review the main types of adoption available. While there are countless permeations, hybrids, and exceptions, in general we can categorize most adoptions into five main categories: domestic public agency adoption; domestic private agency adoption; domestic independent adoption, agency-assisted international adoption, and independent international adoption. In the following pages, we'll briefly review the three main types of domestic adoption and just a few of the advantages and disadvantages associated with each before moving on to the details of international adoption. If you believe one of these methods may be more appropriate for you than international adoption, you'll certainly want to do more research. A smooth adoption begins with choosing the type of adoption that is most appealing and will work best for you.

Public Agency Adoption

Funded by your tax dollars, public agency adoptions are directed by state or county offices and exist to find permanent homes for children when parental rights are either voluntary relinquished or terminated by the courts due to abuse, neglect or other factors. In the United States, most children in this category live in foster homes until an appropriate adoptive family is found. It comes as a surprise to many that of the 520,000 children currently in foster care in the United States, only 117,000 (just over 20 percent) have an adoptive placement plan, meaning that the parental rights have been either relinquished or terminated and the child is eligible for adoption by a nonrelated adult. The majority of children residing in foster care will eventually be returned to their parents or placed with an extended family member.

Table 1-1: Estimates of Adoption Costs

Type of Adoption	Cost
Domestic – Foster Care	$ 0 - $2,500
Domestic – Private Agency	$6,000 - $25,000
Domestic – Independent	$5,000 - $40,000
International – Agency or Independent	$7,000 - $30,000

Couples and singles adopting through a local social service office will be shown photos and biographical information on children they could parent well. Applicants then select the child they are most interested in adopting. They, along with other applicants, are then considered for the same child. A social worker assigned to the child, working in cooperation with the rest of the social service staff, selects the adoptive parents he or she feels is best for the child. Adoptive parents may have to apply for many different children before they are matched with a child.

Many of the children available through foster care may be classified as "special needs" — a broad category used to describe children that may be harder to place because of their age, because they are part of a sibling group, because they may have a physical, mental, or behavioral impairment, or numerous other reasons. In addition, according to the Evan B. Donaldson Adoption Institute (**www.adoptioninstitute.org**), more than half of children adopted from foster care are over the age of 5. Only 2 percent are infants at the time of adoption.

Hopefully, new laws mandating that states act more quickly to make a permanency plan for children in foster care will result in children finding stable, loving, and permanent homes at a younger age. More and more foster children find families every year; 50,000 were adopted in 2000 (that's close to 45 percent of waiting children), and adoptions from foster care have almost doubled in the last five years.

One advantage of adopting through foster care or similar agencies is that many individuals who might not be accepted by a private agency are accepted at state or county social service offices. Foster parents, parents over fifty, gays and lesbians, parents with large families, and those with low incomes are eligible as adoptive parents. In addition, the costs associated with adoption through a social service agency are minimal compared to private or independent adoptions, whether domestic or international. In some cases, subsidies, grants, and other special services may be available to help families with adoption expenses and costs related to the child's care before and after adoption.

The North American Council on Adoptable Children is a nonprofit organization that provides excellent information on adopting children from foster care. For more information, visit its web site at **www.nacac.org**.

Private Agency Adoption

Private agency adoptions, which are regulated by the state public welfare system, are quite different. Most private adoptions are arranged with the birth mother (through the help of a private agency) before or soon after the baby is born. When prospective adoptive parents work with a private agency, social workers provide counseling, conduct several interviews for the home study and arrange child care classes and training on various aspects of adoption. Once their home study is approved, potential parents submit a profile, photos and other information about themselves. The birth mothers, under the supervision of social workers, then choose a family from their pictures and profiles. Not surprisingly, birth mothers tend to choose people that they themselves would have wanted as parents. Young, attractive couples with an active lifestyle and an upper-middle income have the best chance of being chosen. Stay-at-home moms are also preferred.

Once adoptive parents are matched with a birth mother, the terms of the adoption (such as disclosure of information about the birth mother and contact between the birth mother and child) are negotiated. Most girls and women want to be a part of the child's life and want an "open adoption." In an open adoption, all parties agree to an exchange of letters, photos, phone calls, or visits to the adoptive family's home.

However, not all of these plans end in an adoption. While it is still very rare for a custody dispute to arise after an adoption is finalized, agencies report that anywhere from one out of four to one out of six birth mothers/birth fathers are pressured by family members to change their minds before the child is placed or before the adoption is final. Even though the adoption may not be legally considered final, in such cases the prospective adoptive parents may have formed a relationship with the birth mother, paid her medical bills and perhaps even cared for the baby during the supervisory period prior to consummation of the adoption. For some people, the emotional and financial risk involved in adopting a U.S.-born baby may be a lot higher than an international adoption. However, for many, one of the main advantages of a private adoption is that the adoptive parents may receive the child only a few days after birth and may even be present in the delivery room. In addition, adoptive parents who choose to work with a licensed, experienced agency, receive the full spectrum of adoption-related services, including three to five months of postplacement consultation and supervision after the adoption.

To cope with the high demand for babies, some private U.S. adoption agencies have established strict intake rules in an attempt to be fair to the adoptive parents. Childless couples take first priority. Other agencies may even require that the couple be infertile. Prospective parents who are between the ages of 25 and 35 and are without physical disabilities are considered to be ideal. Single parents are not accepted at many agencies. If the adoption agency is religiously affiliated, preference may be shown on the basis of religion.

Independent Adoptions

The last category of domestic adoption is independent adoption, which is also referred to as direct adoption or non-agency adoption. Independent adoptions are regulated by the state legal system. In an independent adoption, the prospective adoptive parents assume greater responsibility for finding the birth mother, negotiating the terms of the adoption, and for arranging a legal, final adoption (usually with the help of an adoption attorney or facilitator). Rather than waiting for an agency to find a match or for a birth mother to choose them from a pool of others, prospective parents pursuing independent adoptions take it on themselves to locate and meet a birth mother. Some place ads in newspapers across the country and install a toll-free line to take possible calls; some list their profiles on existing web sites or create their own; some rely on a network of friends, health care professionals, and clergy; some use adoption facilitators;

and some even purchase billboard space announcing that they are looking to adopt an infant. Once a birth mother is located, contact is made and terms of the adoption are agreed to, the birth mother or parents place the child directly with the adoptive parents with the help of an adoption attorney (usually hired by the adoptive parents). In the United States, more infants are placed each year through independent adoption than through private agencies, although independent adoptions are not legal in all states. Some of the main advantages of independent adoptions are that there are few eligibility requirements (the parents must simply be in compliance with the adoption laws of their state) and the wait may be shorter and less frustrating since the prospective parents have more control over contacting a birth mother. In many states, a court-appointed social worker makes only one home visit prior to the adoption.

Turning to International Adoption

Those who have become disillusioned with the domestic adoption process, who do not meet the requirements for a U.S. adoption, who believe in ZPG (zero population growth), or who simply have a strong desire to adopt a foreign child often turn to international adoption. The number of foreign-born orphans adopted by U.S. citizens rose from 9,356 in 1988 to 19,137 in 2001.

In addition to shorter waits, less stringent requirements, and discomfort with the idea of an open adoption or birth mothers who may change their mind, there are many other factors that may lead individuals and couples to international adoption. One main advantage is that there is no competition for a child. Once you have been approved by the adoption agency and the Immigration and Naturalization Service (INS) and you have prepared documents for a foreign court, you will be given the opportunity to select an orphan or one will be referred to you. If you are using an adoption agency, the U.S.-based international adoption agency's representative will help you find a child or children based on the age, gender, ethnicity, etc. that you requested. Another compelling reason for adopting legally abroad is the fact that the stringent requirements concerning the documentation of a child's status as an orphan by both the U.S. and child-placing governments make custody suits by foreign birth parents virtually unheard of. While such occurrences are extremely rare, everyone in America remembers the outcome of the Baby Jessica and Baby Richard cases, and most U.S. courts still seem inclined to rule in favor of the birth parent's rights rather than the child's rights.

Most importantly, international adoption opens a whole new dimension in your life. Suddenly, you view your child's homeland as yours as well. You pay more attention to news of that part of the world. Your foray into another country and culture becomes a hot news item, too. Word travels fast. New acquaintances of that ethnic group and others are eager to celebrate your family's diversity. Just as suddenly, your adopted child gathers a caring flock of adults and children who become your friends as well.

As the Pulitzer Prize winning journalist, Charles Krauthammer wrote, "Fertility rates in the United States are barely at replacement level."

In 40 years, there would not be enough working young people to pay pensions for the old were it not for immigration. Immigrants are the magic cure, 'the American cure,' for the birth dearth."

Immigrant orphans are doubly magic. They cure their lonely hearts as well as ours. They evoke social change. Infants and children bridge American social divisions of color, culture, and nationality faster than any politician's speeches. After more than a quarter of a century of watching international adoptions, I've been privileged to see a generation of children grow up and take positions in society as educated and responsible citizens. Our family has extended far beyond the confines of a white, middle-class community. We benefited from the companionship of children and adults of other ethnicities and nationalities we otherwise might not have met. Heino and I both feel that the time, money, and energy we expended to raise our family and to establish Los Ninos International Adoption Center has been worth every minute and every penny. Sometimes our house and our office are like a joyful, mini United Nations. Our lives have been enriched beyond all measure.

It's a special blessing to see these happy infants, children, and adults so confident and secure within the circle of a loving family.

Coping with International Adoption: How Are You Likely to Handle It?

Adopting abroad means pleasing a lot of entities. Your state welfare department, your local adoption agency, the Immigration and Naturalization Service (INS), and the presiding judge have an interest in your capabilities as an adoptive parent. Each needs assurance that the adoption will endure.

Each of these entities will give you a list of documents that they require in order to approve your home study, to approve your advance petition to classify an orphan as an immediate relative, and to grant a final adoption decree. If you readopt your foreign-born child in your state of residence, you will also have to meet the requirements of the court in your county.

At this point, you might ask yourself, "Why do I have to measure up to someone's idea of the perfect parent when all I want is to bring a child into my life? Biological parents don't have to go through this!"

Of course, biological parents are not necessarily good at parenting. Most of them would benefit from the type of training you will be receiving. To work successfully with an adoption agency, you will fare best if you are naturally kind, open, trusting, understanding, and flexible in dealing with unforeseen problems. You must be helpful and cooperative during this long and complicated process. In the past, you have probably had to put your trust in other professionals to reach your goals. If you can tell that forming this kind of relationship with your adoption agency is going to be difficult, think about the fact that successful parenthood requires the same kinds of traits.

Here's a summary of some personalities commonly seen in the adoption process. It may help you understand your strengths and weaknesses in coping with the adoption process.

Dreamers — These are sensitive, intuitive people who feel driven to help others. They do not fear the unknown and are willing to explore new pathways. They involve themselves in causes to help humanity. They volunteer to help their agency and make contributions after they have adopted. Dreamers are popular with everyone because they are articulate, loving, and so persuasive that they are able to bring out the best in everyone around them.

Behavior: The Dreamer looks at international adoption in terms of the big picture and does not bother with the details. Unfortunately, they can set themselves up for disappointment if they are not realistic about the requirements or about the child of their dreams. However, dreamers make good ambassadors on their adoption trips. If they travel with a group and find a problem abroad, they quickly act as mediators to help find solutions.

Tips for Dreamers: Make certain that your ideas about the adoption process, your dreams of the child, and your perceptions of the trip abroad are realistic. Talk to the agency director in person and visit with other families who have recently adopted before you apply. Be certain that you are not under any illusions or assumptions. Your dream of a child must match the reality of an institutionalized child — in appearance and behavior. Reread all of the information you have been given by your agency to make certain that you know what will happen in each step of the process.

Organizers — Stable and conservative, organizers are always well prepared. They are always on time, dependable, reliable, and make their environments orderly and structured. Organizers have strong opinions. They uphold policies, procedures, and rules. They support established social norms and traditions. They take on a lot of responsibilities and like to take care of others, which makes them good candidates for adopting a child.

Behavior: Organizers send perfectly prepared documents to their adoption agency in record time. They answer the questions in their international parenting courses thoroughly. They are likely to advise their adoption agency on how to improve their delivery of services. The organizer's biggest problem is in trying to accept some of the vagaries of international adoption regarding waits and schedules. They need to know on a regular basis how they stand in the waiting pool. Once they have been assigned a child, they want a schedule of events for each day they are abroad, even though these appointments are not usually finalized until they are abroad. They become frustrated and tend to become outraged when changes occur.

Tips for Organizers: Make an outline or a flow chart of the sequential adoption steps you have already accomplished. Ask pertinent questions of the adoption agency staff to track your progress. If you are suddenly told something in the process has changed, think about how your cooperation is helping your family, the staff at the agency, and especially your future child. Ask your agency for a copy of The Adoptive Parent Preparation System published by the Joint Council on International Children's Services (**www.jcics.org**) by e-mailing them at **jcics@jcics.org** ($30.00). Envision a clear picture of the end result — when you are back home with your child in your arms.

Risk Takers — Risk Takers are resourceful and practical. They have great problem-solving skills and thrive in a crisis as well as in situations where the outcome is unknown. They make friends easily because they are charming, witty, and exciting. Risk takers live for today and dislike having to live by a time clock or a schedule.

Behavior: The Risk Taker is not very well organized when it comes to documentation. They tend to skim their agency's written directions and instructions rather than studying them. However, they are practical. They need to know their status in the waiting pool at all times. They love to discuss, to argue, and to rework their adoption plans. The wait for the referral of a child is extremely frustrating to them. They want to dispense with all the red tape and just go!

Tips for Risk Takers: Rewrite your adoption plans. Discuss alternatives to your original plan with your adoption agency staff whenever you feel the need to do so. They will help you readdress each issue. Would another country be more suitable? What positive activities can you latch on to during your wait for a refer-ral and a court date? Reward yourself each time you progress through a step. Once you are satisfied with your adoption plan, at least for the time being, com-plete your international adoptive parenting training. Then look at the tips given to the Organizers.

Thinkers — These are the folks everyone calls "workaholics" because they live for the pursuit of information and self-improvement. They look at internation-al adoption in terms of the big picture, such as international treaties and demo-graphic changes. They come up with a lot of theories. Adopting a child brings out their playful side and gives them a reason to loosen up. They think big — although not necessarily realistically. Their calls to the adoption agency are logi-cal and quick. They mostly want to know where to find objective information.

Behaviors: Thinkers are analytical and examine cause and effect. They are concerned about how international adoptions are viewed in developing "sending countries." They think about the social change affected by international families in developed, receiving countries." They are frustrated at the dearth of informa-tion provided by adoption agencies. Thinkers want books, social studies, and research.

Tips for Thinkers: Your adoption agency may not have enough material or manpower to satisfy the scope of your intellectual needs. University social sci-ence libraries; the Joint Council on International Children's Services (**www.jcics.org**); Adoption/Medical News (**www.adoptionmedicalnews.com**) ; the National Adoption Information Clearinghouse (**www.calib.com/naic**) and numer-ous other Internet sites such as **adoptionstatistics.com** will provide you with a wealth of up-to-date information. Two documents you may wish to obtain from JCICS are the Intercountry Adoption Act of 2000 and the Hague Convention on the Protection of Children and Cooperation in Respect of Intercountry Adoption.

Evaluating Motives for Adoption

Despite all of the advantages, international adoption is not for everyone. As with a biological birth or any other adoption, the parent and child are entering a life-long relationship. Adopting a foreign child means that your family will become intercultur-al and perhaps interracial. Furthermore, your family will remain changed for all future generations as your child grows up, forms friendships, dates, marries (perhaps a differ-ent minority), and begins a family of his or her own.

Before even beginning the process of international adoption, potential adopters need to examine their motives and carefully consider the challenges of adopting and raising a foreign-born child.

A skilled social worker can lead prospective adopters to decide whether or not their abilities and motives are sufficient for a long-term transracial relationship. For example, one of the first questions a social worker might ask ("Why do you want to adopt a for-eign child?") may bring forth a straightforward answer, an around-the-bush answer, an angry retort, or even a shocked or baffled silence.

One of the most frequent responses to the question is, "We are an infertile cou-ple." More than half of all international adoption candidates are unable to bear a child. New technologies encourage would-be parents to continue their treatments for many years. Sometimes a woman doesn't consider adoption until she is in her late thirties or early forties. Unfortunately, at that point she is over the age limit to adopt an infant from some foreign countries.

A social worker interviewing an infertile couple may want to discuss how the couple feels about their inability to produce children. Are they angry or resentful that they must seek help? Authorities on the subject of infertility believe that infertile parents are not able to cope well with parenthood until they learn to handle the emotional stress of infertility and to resolve their dreams of producing children.

Some other common responses to the question "Why do you want to adopt a foreign child?" are listed below:

We prefer to put our money toward adopting a child rather than spending it on high-tech infertility treatments.

We don't want to get involved with local birth mothers.

We've had several domestic adoptive placements fall through.

We're worried about possible repercussions with the open adoptions that are common in domestic placements.

We don't meet the age, length of marriage, religious, or other requirements of U.S. adoption agencies.

We don't want to wait two to three years for a baby.

We prefer to adopt rather than produce a child in an already overpopulated world.

We believe in ZPG (zero population growth) philosophy: produce two children and adopt the rest.

I am still nursing my toddler; I want to adopt a tiny baby to nurse.

We want to adopt from _____ (country) because there is less prejudice toward people of that nationality than toward other nationalities in our locality.

I am single. Local adoption agencies will not place a U.S.-born baby with me.

I have a medical problem that prevents another pregnancy.

Our family has all boys and no girls; or all girls, no boys.

We are capable of dealing with medical disabilities. We would like to adopt a handicapped child.

I have a history of stillbirths and miscarriages.

Most of these responses exhibit a responsible sincerity, and few seem likely to end in failure. Whereas the responses listed below may be given in all sincerity, their potential for failure is higher.

We want to adopt a child orphaned in Afghanistan because of the war; in Honduras because of the hurricane; in Mexico because of the earthquake; and so on. (Every child deserves a parent and should not have to feel grateful for being saved. In addition, children orphaned or made homeless by disaster are not necessarily available for adoption.)

We want to try to get pregnant and adopt at the same time. Then we'll go with whatever happens first. (This is irresponsible. Both choices are highly stressful. The couple needs to decide. To turn down the referral of an orphan because of a pregnancy can delay the orphan's placement with a different family for many months.)

One of us was medically sterilized through a vasectomy or tubal ligation.

We want a child to enhance our marriage. (OK, if they don't mean to save the marriage.)

We want a child of every race. (Child collectors? Liberals out to prove their viewpoints?)

Our child died. (Counseling is needed to be certain the parents do not expect an identical replacement for the dead child.)

We want an older child because we hate the loss of sleep and the mess connected with baby care.

We want a playmate for our only child. (The children may not be able to get along with each other for a year or more.)

We want an older child, handicapped child, or sibling group unlikely to be adopted by anyone else. (Idealists who expect gratitude and recognition?)

Some of the most important questions, however, cannot be answered with any degree of certainty: Will the child feel that there is something wrong with him because his biological mother rejected him? Will the adoptive parents and child grow to love each other? Will racial prejudice appear only after the child joins the family? Will the family stay together throughout the child's growing-up years? Adopters must learn to know themselves before they create a family in the hope of living happily ever after.

Adoptive parents must be able to acknowledge that their foreign-born children will always have a unique situation. Coping with the fact that they have another set of parents somewhere and that they are racially and/or culturally different from you can be difficult during childhood and adolescence. Counseling and/or family therapy are sometimes necessary. Adoptees end up explaining their adoptive status throughout their lives, even as adults.

The majority of foreign adoptions within our experience have been successful placements. However, children older than two, handicapped children, and sibling groups present a greater challenge to a harmonious family adjustment. The most successful placements of children more than two years old occur when the parents fulfill the child's needs without expecting anything in return. These parents adopt knowing that the child may not be able to love or trust them for many years. If you are considering adopting a child more than two years of age, remember that he or she already has a personality, memories, habits, and probably a different language.

An Overview of this Book

In addition to examining individual motives, potential adopters need to have a clear understanding of the international adoption process itself and the legal requirements, expenses, and potential bureaucratic headaches that can be part of the process. This book is designed to do that by first giving an overview of the international adoption process (Chapter 3) and then providing the information for a step-by-step approach to conducting a successful international adoption (Chapters 4-15) should you decide to pursue this route. Samples of most of the documents needed for an international adoption are included at the end of the chapter in which they are discussed.

The last half of the book is a Compendium of the adoption laws and requirements for most countries participating in international adoption. For each country listed, the Compendium includes a summary of the adoption laws for that country, the central authority in charge of adoption, the address and phone number for the U.S. visa issuing post, and, if available, the number of orphans immigrated into the United States from that country. In addition, the Compendium also includes basic information on geography, demography, language, currency, and major religions.

How to Adopt Internationally also includes an Appendix and a Bibliography. The Appendix includes a collection of resources and contacts that may be helpful during the adoption process, including information on adoptive parent support groups and contact information for state licensing agencies that supervise adoption agencies. Although care was taken to include the most recent information available, phone numbers, addresses, fees for filing INS forms, etc., change frequently. You can find updated information for most of these items on the Internet. We include web site addresses along with other information when possible.

The Bibliography includes a list of recommended books on cross-cultural, interracial, and special needs adoption; magazines and newsletters of adoptive parent groups; information on travel and foreign languages; and other resources that may be helpful as you research and pursue an international adoption.

CHAPTER 2

Parents' Journals

Before moving on to the more practical proceedings of international adoption, we've provided a few excerpts from the journals of four sets of adoptive parents. We've tried to include selections that represent different parts of the world and different adoption situations. As you read these journals, keep in mind that every adoption is a different experience. Even parents who use the same agency and return to the same country and same orphanage to adopt a second child may have a very different experience than their first trip. The following pieces provide just a glimpse of a few of the unexpected joys and bureaucratic mishaps that are common in international adoption.

In one, a single mother-to-be strikes out to adopt an infant from Russia and ends up with a series of surprises — each as wonderful as the first. In another, a couple adopts an infant son from Vietnam in the midst of bureaucratic changes, and, in another, a couple adopts "virtual twins" (unrelated orphans the same age) from the Ukraine. In the last selection, a couple with two older children, adopted as babies, return to Honduras to introduce their children to their birth country.

Journal from Russia

When I began the adoption process, I was 30 years old, newly divorced, and ready to become a parent. Like many prospective parents, I had a vague picture in my mind of the child I hoped to adopt. I wasn't set on the gender, but as I began the process, I was picturing an infant under one year old. My, how that changed!

As soon as I was "paper ready" and had been placed on the list of waiting parents, my agency's newsletter arrived at my home. Like all waiting parents, I devoured each issue of the newsletter. As in every issue, this one contained photographs of waiting children. But this issue was different because it contained a photograph of MY children! I knew it the moment I saw them. Sergei and Alexandra were four-year-old twins. Their

blue eyes twinkled and their grins were infectious. Somewhere, deep inside my heart, I knew we were meant to be together. The moment I saw the twins' picture, the image of adopting an infant under one vanished from my heart and was replaced by this adorable duo.

Things happened very quickly. Soon after seeing Sergei and Alexandra's photograph, I requested and received their information and formally accepted their referral. In September, just two weeks after accepting the referral, I was on my way to Russia to adopt my son and daughter.

Though the adoption journey is usually filled with joy, there are sometimes unexpected twists along the way. Therefore, families are advised to be flexible. I am the poster child for flexibility.

The first surprise occurred when my friend Karen, who was scheduled to travel with me to Russia, was unable to go. Her visa to enter Russia had been "misplaced" by the overnight delivery company, and she could not travel without it. So at the last minute, I boarded the plane alone. Despite my fears, the trip went fine. I was mildly afraid I would arrive in Moscow, unable to speak Russian, and somehow miss my LNI representative at the airport. This fear was put to rest by Tarek, who spoke English and met me at the airport with a sign bearing my name. He delivered me to the home of the wonderful and nurturing Tamara, with whom I would be staying. Tamara did not speak English, but her compassion was apparent.

My inability to communicate with Tamara led to an amusing dilemma. Though Tamara gave me a tour of her lovely apartment, she forgot to show me the bathroom. As the evening wore on, I found it necessary to find the facilities. But when I tried to express this to Tamara, it was clear to both of us that some translation help was needed. So Tamara called a friend who spoke English, and when she thrust the phone at me, I explained my situation to her male friend. Within moments we had the problem solved! I was a bit embarrassed, but mostly relieved!

While I was traveling, the LNI staff were helping my friend Karen make plans to join me. Her visa was found shortly after I left for Moscow. My agency staff even returned to the office in the middle of the night to communicate with Sasha, the Moscow coordinator, and make plans for Karen to meet up with me in Russia. And everything went like clockwork.

After a good night's sleep and a great sightseeing tour of Moscow, I boarded a plane to Saratov. I was met upon arrival by LNI's coordinators in the Saratov region. The translator, Nick, spoke perfect English. And I am glad, for what happened next was very shocking!!

The first question Nick asked me was why I had chosen to give my son the middle name of Marie. You see, I had decided to keep Alexandra's first name and give her my mother's name, Marie, as her middle name. I quickly explained that Marie would be the middle name for my daughter, not my son. This conversation was very confusing to Nick. He wondered why I mentioned a daughter, when I was there to adopt twin sons! Identical twin boys?! My first thought was that Nick had me mixed up with another family. After all, I had the medical records, photographs, and even a video of my adorable blonde twins. But Nick calmly explained to me that Alexandra was Alexander. Somehow, there had been a translation error in the records. I was in shock!

I was scheduled to spend that night in Saratov and then travel the next day to the city of Volsk, where the boys' orphanage was located. Since Volsk is three hours away from the city of Saratov by car, I would be allowed to complete the adoption process in one day. I would meet the boys in the morning, then go to court to finalize the adoption. We would ask the judge to waive the ten day waiting period, and if everything went as planned, I would pick the boys up in the afternoon and we would return to Saratov.

I have to admit that the night before the adoption was a sleepless one for me. I had spent the last several weeks planning for a boy and a girl. I never considered NOT adopting the two boys (although that certainly would have been an option, considering the translation error); I just felt numb. The host family I stayed with in Saratov had a Schnauzer named Linda, who seemed to sense that I needed a friend. I hugged Linda close that sleepless night as I pondered the new life that lay ahead of me…with my two boys!!

The next morning as I prepared to leave for Volsk, I had a chat with Lena, my hostess. She told me that she had seen my sons a few days before and that they asked her when their mother was coming to get them. They told her it was taking too long. They also told her they hoped I would bring Mickey Mouse watches. They said they had always wanted Mickey Mouse watches! It dawned on me at that moment that these two little boys were waiting anxiously for me. And from the sounds of it, they were totally ready to have a mom. This thought lightened my heart. And I eagerly prepared for the journey to Volsk.

When we arrived at the orphanage in Volsk, we were taken to a large, attractive room, where the boys would be introduced to me. I had a toy car for each of them. I was sitting on the floor when the boys entered the room. Their pictures had been adorable, but they were so much more beautiful in person! They were four years old, but they were small for their age. They were dressed identically, and they had tiny crosses around their necks. When they saw me, they both exclaimed, "Mama!" Then they ran to me and simultaneously kissed me on the cheek. I cannot describe the joy that coursed through me at that moment. All the confusion I felt about the mix-up vanished. And I knew that everything had happened just the way it was meant to. As a single mom, I probably would not have set out to adopt two four-year-old boys. But adopting them turned out to be the greatest gift I've ever received.

After the adoption was finalized in Volsk, the rest of our trip was a breeze. My friend Karen caught up with me in Saratov, just after we returned from Volsk. She had stayed with Tamara in Moscow, and she found her to be just as charming as I did. The only thing that puzzled her was why Tamara showed her the bathroom so many times!

Update: It has been almost five years since I adopted the boys, and they are about to turn nine. They are doing great. They bonded instantly with me and with my family. They learned English very quickly and were fluent within a few months. They never had any of the adjustment issues that some people worry that older children will have. And because they were a little older, they seem to really appreciate their happy lives.

Alexander is called Alex now. He is a great reader and writer, as well as a truly gifted artist. He loves karate and swimming. His voice gets an octave deeper when he's trying to sound grown up, and he is already very interested in girls! Sergei is called Seth these days. He is an excellent mathematician. We think we have a budding accountant on our hands. He is kind-hearted and funny and full of questions. And something exciting happened in our lives a couple of years ago. We met a wonderful man named Darin Alley and "we" married him last June. He adopted Seth and Alex in December 2001. So our story has another very happy ending...or maybe just another wonderful new beginning.

— Sara Alley

Journal from Vietnam

Eleven months after being entered on the agency waiting list for a baby from Vietnam, I am on a plane to Hanoi, the capital city in north Vietnam. Although the early parts of our adoption process were textbook perfect, the last three months have been chaotic.

Through the spring and summer, we watched our gradual climb to the top of the waiting list and then in July, the agency calls. They anticipate another set of referrals from Vietnam in a few weeks. Although we are only #7 on the waiting list, we are the first couple who will accept the referral of a boy. If a boy is included with the next set of children, he will be ours.

But instead of the referral, the next call from the agency is bad news. The Vietnamese government has announced that it plans to make changes to its international adoption laws to more closely safeguard its children. While the new laws are being written and implemented, a moratorium on adoption will likely be put into place. While some provinces will continue placing orphans and processing adoptions until the moratorium is formally announced, it appears that our province will suspend new adoptions effective immediately. After coming so close, we are stunned by the news.

Our agency gives us the choice of moving to another program, but we decline. We need time to recover and adjust. Duane and I decide to hold off on any major decisions until the end of the year.

It is therefore with complete surprise that two months later, in mid October, we get the news that our agency has been cleared to process one more set of referrals from Vietnam. They are careful not to raise our hopes too high, but they think there could be a child for us.

And then a few days later, he arrives. A grainy, black and white image slowly emerging from the fax machine. Duane and I watch pages and pages of official documents (most in Vietnamese) roll through the fax – a birth certificate, a translation of the birth certificate, some sketchy medical information, a letter from his birth mother, some forms from the orphanage — and then, at last, a series of photos.

We are surprised at how young (just two months old) and how beautiful, happy, and alert he seems. He is smiling in almost every photo and his eyes catch and engage the camera in a way that makes him seem much older. We are charmed.

A short month later, I'm on a plane for Hanoi to deliver our dossier. Duane will join me in another week and we hope to complete the adoption and immigration process by early December. There is still an air of uncertainty that looms over the adoption. Due to the pending changes, we are traveling without a date for the Giving and Receiving ceremony, an unusual circumstance for adoptions from Vietnam. It's not clear how the process will proceed or exactly how long it will take.

A day after my arrival, I am on the road to Hoa Binh to meet my son and deliver the dossier.

Although the village of Hoa Binh is only 80 kilometres from Hanoi, it's a two-hour car ride up a narrow, semi-paved road shared by bicycles, water buffalo, cyclos, women carrying yoked baskets, mopeds, and cars. Farmers use the heat of the pavement to dry crops of cassava, a process that takes up about 1/3 of the narrow road. The remaining two-thirds is politely shared through an intricate, unwritten system of road etiquette that involves a lot of beeping horns and ringing bells.

The drive to Hoa Binh is picturesque. The mountains in this part of the world are hard to describe. Some, like the one Hoa Binh sits upon, are like the mountains we think of. Large domed figures with gradual inclines that you could climb or drive up. But most of the ones here are like giant, limestone stalagmites that leap straight up from rice paddies. The building style is the same, both in and out of the city — one room structures stacked 4, 5, and 6 stories high. When the mountains and buildings are pushed together, it looks like a page from Dr. Seuss.

The Hoa Binh Social Protection Center is a simple, but beautiful complex nestled in a small valley up high, surrounded by even more mountains. The driveway is lined with trees and blooming oleander.

The center is a cinder-block square of open-air rooms built around a paved courtyard filled with potted trees and rusting playground equipment. Bright green butterflies cover the trees. The center houses about a dozen infants, 15 older children and about 30 elderly or disabled villagers. The baby rooms line one side of the complex.

You would think after staring at his picture for weeks, I could have walked right up to our baby. That's how I imagined it would happen. But with the temperature dropping down into the mid 70s, the babies are wrapped and swaddled like villagers in outer Mongolia. Ben Thu is in the very last room on the right. By the time I get to him, I have given up guessing.

He is wearing a heavy yellow sweater with a pair of too big pants pulled up to his armpits. The nanny swaddles him in additional towels and then ties a tiny bandana around his neck and pulls a hood over his head before she hands him to me.

He is awake and alert for the first few minutes, but obviously already tired. We talk for a bit, I kiss him a billion times, and then we walk up and down the veranda until he falls asleep in my arms. We walk from one end of the veranda with western classical music drifting out of the first baby room to the far end with traditional Vietnamese music piping out of the last room. It's an appropriate soundtrack for East meets West.

At 3½ months old, he's still a tiny fellow — barely 9 pounds — but despite a rattling cough and an eye gooped with infection, it's obvious that he's healthy, strong and alert.

How do you describe a baby you held for 20 minutes through four layers of swaddling? He is more solemn than I expected and very watchful. He liked to be walked from room to room to look at the other babies. If you pull his hood back, you can cup the back of his head and it is warm and soft and his hair is silky smooth. When you kiss his face, you can feel his eyelashes tickle your cheek. And he smells like the village of Hoa Binh — a sweet mixture of mountains and baby formula and small fires of green bamboo. And then there's the very best part. If you stare straight into his eyes and rock him back and forth, and smile and call his name, he'll give you a tiny smile back. And when he smiles, it's Christmas.

Each baby room is an open-air, cinderblock room with blue walls, green and white tile floors and two hard, wood beds with a thin bamboo mat for a mattress. The babies are either on the bamboo mat or in a nanny's arms. Although all of the nannies share in the care of the babies, each is assigned to specific children. Ben Thu's nanny is named Hong. She is shy with me, but wonderfully outgoing with the babies. Any time a baby begins to fuss, she leaps on the bed with both feet and then drops over the baby and begins tickling and singing and kissing them. The babies love it!

It isn't as hard to leave him as I thought it would be. His surroundings are spartan, but I can see that he gets more love and attention than I ever would have imagined. It's obvious that the nannies are truly in love with their little charges.

In another week, we make a second trip to the orphanage, and this time Duane is able to come. I watch his father hold him for the first time and it's almost as sweet as holding him myself. The two of them find a quiet spot outside and stare into each other's eyes for the longest time. I try to give Duane time alone with him and then the three of us sit together and watch the orphanage routine and chat with the other new parents, our facilitator and the nannies. The nannies call our son Thu Em (Little Thu or Little Autumn).

Although waiting for the formal date for the Giving and Receiving ceremony is stressful, after meeting our facilitator, the province officials and orphanage director, we feel confident that it will happen. We just don't know when. We are aware that the confusion and delay caused by the pending changes have brought an unexpected blessing — time. Time we are able to spend at the orphanage, getting to know our baby and soaking up the sights and sounds of the place he spent his early months and time getting to know Vietnam and some of its people. In between the two trips to the orphanage, Duane and I prowl the streets of Hanoi and make day trips to surrounding areas. We are in love with Vietnam from the start and we memorize as much as we can, knowing that our memories will someday become an important part of our son's identity and understanding of his birth country.

We are on a day-trip to Halong Bay with two other sets of waiting parents (a couple adopting their second son from Vietnam and a single mom adopting her second daughter) when the news comes. Duane and I are perched on the roof of the boat's cabin soaking up the sun, sea air, and the awesome beauty of Vietnam's most famous destination, when we hear clapping and cheers erupt from below. A cell phone brings the word that the Ministry of Justice has set the Giving and Receiving for the next day.

Early the next morning, we make one last trip to the orphanage and nervously wait at the entrance to the complex. And then from a narrow alley, three women emerge, each carefully balancing an umbrella to block the sun's rays from the baby in her arms. We recognize Hong right off. She walks straight to us and without a word, gently transfers Ben Thu into my arms. I stare at him trying hard to comprehend the importance of the moment. And when I look up again, Hong is gone.

A few days after the Giving and Receiving, we are on a plane to Ho Chi Minh City to complete the U.S. immigration process. Lifting off from the ground with Ben Thu in my arms, I find myself crying for the first time. I cry for his mother and for him and for the country he will never know in quite the same way, despite all of our good intentions. I cry for all he has lost in such a short life. And I cry for all that the three of us have just gained.

— Karee Galloway Bidwell

Journal from Ukraine

December 26: I spent many hours these last few months daydreaming about what the children will be like — ages, personalities, looks and so on. At some moments, I can't wait to wrap my arms around them and just love them. At other times, I am very nervous and wonder if we're doing the right thing. Bruce and I have been married for seven years and we married late — both in our middle thirties. We are very set in our ways as a childless couple. But both of us feel the need for having children. We feel we have been missing a big part of life.

December 27: We arrive in Kiev. Our driver is waiting for us and takes us to the apartment of Marina and Alexander. When families come from other countries, they provide their apartment for a daily fee of $70.00. This includes Marina's very simple, but tasty cooking. She has offered to do our laundry and ironing.

December 28: We appear before the director at the Adoption Center. She is stern and does not smile. After asking us a couple of questions — including why we didn't contact her directly instead of using the agency and why we are here during the Ukrainian New Year holiday. Her assistant shows us informational sheets on three toddler girls. Then she leaves and returns with sheets on two younger children, both less than 18 months old. Their orphanage is in Pryluky, about two hours from Kiev. Both are healthy. Bruce and I are delighted and agree to meet them.

When we arrive in Pryluky, our first stop is the Ministry. We need their permission to visit the orphanage. At the orphanage, our guide gets the key from the director and opens the reception room for us. A nurse comes in and explains that the children

are napping, but they will wake them up and bring them in. A few minutes later, the door opens and two nurses, each holding a child, walk in. I can't take my eyes off the children.

The boy has blonde hair and blue eyes and the girl has light brown hair and brown eyes. They are introduced: Nazar, a male, born July 30, 1999, and Ganna, a female, born August 21, 1999. Only three weeks apart! Nazar comes right to us, but Ganna is shy and starts to cry when either of us get near.

Our guide explains that she is frightened. We play with Nazar, who is not shy at all. He has a happy disposition and is eager to play. Ganna is a different story. Every time I come near her or even make eye contact across the room, she whimpers and cries. Her nurse comforts her with singing and rocking. We learn that Ganna had a broken leg and the cast was only recently removed.

After too little time with Nazar and Ganna, the critical question comes up — do Bruce and I want to adopt them? I feel put on the spot, but Bruce and I look at each other and answer, "Yes!" At last, we are parents — or at least, almost parents.

Before leaving Pryluky, we make one last stop — the courthouse — so that our guide can speak to the judge and set a court date, which turns out to be January 3.

December 29: At the Notary Office, we supply names for both children for new birth certificates. The childrens' new names will be recorded on the certificates as well as ours as the new parents. We decide to use the names we chose for the kids. Ganna will become Katherine Evangeline and Nazar will become Luke Augustus.

January 3: The judge reads a statement that includes our names occupations and birth dates. Also included are the names of each child — first the birth name and then the new name. It's funny to hear our names pronounced with a Ukrainian accent. Especially the pronunciation of Augustus. It sounds like Ah-oo-goose-toose.

At one point, the judge asks Bruce a lot of questions including who is the head of the household. Bruce and I both point at the other. The judge laughs. Then he asks me the same questions. He also asks me what the population of Ukraine is. All through the court proceeding, the judge has a good sense of humor. Then he says he would consider the matter and render his decision in ten minutes. When he returns he reads a statement that grants Bruce and I custody of the children until the end of the day ten day waiting period (at which point we become the legal parents).

January 17: Before falling asleep, Bruce and I talk about how much our lives have changed for the better and how much we look forward to another day and another and another, just raising our kids and becoming a family. Despite our anticipation and excitement, exhaustion takes over — we both sleep. We're ready to begin our new life as parents — what a truly excellent word!!

May 18: Katherine and Luke have changed so much. Katherine will sit still for a book as long as Mama keeps reading. She says about 40 words. She loves to dance and is fearless in the swimming pool.

Luke is very affectionate and exuberant. Every waking moment is action-packed until he sleeps. Luke says about 15 words but he understands what we say and can follow two-part instructions.

We are enjoying our "virtual twins." They are quite a handful at times, but I can't remember what life was like before them or imagine what life would be like without them. They make me feel complete.

— Maureen Menzer

Journal from Honduras

It's a beautiful day for flying. A bright, tropical sun dominates a sky peppered with a few puffy clouds, no turbulence, and a gorgeous view of the world below. We left Miami only hours ago, passing over the beautiful, blue Caribbean Sea. As we descend, the mountains, meandering red dirt roads and rural countryside of Honduras, in Central America, come clearly into view.

Approaching the airport in Tegucigalpa, the capitol of Honduras, the American Airlines pilot reminds us for the third time not to worry about the steep banking maneuvers and sudden drop in elevation we are about to experience. "We do this trip every day," he says. Tegucigalpa is in a valley. The airport is at the bottom of the valley and is boxed in by steep hills on three sides, and a sheer drop-off at the end of the runway on the fourth side. Without a doubt, landing at this airport requires some sophisticated piloting skills.

My heart is in my throat and the tears come remembering the other trips to Honduras (and the same roller coaster landings) to meet my beautiful babies. This time, though, it feels good to be coming back, this time as a family, without all of the anxiety connected with the foreign adoption experience.

On this trip, the questions are not: Will they be healthy? Will I know how to take care of them? What will they look like? Will all the paperwork be in order? How long will it take, and will we be successful getting them home with us? Today, the question racing through my mind is: how will our children react to their birth country seen for the first time in their memory, from the perspective of normal, American kids who began their lives in Honduras?

Before we left, Carolyn, who is eleven years old, wanted to see the picture of her birth mother that I have kept for her. Carolyn is just beginning to care about her emerging adolescent appearance. She was very curious about her birth mom's general appearance and wanted to make a comparison to her own features. Just in case she saw her birth mother on the street, Carolyn wanted to be able to recognize her! We have no picture of Michael's birth mother. At nine years old, he has no interest yet in his birth family, and he's not all that excited about traveling to an unknown place so far from home.

The children are very different from one another. Curious and adventuresome, our daughter is always ready to try something new and different; especially the unusual and exciting. Michael, on the other hand, likes things to stay as they are. He needs prodding and reassurance to try something outside of his routine. Our Honduran friends call him "timido." Yet, I am very proud of the thoughtful way they each, in their own way, approach new experiences.

Carolyn and Michael know all about being adopted. Before they were old enough to understand, we talked openly to them about adoption as another way of creating a family. They know all about our trips to Honduras to adopt them - two years apart. In our home, adoption is a normal part of our lives — our family story.

The idea of Honduras is familiar to the children. They know about Honduras from our adoption stories, photo albums, passports and books. From souvenirs and artifacts kept in our home. They know something of their heritage and beginnings from the conversations we've had. Until now, though, they know only what we have shared with them. Beginning today, they will put shape and form and color to their own experiences of Honduras. They will hear Spanish spoken all around them and see lots of people who resemble them.

Then, of course, there's the book: "*Carolyn's Story: A Book about an Adopted Girl,*" my husband Perry wrote with Carolyn last year. Written in the first-person, the book gives readers a personal account of why Carolyn was adopted and how she feels knowing she has two sets of parents. In her own voice, Carolyn explores how being adopted makes her feel, and shares her thoughts about birth parents, different kinds of families, her brother, being connected to two cultures, and some of the challenges she faces as an adopted child.

The book has received widespread attention. It made its way to the desk of James Creagan, the American Ambassador to Honduras, who liked it so much he arranged for us to present a copy to Sra. Bessie Watson de Reina, the First Lady of the Republic and the person who finalizes Honduran adoptions by signing the adoption paperwork. We are honored by the invitation, and the timing seems right to reintroduce Carolyn and Michael to their birth country.

Seen from the sky, Carolyn is surprised by the simplicity of Honduras. A few small houses dot the hillsides. Roads look more like winding paths. There are no freeways. It's very different from the American cities she has been flying over. This is definitely not Minneapolis, where we live, or Chicago or Miami.

Finally, we touch down and I breathe a sigh of relief. I am back in Honduras, back to the beginning of parenthood for me. This is my fourth visit. It doesn't seem like nine years have elapsed since we came to meet Michael. The forward door opens and a blast of warm, Honduran air fills the cabin. I remember the smell, and it brings back a flood of memories. Everything is the same, everything is different.

Being a parent has changed me immeasurably. I struggle to remember who I was only nine years ago. The focus has shifted. It's not just on Perry and me. It's also on these two malleable children — our kids — and ensuring a positive, memorable life experience for them. In a way, I feel they are on home turf. It is Perry and I who are the foreigners. Even though we're their parents, we can't know what they are feeling, or how this trip will affect them in the years to come.

There is no jetway. As we descend the stairs to the tarmac, we see our first armed guards. Carolyn comments only that the airport is small. She is down the steps in a flash, anxious to get on with her visit. As with most of life's big experiences, I'm hesitating, backpedaling for a moment before being able to move forward down the steps, back to the past, into Honduras.

We are met outside customs by our dear friend, Dr. Orison Velasquez, a pediatrician who befriended us when we first met Carolyn (Honduran adoptions require two visits, the first by both parents to initiate the proceedings, and a second, some months later, to finalize the process. One can also stay in-country between visits. Either way, it's a convoluted, lengthy and nerve-wrecking process.).

During our first visit, Carolyn, at 2 months, was hospitalized for several days for a serious ear infection. Dr. Velasquez discovered the infection before it became a case of meningitis. He also helped us negotiate our Honduran hospital experience. In Central America, the nurses only take care of a patient's medical needs. The family is required to take care of a patient's comfort. So, Perry and I lived in the hospital with our new baby, feeding her and changing her. Adopting Carolyn required a hospital experience after all! We feel very fortunate to have Dr. Velasquez as a friend, and have invited him to go with us to meet the First Lady.

Traveling through the city, Perry and I are aware of how much has changed — and how much has remained the same. Honduras is a very poor country, with a literacy rate of only 50%. There are new cars and trucks on the street; far different from the broken down wrecks we remembered. There appears to be some new construction (a sign of economic growth), and the cars and taxis are just as noisy as they were nine years ago.

The kids are all eyes and ears. Carolyn is like a sponge. Happy to be coming back to her birth country, she is absorbing each new sight and sound with delight. She is proud of her heritage and in that we feel successful!

Michael is very concerned about the little boys his age who offer to load luggage at the airport, and the other young children who are helping their parents sell goods on the street. He is worried about them not wearing shoes, being dressed so poorly and not being in school.

This feel for the street life affects both the children. We don't live in the city, so they are a little intimidated by the many people milling about in the streets, by beggars, and by the presence of soldiers with automatic weapons who protect buildings, especially the banks. Carolyn says the soldiers make her feel safe. Michael says the guns make him nervous.

Carolyn notices the razor wire and glass shards imbedded on the tops of walls surrounding many nice homes and buildings. We explain that people have to protect what they have from thieves.

This trip is a birth country adventure, but it's also a family vacation. More than anything, it is a time to have mom and dad's undivided attention. A relief from the everyday routine of home and school. It's foreign, it's different, it's fun. Just like any foreign travel experience, it changes and enriches us. We appreciate all the comforts and choices we have at home. We'll continue to encourage Carolyn and Michael to learn Spanish, so that the next time someone in Honduras speaks to them, thinking they're "local," they will be able to answer (and translate for their parents, too).

Carolyn realizes we have too many choices; that life can be far more simple than the American way of life. Here, people take life at a more leisurely pace and seem to have time for each other. They don't seem to be rushing around so much. That feels good.

The kids are each keeping a journal to record their thoughts and feelings about the trip. Carolyn writes in her journal that she loves Honduras and feels like she never left. It's difficult to respond to this information. We know in our hearts she would not have the life she enjoys had she remained in her birth country, but we haven't discussed that with her in detail. From our perspective, her comments are a response to being on vacation; safe and secure among family and friends. She felt the same way about Disney World.

We are treated with great kindness by our friends in Honduras, obviously proud of their country and anxious to please. We are grateful for their help. In typical kid fashion, Carolyn decides she'd like to live here for awhile. We have to remind her that if she lived in Honduras she wouldn't be on vacation all the time! Carolyn can't possibly know what a struggle life is for most people in such a poor country. I do wonder, though, is she connecting, in some fundamental way, to her first six months of life in Honduras?

Our second day in Tegucigalpa. We put on our best clothes for our meeting with Mrs. Reina. Dr. Velasquez picks us up at the hotel and we drive to La Casa Presidential, the Honduran White House, for the big event. Two officials from the American Embassy are there to join us for the presentation. Security is tight; even for the diplomats. We have to pass through metal detectors and surrender our passports for special badges. Perry and Dr. Velasquez are frisked for weapons, which impresses the kids. It's all very official.

During the buzz of activity, I keep remembering why we're here. We feel it is important for the First Lady, and all Hondurans, to see that the children are part of a healthy, happy family; well-cared for and just a couple of normal kids. Carolyn understands the significance of the event. Michael is uncomfortable wearing a coat and tie, and sitting still for 45 minutes. He really wants to wear sandals instead of his new shoes.

We are ushered into Sra. Reina's private office, a spacious, well appointed-but comfortable- room with a banquet table at one end, and a private sitting area at the other.

Tuxedoed butlers with white gloves descend upon us, offering cookies, finger sand-wiches and drinks. The kids become bug-eyed. Perry remarks quietly that this is a spin on the "Prince and the Pauper" story. It gives us pause to watch these well-mannered children, returning to their birth country under circumstances very different from what would have been their life, had they stayed.

Sra. Reina enters and we all stand and introduce ourselves. She is very gracious, fluent in English (thank goodness!) and appears to have all the time in the world to spend with us. The butlers make yet another pass with refreshments and finger food. She invites Carolyn to sit next to her on a loveseat and begins chatting. She speaks directly to the children, asking them about their lives, school and home. Carolyn pre-sents Sra. Reina with a copy of our book. Inside, we have written a personal message to her and the people of Honduras. Sra. Reina acknowledges that she has read the book and is most impressed. We hope that in some small way, we can influence the stream-lining of the Honduran adoption process. There are so many kids in need of parents, and so much joy in parenting these kids.

Maybe our book, our trip, our visit with Sra. Reina will counter the fear and mis-information generated by the media: stories of kidnappings, placement of these kids as domestic servants or, worse, bringing them to North America to harvest their organs for medical experiments. We don't know whether these stories are true, but we do know many successful adoptive families with Latin American children. We are one of those many families.

From the smile on her face I can tell that we have accomplished our objective: She knows that Carolyn and Michael are bright, thriving children, who are loved and well-cared for. After 45 minutes of delightful conversation, Carolyn invites her to visit us in Minnepolis. Sra. Reina then presents the children with gifts! What a pleasant surprise. We pose for photographs and she kisses the children good-bye. That night we celebrate at dinner with Dr. Velasquez and his family. Such wonderful friends. There is a reporter to interview us from Canal Cinquo,the top TV station in Honduras. The reporter asks us all sorts of questions about our trip, and about adoption. It is obviously difficult for Hondurans- who say they can spot a Salvadorian or a Nicaraguan at 100 paces- to understand how our kids could be so easily accepted by our families, friends and com-munity. Perry explains how eagerly our families awaited the kids' arrival. How their grandmother's indulge them, like grandmothers everywhere. How they have so many friends at school, in cub scouts and girl scouts and on their baseball teams.

I tell the reporter that all Americans come from somewhere else. Along with the Swedish, Danish, Norwegian, German and Eastern European branches, our family tree now has a couple of Honduran branches. She is understanding, but is still somewhat puzzled by this acceptance. The story appears on the news that evening. Clearly, she got it! It's a warm, fuzzy human interest piece about our family's trip with the kids to show them their birthplace. It is a positive adoption story with soft music underscoring the narrative. Success!

Tomorrow we leave for home. We have made a connection to this place and we talk about coming back "next time" to see other parts of the country. Now, Honduras is more than picture postcards, stamps, artifacts and parents' memories. At last, the kids have their own impressions and souvenirs, which include several CD's of popular Honduran music to enjoy at home.

I know that our kids will encounter challenges as they grow up because they are Latin American and adopted. Carolyn has already endured questions and comments about her skin color and whether Michael is her "real" brother. Like all parents, every-where, I worry about my kids and their future. As adoptive parents of foreign-born children, we face special challenges. How do we live and thrive in a bi-racial, bi-cultural family? How do we raise our kids to be Americans, yet take pride in their cultural heritage and grow up with high self-esteem? These are questions we began to answer by making our journey to Honduras.

Upon reflection I realize what I already knew. The adoption of our two babies from Honduras turns out to have been easy. Raising them to be good citizens of the world and addressing cultural and identity issues is the hard part. Our trip to Honduras was an experience we will never forget. But it's good to be home. Our journey continues.

— Mary Jane Miller

CHAPTER 3

Understanding International Adoption: An Overview

Should you decide to adopt internationally, it is in your best interest and that of your future child to learn the adoption procedures both in the United States and abroad. You will be handling much of the paperwork in cooperation with your U.S. social worker and your international agency or attorney. Your function is that of expediter. Endless delays can be avoided if you take responsibility for the paperwork shuffle; always know who has your papers, why they have them, and what happens next. While most adoption agencies, here and abroad, have years of experience in handling foreign adoptions, a few foreign adoption sources cited in the Compendium are not yet familiar with foreign adoptions; in fact, the same is true for some of the private and public agencies in the United States. And yet, some of them may be involved in processing your paperwork. The more you know about the process, the more likely it is that your experience will go smoothly.

One of the best ways to become familiar with the adoption process itself and to understand the issues facing both the parents and children of international adoption is to attend orientations or educational seminars. These are typically sponsored by private, licensed adoption agencies to provide potential adopters with information on how the home study is conducted and to give an overview of the U.S. immigration and foreign adoption process. Adoptive parent support groups may also sponsor seminars and usually invite all of the adoption agencies to participate. (See Appendix for a list of adoptive parent support groups.) At seminars for international adoption, adoptive parents usually bring their children and speak about their experiences. Prospective adoptive parents find out about seminars by word of mouth, by keeping in contact with local agencies, and through public service announcements on television, radio, and newspapers. Attend as many seminars as possible before selecting an agency. Information more specific to you and your personal situation may require an individual consultation. International adoption professionals with degrees in social work or human development can give you the attention you need to make an informed decision.

Step 1
Learn all you can about international adoption from available resources. Attend orientations and seminars hosted by adoptive parent organizations and private adoption agencies.

The Internet and Adoption: A World of Information, But User Beware

I adore the Internet. Need a State Department or INS form? Download it with the click of a mouse. Heading to Moscow? Travel information is at the touch of your fingertip. Need to know your status in the waiting pool at your adoption agency? Visit their list serve or e-mail your agency contact.

Yes, the Internet can be a wonderful place, but the naive user can easily be led astray. Unfortunately, it's just as easy to find misinformation or out of date postings on the Internet as it is to find information.

To help provide some direction, we've tried to include the Internet addresses for helpful, active web sites throughout the book. Of course, you'll find many other helpful resources on the Internet as well, but these sites are a good place to begin your research. In fact, you might even start now by taking a look at the web sites of just a few of the organizations dedicated to helping individuals learn more about international adoption.

Joint Council on International Children's Services (**www.jcics.org**)

The Evan B. Donald Adoption Institute (**www.adoptioninstitute.org**)

National Adoption Information Clearinghouse (**www.calib.com/naic**)

International Association of Voluntary Adoption Agencies (**www.iavaan.org**)

Comeunity Adoption Parenting Support (**www.comeunity.com**)

Adoption.com (**www.adoption.com**)

Adopting.org (**www.adopting.org**)

U.S. Department of State (**www.travel.state.gov/adopt.html**)

In addition to general information sites like the ones listed above, many sites are devoted to providing information and support to families adopting from specific countries or regions. A few of these are listed below.

Eastern European Adoption Coalition (**www.eeadopt.org**)

Families for Russian and Ukrainian Adoption — including neighboring countries (**www.frua.org**)

Families with Children from China (**http://catalog.com/fwcfc**)

Families with Children from Vietnam (**http://fcvn.org**)

Latin America Adoptive Parents Association (**http://lapa-nnj.com**)

Despite the multitudes of great and timely information made available through the Internet, unfortunately the Internet has also opened the door to a variety of ethical dilemmas. One frequently questioned issue is the photo listing of waiting children. A waiting child is defined as one who is school age, handicapped, or whose sibling group or race has hampered placement into an adoptive home. Some countries, such as Bolivia and Russia, will not allow U.S. agencies to photo list their children because of critical stories calling it "baby-selling." Although the issue of photo listing has been blown out of proportion, the use of this medium to find families for orphans can create serious problems. However, most problems that result from photo listings are due to a lack of knowledge regarding social and legal issues. Some prospective adoptive parents impulsively search for an orphan before they have completed the preliminary steps of INS clearance, home study approval, and the compilation of supporting documents. In turn, overeager or inexperienced adoption facilitators may be so anxious to make a placement that they refer a child to parents who are neither approved nor prepared to adopt internationally. Such scenarios are adoption disruptions waiting to happen! An important part of the home study process is designed to help people understand their own capabilities and motives regarding an adopted child so the agency can make an appropriate referral.

Another potential problem arises in some adoption newsgroups or list serves. Newsgroups are typically created by volunteer, postadoptive parents to provide support and information to others going through the adoption process. Their words of encouragement and responses to general adoption questions have been a blessed relief to countless prospective adoptive parents. Unfortunately, some individuals also use newsgroups to post hostile and erratic messages berating the INS, foreign governments, or U.S. agencies for not rubber stamping them through the process. One of the biggest dangers in posting such messages is that they can just as easily be read by officials in foreign countries! In addition, some of the more specific questions posed to newsgroups — particularly those regarding state and INS procedures or child-placement policies — are best directed to the adoption agency handling the case. The requirements and procedures for a foreign adoption can change quickly. Your agency is the best source of information for staying on top of these changes.

For a list of most of the active country-specific list serves for adopting and adoptive parents, visit **www.comeunity.com/adoption/listservs.html**.

In addition, begin learning all you can about international adoption from other sources, such as books, newsletters, magazines, videos, the Internet (see nearby box), on-line adoptive parent groups and local adoptive parent groups. The typical adoption candidate has access to the Internet and orders books on-line about adoption, parenting, and the country from which he or she is planning to adopt. A list of recommended publications is found in the Bibliography. The National Adoption Information Clearinghouse (NAIC) also offers a series of publications on various aspects of the international adoption process. Many of these publications are free. Write or call the NAIC at

330 C Street, S.W.
Washington, DC 20447
Tel: 888-251-0075 (toll-free)
Web site: **www.calib.com/naic**

International adoptions occur in eight major stages:

1. Preliminary Home State Approval (Chapter 5)

2. Preliminary INS Approval (Chapter 6)

3. Application to a Foreign Adoption Source (Chapter 7)

4. Receiving Referral of the Child (Chapter 8)

5. Filing the Orphan Petition (Chapter 9)

6. Travel Abroad (Chapter 10)

7. Adoption, Emigration, Immigration and Citizenship (Chapter 12)

8. Postplacement Procedures (Chapter 14)

Twenty-three steps are dealt with, from agency registration to U.S. citizenship (see Table 3-1). These steps are highlighted, beginning in this chapter and ending in Chapter 14.

It is best to follow the steps in the order they appear, whenever possible. Based on our experience and that of the many adoptive parents we have guided, prospective U.S. adopters who try to alter this approach will encounter serious difficulties along the way.

Requirements for Adoptive Parents

Most prospective adoptive parents are pleased to see that the basic requirements for an international adoption are less stringent than for a domestic adoption. Although the requirements may vary according to the international adoption agency and the child-placing country, in general, single persons and couples married one year or more, between the ages of twenty-five and fifty-five, with or without children, of all races and religious affiliations, as well as persons who were previously divorced can find adoption agencies and foreign programs who will gladly accept their applications. In addition to expediting documents and traveling abroad if required, prospective adoptive parents must be able to prove that they can afford the expenses associated with completing an international adoption as well as supporting the child once the adoption is complete.

In addition to meeting the requirements of the adoption agency and the child-placing country, prospective adoptive parents must also meet the requirements of the Immigration and Naturalization Service (INS). The INS requires that at least one spouse be a citizen of the United States and that the household income be 25 percent above the poverty level. The INS seldom approves welfare recipients, unmarried heterosexual or homosexual couples, or persons who have been convicted of a felony or certain types of misdemeanors.

Adoption by Unmarried, Heterosexual Couples

Some states issue a Certificate of Informal Marriage to couples who qualify according to common-law marriage guidelines. The couple must prove through paid receipts the date they first cohabited and presented themselves as married. This certificate may not be accepted in every court abroad. Before you apply to an adoption agency, verify that this certificate is acceptable.

TABLE 3-1 : STEPS IN THE INTERNATIONAL ADOPTION PROCESS

Step 1   Learn all you can about international adoption from available resources. Attend orientations and seminars hosted by adoptive parent organizations and private adoption agencies.

Step 2   Collect agency information.

Step 3   Choose an international adoption agency.

Step 4   Choose the agency that will conduct your home study (if different from your international adoption agency).

Step 5   Initiate home study by applying to appropriate agency.

Step 6   Obtain documents required for home study.

Step 7   Prepare documentation required for Form I-600A (Application for Advance Processing).

Step 8   File Form I-600A (Application for Advance Processing).

Step 9   Apply for a passport.

Step 10   Select an adoption program in a foreign country.

Step 11   Obtain documents required for your foreign dossier.

Step 12   Obtain translations for documents in your foreign dossier.

Step 13   Obtain notarization, verification (or apostille), and authentication of documents in your dossier.

Step 14   Prepare for the referral of your child.

Step 15   Obtain visa or tourist card (if necessary) for travel to your child's country.

Step 16   File Form I-600 (Orphan Petition) if this is to be filed in the United States. (This is usually filed abroad if the adoption is finalized in the child's country and both parents travel to meet the child.)

Step 17   Prepare for your adoption trip.

Step 18   Meet your child.

Step 19   Obtain the guardianship or final adoption decree.

Step 20   Apply for the orphan visa and file Form I-600 (Orphan Petition) if this was not filed earlier.

Step 21   Participate in postplacement supervision.

Step 22   Readopt your child in your state of residence.

Step 23   Obtain proof of citizenship for your child, or file for U.S. citizenship if your child's adoption was not final at the time he or she entered the country.

Couples have tried to get around the marriage issue by choosing one partner to adopt abroad as a single. Some adoption agencies may cooperate and write two home studies, although this is viewed as unethical by most authorities. One study covers the single prospective parent; the other covers them as a couple. After the placement abroad, the other partner adopts the child in their county of residence. Whether the partners are successful in taking equal responsibility for the child is up to the judge's discretion. A consultation with an attorney is indicated before you initiate the first step.

Adoption by Same-Sex Couples or Single Homosexuals

We are not aware of any foreign, child-placing country with a stated policy in favor of adoption by gays and lesbians. More in-depth research may show some exceptions, however.

Homosexual couples have also tried to get around the issue with the same tactics as unmarried heterosexuals. Many adoption authorities in the United States are concerned about hiding this information and consider these methods fraudulent.

China has severely limited single applicants and will only place with those who convince the authorities of their heterosexuality with a written statement. Vietnam is considering a similar course of action.

Agency-Initiated and Parent-Initiated Adoptions

There are two major types of legal foreign adoptions: agency-initiated adoptions and parent-initiated adoptions (also known as direct or independent adoptions).

In an agency-initiated foreign adoption, prospective parents work with a U.S.-based international adoption agency, which handles paperwork and communications and obtains the potential match of a child through a child-placing agreement or contract with a foreign source. (More detailed information on the assignment and referral processes used by different countries is included in Chapter 8.)

Once the adoptive parents have accepted the formal referral, suggestion of a child or an invitation to travel, the U.S. agency coordinates their adoption travel. The agency and its bilingual representatives take responsibility for assisting you with the child, your lodging, and obtaining the final adoption decree and the child's passport and exit visas. They will also provide the documents required for the orphan visa by the American Consulate. (A more detailed description of the different types of agency-initiated adoptions is given in Chapter 7. Many of these differences are based on requirements of the child-placing country)

Parents do not have to travel to some countries. For example, Korea and India arrange proxy adoptions and allow for escorts to bring the child to you. The U.S. adoption agency is the guardian of the child until you adopt about six months later. Guatemala also permits adoption by proxy; when the final decree is issued, the child can be brought to you. The most obvious problem with this type of escort arrangement, however, is that the child becomes part of your family sight unseen.

In a parent-initiated, international adoption (also known as an independent or direct adoption), prospective parents obtain a home study from a licensed adoption agency or social worker. After this point, they are on their own as far as filing with the INS and preparing a dossier of documents for the court abroad. The adoptive parents are solely responsible for selecting and securing a foreign lawyer or agency that will, in turn, refer a child to them. They will also need to know and understand the adoption procedures in that country and how to coordinate the adoption with the U.S. immigration requirements.

The foreign agency, government staff, or lawyer arranges for the adoption hearing in court and tells the adoptive parents when to take their adoption trip. After that, the parents are again on their own. They must take full responsibility for the child as well as for obtaining the proper documentation for the child's adoption, passport, and orphan visa.

While independent international adoptions are certainly possible, the risks are much higher than in agency adoptions, which are regulated by the state. In addition, many foreign countries do not allow independent adoptions. According to the National Adoption Information Clearinghouse, the risks of an independent adoption include involvement in the black market; loss of confidentiality; infringements upon the child's privacy; inadequate medical information; the possibility of outright fraud; and the lack of proper documentation of the child's status as an orphan.

The safest way to adopt a foreign child is to involve a licensed adoption agency or social worker (if individually licensed) in your state of residence and adopt the child through an international adoption agency or public welfare department abroad. (A more detailed discussion of selecting agencies or other adoption professionals to assist you is provided in Chapters 4 and 5.) Over the years, we have heard of many sad cases in which a missionary or foreign lawyer, rather than an international agency abroad, found a couple a child but was unable to obtain the birth documents needed for a U.S. orphan visa in order to immigrate the child. The prospective adoptive parents send money abroad for years in the hope that the child can be legally immigrated. We usually meet them when they have given up hope and want to start over with an agency-initiated adoption.

U.S. Safeguards for Foreign Adopted Children

Any adoption can be a legally complicated affair, but in international adoptions the typical issues are compounded by U.S. immigration requirements, the legal requirements of the country from which the child is originating, and the requirements of the state in which the child will ultimately live.

Immigration and Naturalization Service (INS) laws are strict. Adopters must have documents to prove their identities, whom they are married to, whom they are no longer married to, and how much money they have to support a family. INS will not approve advance applications for the orphan petition until the adopters get FBI clearances to prove they have no criminal records. U.S. immigration laws are designed to prevent criminal activities by foreign and U.S. citizens who are involved in the adoption process. Without a doubt, unscrupulous persons with criminal intent would import large numbers of children if they could.

A number of legal and procedural safeguards have been enacted by the federal and state governments to ensure the success of foreign adoptions by U.S. citizens.

On the federal level these actions include:

- A home study performed by a licensed agency or a licensed social worker affiliated with an agency in the adopter's home state.

- A statewide check for criminal and child abuse records on each adoptive parent.

- Fulfillment of INS orphan immigration petition requirements.

- An FBI check of every preadoptive parent.

- Adherence to good practice, intercountry adoption guidelines established by the U.S. Departments of Health, Education, and Welfare.

- Automatic U.S. citizenship for every legally immigrated orphan who was adopted abroad and enters the United States on an IR-3 visa. If an orphan enters the United States with an IR-4 visa, a readoption or reaffirmation of the adoption in the home state of the adopters must occur before the child is eligible for U.S. citizenship. (See Chapter 12 for a more detailed discussion of the different types of orphan visas issued by INS.)

Those actions on the state level are as follows:

- Postplacement visits by a licensed social worker.

- A social worker's recommendation for adoption, readoption or reaffirmation. A complete discussion of readoption and reaffirmation is included in Chapter 14. (This step will not be necessary after U.S. ratification of the Hague Convention.)

- Issuance of a new birth certificate (in most states). This may also not be necessary after the U.S. ratification of the Hague Convention

Finally, we cannot leave this section without a comment on the children born in the United States who are adopted by non-residents. As mentioned earlier in Chapter 1, there is no public or private attempt to collect comprehensive data on private adoptions in each state. Nor is there any record of U.S. born children who are adopted by citizens of another country. It's estimated, however, that 100-300 children leave the United States on a U.S. passport each year to be raised in another country. (Canada alone reports the immigration of close to 100 U.S. born children adopted by Canadian citizens each year.) While numerous controls are in place for adopted children who enter this country, none are in place for those who leave. The Hague Convention (see following section) includes provisions to protect American children departing the United States after being adopted by a citizen of another country.

The Hague Convention

An international convention known as the Hague Conference on Private International Law was concluded in May of 1993. At the conclusion of the last session, the final text of an international treaty (known as the Convention on Protection of Children and Cooperation in Respect of Intercountry Adoption) was passed. The intent of this treaty is to set standards and procedures designed to protect the interests of the children being adopted as well as those of the birth parents and the adoptive parents. The standards set forth in the final version of the Convention will apply to all adoptions between countries that have ratified the Convention. However, the treaty does not prohibit countries party to the Convention from setting additional requirements and standards for children leaving their country.

Table 3-2: Countries Ratifying The Hague Convention

Country	Signature	Ratification, Acceptance, Approval, or Accession*	Entry into Force
Albania	09/12/00	R—09/12/00	01/01/01
Andorra	01/03/97	A—01/03/97	05/01/97
Australia	08/25/98	R—08/25/98	12/01/98
Austria	12/18/98	R—05/19/99	09/01/99
Belarus	12/10/97		
Belgium	01/27/99		
Bolivia	03/12/02	R—03/12/02	07/01/02
Brazil	05/25/93	R—01/10/99	07/01/99
Bulgaria	05/15/02	R—05/15/02	09/01/02
Burkino Faso	04/14/94	R—01/11/96	05/01/96
Burundi	10/15/98	A—10/15/98	02/01/99
Canada	04/12/94	R—12/19/96	04/01/97
Chili	07/13/99	R—07/13/99	11/01/99
China	11/30/00		
Colombia	09/01/93	R—07/13/98	11/01/98
Costa Rica	03/25/93	R—10/30/95	02/01/96
Cyprus	11/17/94	R—02/20/95	06/01/95
Czech Republic	02/11/00	R—02/11/00	06/01/00
Denmark	07/02/97	R—07/02/97	11/01/97
Ecuador	05/03/94	R—09/07/95	01/01/96
El Salvador	11/02/96	R—11/17/98	03/01/99
Estonia	02/22/02	A—02/22/02	10/01/02
Finland	04/14/94	R—03/27/97	07/01/97
France	04/05/95	R—06/30/98	10/01/98
Georgia	04/09/99	A—04/09/99	08/01/99
Germany	11/07/97	R—11/22/01	03/01/02
Iceland	01/17/00	A—01/17/00	08/15/00
Ireland	06/19/96		
Israel	11/02/93	R—02/03/99	06/01/99
Italy	12/11/95	R—01/18/00	05/01/00
Latvia	05/29/02		
Lithuania	04/29/98	A—04/29/98	08/01/98
Luxemburg	06/06/95		
Mauritius	09/28/98	A—09/28/98	01/01/99
Mexico	05/25/93	R—09/14/94	05/01/95
Moldova	04/10/98	A—04/10/98	08/01/98
Monaco	06/29/99	A—06/29/99	10/01/99
Mongolia	04/25/00	A—04/25/00	11/30/00
Netherlands	12/05/93	R—06/26/98	10/01/98
New Zealand	09/18/98	A—09/18/98	01/01/99
Norway	05/20/96	R—09/25/97	01/01/98
Panama	06/15/99	R—09/29/99	01/01/00
Paraguay	05/13/98	R—05/13/98	09/01/98
Peru	11/16/94	R—09/14/95	01/01/96
Philippines	071795	R—07/02/96	11/01/96
Poland	06/12/95	R—06/12/95	10/01/95
Portugal	08/26/99		
Romania	05/29/93	R—12/28/94	05/01/95
Russia	09/07/00		
Slovakia	06/01/99	R—06/06/01	10/01/01
Slovenia	01/24/02	R—01/24/02	05/01/02
Spain	03/27/95	R—07/11/95	11/01/95
Sri Lanka	05/24/95	R—01/23/95	05/01/95
Sweden	10/10/96	R—05/28/97	09/01/97
Switzerland	01/16/95		
Turkey	12/05/01		
United Kingdom	01/12/94		
United States	03/31/94		
Uruguay	09/01/93		
Venezuela	01/10/97	R—01/10/97	05/01/97

* An R designates ratification, while an A designates accession

By 2002, thirty-five countries had ratified the Convention. (See Table 3-2.) Twelve countries had joined by acceding to the Convention and thirteen countries (including the United States) had signed the Convention but had not yet ratified it. By signing the Convention, the country expresses, in principle, its intention to ratify. However, the signature does not, in any way, oblige a country to take further action toward ratification. More up-to-date information on those countries that have ratified, signed, or acceded to the Convention can be found on the Hague Conference's web site: **www.hcch.net/e/status/adoshte.html**. (Note: The text of the Hague Convention consistently refers to "states," which, in this case, refers to individual countries.)

CHAPTER 4

Choosing the Right Agency

In the years following World War II, when U.S. citizens were first trying to adopt abroad, it was difficult to find a local agency to conduct pre- and post adoption services. The first U.S.-based international agency was Holt International Adoption Services of Eugene, Oregon, which was founded in the 1950s. That agency made arrangements with private agencies in various states to provide services to Korean orphans being placed through Holt. However, prospective adoptive parents who did not fit the requirements for Holt because of their age, length of marriage, or religious beliefs had a difficult time finding alternatives.

International adoption nowadays is a completely different story. So many agencies exist and so much information is available that potential parents are overwhelmed.

Most potential adoptive parents find an international adoption agency by word-of-mouth, through recommendation by their local, domestic adoption agency or parent group, by researching all available books on the subject, and by searching the Internet and requesting literature and additional information from agency web sites. In addition, adoption information and referral services have popped up in many states to help adoptive parents find the most suitable agency for their needs. Annual adoption conferences are held in many states. This gives preadoptive parents the chance to talk to more agencies, both local and out of state, and to take home their literature. Most local agencies hold their own seminars or orientations to present an overview of their services.

Several directories of agencies and services are also available. One excellent source for this kind of information is the *Report on Foreign Adoption*, published by International Concerns for Children, Inc., a nonprofit organization that provides comprehensive, up-to-date information on international adoption for interested individuals. The report includes 10 monthly updates and also includes a list of reputable, licensed and experienced agencies with no history of major litigation. Visit **www.iccadopt.org** for more information on ICC and the *Report on Foreign Adoption*.

Step 2
Collect agency information.

In addition, the National Adoption Information Clearinghouse offers the *National Adoption Directory*, a 300-page reference, that can be downloaded for free from the NAIC web site (**www.calib.com/naic**) or ordered by mail for $25.00. In addition, the site offers an online *National Organizations Directory*, updated daily, that allows you to search by state for adoption agencies, officials, support groups and more. Other resources for beginning your search for a reputable international adoption agency include the Joint Council on International Children's Services (**www.jcics.org**), which maintains a list of member agencies.

Many adoptive parents turn to the Internet and email the agencies they are interested in from the listings. Just a few of the widely used sites for contacting agencies include **adoption.com**; **adoption.org**; **adopting.org**; **parentsoup.com/adoption**; **childofmydreams.com**; **comeunity.com**; and **rainbowkids.com**. Since adoption agencies must pay fees to be listed in many of the print and web directories, you won't find every reputable, nonprofit, licensed international adoption agency listed in every resource. In addition, some commercial directories list any agency that pays them, even though the agency may be unlicensed, nonaccredited, inexperienced, and may have a string of complaints against them. Just because an agency is listed doesn't mean it's reputable. In order to affirm the reliability of the agencies you prefer, contact the state licensing specialists who supervise adoption agencies or check it out with International Concerns for Children (**www.iccadopt.org**). The Appendix includes contact information for each of these organizations.

It's not necessary to choose an international adoption agency that is located close to where you live or even in your own state. Los Niños International Adoption Center (**www.losninos.org**) provides adoption services to residents in Texas and to residents of states where LNI networks with other licensed adoption agencies. Many other U.S.-based international adoption agencies also network with private adoption agencies in other states.

Choosing an International Adoption Agency

Once you have gathered information on the agency or agencies you are interested in contacting, you may wish to prepare a list of questions for each one. That done, you can ask the questions not covered in the literature by phone, e-mail, or in person. Since some agencies work with several different countries, the answers to questions regarding requirements, waits, and fees may differ according to country. In addition, each agency should be able to provide you with names and telephone numbers of postadoptive parents who enjoy discussing their adoption experiences. What follows is a sample of some helpful questions for evaluating an international adoption agency.

After the regulations for U.S. agency accreditation have been issued for compliance with the Hague Convention, all U.S. agencies who want to work in intercountry adoption must apply for such accreditation. After the United States ratifies the Hague Convention, only accredited agencies will be allowed to continue to place orphans internationally.

International Agency Administration

Q: Is your agency licensed and nonprofit? Which government body licenses you?

Q: Who directs the agency — human service professionals, business administrators, or lawyers?

Q: How many years have you been placing children?

Q: May I have a copy of your contracts for adoptive parents?

Q: Who helps me prepare a dossier of documents for the child-placing authorities?

Q: What types of preparation, education and support services do you provide before, during and after the placement of a child?

Q: Are you licensed, approved or accredited by the foreign governments in countries where you have programs? In which countries is this necessary?

Q: Do you have bilingual staff abroad to obtain the referral of a child and to assist the adoptive parents while they are there?

Q: May I have names of people who have recently adopted from _____ (country)?

Placement Procedures

Q: How many children did you place last year?

Q: What are the ages and nationalities of the children you place?

Q: What is their general state of health?

Requirements for Adoptive Parents

Q: What are your requirements for adoptive parents, relating to age, income, religion, marital status, living arrangements, length of marriage, divorce, state of health, or records of a legal misdemeanor?

Q: What is your policy regarding single applicants?

Q: Which countries do you think might accept my application?

The Referral of a Child

Q: After my dossier is completed, how long is the wait for a girl/boy of ____ years of age from _____ (country)?

Q: How will a child be assigned to me?
    a. Will I get a referral with written information and a video?
    b. Will I get the suggestion of a referral without written information?
    c. Will I be sent an invitation to select a child abroad?

Q: What happens if I don't feel I can accept a. or b.?

Q: Once I accept a referral, how long will it be until I can travel to _____ (country) to adopt and immigrate the child? Will that be one trip or two?

Q. Will orphanage professionals describe the health, schedule, and behavior of the child to me?

Q: How long will I need to stay abroad?

Q. If I choose a country where the child will be escorted, how long does it take for the child to be brought to me?

Q: What happens if the child becomes too ill to be adopted before or during my stay?

Q. What happens if I decide I don't wish to adopt that particular child?

Q: What happens if we can't adjust to this new child?

Q: What arrangements will your agency make if the child doesn't like us?

Expenses
Q: What is the total cost for an adoption from _____ (country)?

Estimating the Costs of an International Adoption

The costs of an international adoption vary greatly depending on the agency you use, the range of services provided, the country from which you adopt your child, the cost of travel, present exchange rates for the U.S. dollar, and a host of other factors.

The average cost for international adoption services in 2002 was between $18,000 and $30,000, which included agency fees, dossier and immigration fees, as well as the orphanage donation, legal work, and travel. The only way to get a firm handle on what an adoption will cost is to keep track with a sheet of estimated expenses (see nearby table). Whatever the figure you arrive at, the amount will be trifling in comparison to the costs of actually raising the child. (The Department of Agriculture predicts that a family with a child born in the year 2001 will spend $169,921 to raise that child over the next 17 years.)

Although an international adoption agency should be able to provide exact figures for costs such as the agency's international processing fee and the foreign program fee, other costs such as document preparation and travel may vary considerably according to the adoptive parents' individual situation and the country from which they are adopting. For example, a single or a couple in Pennsylvania who adopt through a U.S.-based international agency in Texas will know ahead of time what the pre- and postadoption fees will be for their adoption agency in Pennsylvania. However, the costs of obtaining their certified documents and getting them translated, notarized, and verified and authenticated or apostilled, will differ, since a typical single will have fewer documents than a married couple who were both previously divorced.

Think You Can't Afford Adoption? Think Again

More than $25,000 may be available to you if you decide to adopt! A plethora of adoption loans, benefits, and grants await you. Or, you can borrow on funds you have squirreled away and use your adoption tax credit to offset the loans you'll be paying back.

Here's just a few of the financial benefits that may be available to you, should you decide to adopt.

State tax benefits: Many states offer adoption tax credits, deductions, subsidies, or other benefits. Some of these may apply to international adoption. Individuals adopting children who can be classified as "special needs" may be eligible for additional benefits. Ask your adoption agency, social worker or contact your state's department of taxation for a full explanation of benefits. In addition, the North American Council on Adoptable Children maintains a web site (**www.nacac.org/sub-sidy_stateprofiles.html**) that summarizes various state tax benefits and lists contacts for more information.

Federal tax benefits: An income tax credit of up to $10,000 per child is available for qualified adoption expenses paid or incurred by the taxpayer. The full $10,000 may be available to qualified taxpayers with an adjustable gross income of less than $150,000. The credit is gradually phased out for taxpayers earning more. For more information, download Publication 968 "Tax Benefits for Adoption" from the IRS web site (**www.irs.gov/forms_pubs/pubs.html**) or request a copy through mail by calling 800-829-3676. Check with your tax advisor for more information on eligibility for this credit.

Adoption loans: Many banks offer a variety of loan plans to waiting parents, such as home equity loans, second mortgages, and special adoption loans (low-interest unsecured loans). The National Adoption Foundation Loan Program offered through MBNA (**www.nafadopt.org/NAFPrograms.htm**) or (888-627-8767) is one popular loan program that can be used for a wide variety of adoption-related expenses. A second program is First Union Bank's adoption loan program (888-314-5437). Information about other loan programs can be found through the Internet, a financial advisor, your adoption agency, or other adoption resources.

Family loans: Ask for a gift or an interest-free loan from family members. If that fails, offer to pay a higher rate on a personal note than your family member receives on a certificate of deposit.

Military adoption benefits: The military will reimburse active-duty personnel for up to $2,000 per child for some adoption-related expenses. Check with the National Military Family Association (**www.nmfa.org**), a tax advisor or military personnel for more information.

Employer benefits: Some companies reimburse employees for adoption-related expenses of up to several thousand dollars. Ask your company if any such benefits are available or contact the National Adoption Center (800-862-3678) for a list of employers providing benefits and materials to guide you in requesting adoption assistance from your employer if no benefit program is in place. On-line, you can visit **www.adopt.org/datacenter/faces/emplist.html** for a list of companies offering adoption benefits and the types of benefits available.

Grants: Adoption grants are available to qualified prospective parents. Contact the National Adoption Information Clearinghouse at 888-251-0075 for their list of "Organizations that Provide Grants" or visit **http://kids4us.org**

Other Options: Borrow against your 401K, pension plan, life-insurance policy or company profit-sharing plan. Use credit cards for cash advances (make sure you can live with the interest rate!) or to pay for plane tickets and travel expenses. Use interest-free offers aimed at attracting new credit card customers to your advantage—just be sure to keep track of interest-free deadlines and the resulting interest rates.

Table 4-1: Estimating Adoption Expenses

The fees listed below are estimates only and will vary according to the agency you work with, the country you adopt from, and your individual situation. We've made these estimates based on the fees charged by adoption agencies with which we are familiar. To determine your approximate cost, select only the expenses that apply to your individual case or choice of country. Most countries have a widely varying rate of inflation that is generally much higher than in the United States, as well as fluctuating exchange rates.

Preadoption U.S. Agency Fee

Registration with agency. . . . . $50 to $600

Home study fee. . . . . $600 to $2,500

Agency fee for services. . . . . $3,000 to $6,000
(Some agencies do not list this fee separately, but combine it with the program fee.)

Other Adoption-Related Expenses Incurred in the United States

INS filing fee Application of Advance Processing (I-600A) $460
(There is no filing fee for the Orphan Petition if done in the
same year as the application.)

Fingerprinting. $50
(Fee applies to each member of family over age 18.)

Certified copies of birth, marriage, and divorce certificates $10 to $60
(Fees range from $5-$10 per document.)

Notarization, apostille, or verification fees . . . . $400 (average)
(Varies according to state and number of documents.
Most states charge $10 per document.)

Translations of documents . . . . $500 (average)
(Averages $300-$1,000 when done in the United States. If done overseas,
costs vary and are often included in the program fees.)

Authentication of documents by the foreign consulate. . . . . $800 (average)
(Ranges from $600 to $1,500. Only in countries that do not require apostilles)

Program fee for child . . . . $3,000 to $30,000
(If agency fee for services is separate.)

Travel-Related Costs

One round-trip ticket per person traveling . . . . $600 to $2,000
(Varies tremendously depending on country traveling to,
time of year you are traveling, and type of ticket you buy.)

One-way ticket for child to United States. . . . . $200 to $900
(Tickets may be as low as $200 for infants and children up to age two. Tickets for
children age three and older generally cost about ninety percent of the adult fare.)

Food and lodging . . . . $100 to $150 (per day)
(Varies depending on whether stay is in a major city,
an average hotel, or with a family.)

U.S. consular service Orphan Visa fee. $325

Orphan's photos for passport and visa . . . . $25 to $35

Orphan's passport . . . . $25 to $100

Postplacement Expenses
Postplacement supervision. . . . . $800 to 2,500
(Varies according to agency and whether international agency
or network local agency conducts supervision. Also varies
according to the number of supervision contacts required.)

Legal fees for readoption. . . . . Fees vary
(Legal fees may vary tremendously. Call a lawyer in your state for an estimate.
If you are conducting a *pro se* adoption (adoption without a lawyer), you will
only be responsible for court fees.)

U.S. Citizenship Application filing fee. $145
or
U.S. passport for child. $70

*Possibilities for Additional Costs:
Other less common costs that may come into consideration, depending on the
country and the type of program you choose, include the costs of foster care for
the child, escort fee for bringing the child to the United States if you do not travel overseas, medical expenses for a sick child that needs attention overseas, fees
for transferring INS paperwork if you change foreign programs, fees for professional handling of documentation, fees for obtaining visas (required for Bolivia,
China, Kazakhstan, Russia, Ukraine, Vietnam), etc.

One of the most expensive parts of many adoptions is travel. The costs of air travel, hotels, food, and transportation within the country will vary according to the part
of the world you are traveling to and the exchange rate at the time of your trip.
Miscellaneous expenses such as fees for photos and the medical examination required
for the orphan visa will vary as well. A good, up-to-date guidebook will help you estimate most of your travel expenses. The guidebook will also provide information about
tipping and whether or not small gifts are expected by officials.

One of the easiest ways to calculate travel expenses is to talk to several adoptive parents who have recently returned from their adoption trip. However, since we all have different spending and saving habits, you may find a difference of several thousand dollars.
Some folks spend hundreds of dollars to phone home every day, or even include the cost
of expensive souvenirs in their accounts of travel and adoption expenses.

Financing Adoption

When considering adoption, many people initially balk at the cost and wonder how they could possibly ever afford such a thing. Others think that such high costs must mean they're "buying" a baby. However, as they research the process, what they'll find is that adoption fees go toward professional services and orphanage donations. Payments to birth mothers are strictly forbidden by INS. It's the rare individual who can dip into his or her pockets to make one lump sum payment for adoption services. Most individuals finance adoption by a variety of means and a combination of loans, savings, tax credits, and gifts and other methods of creative financing (see nearby box).

While international adoption is costly, the fees can be paid over a series of months. Payments are due in increments as you move through the process. Be sure you know what all of the fees will be (excluding travel) before you begin the process.

Evaluating Your Options

Choosing an adoption agency is an act of faith. The agency assumes a lot of responsibility toward coordinating an adoption. Trust is the key word. And a lot of paperwork.

Warning signs that may make you decide against using a certain agency boil down to communication, administration, and finances. Was your initial phone call, fax, or e-mail requesting information during business hours responded to within a reasonable period of time? If not, the agency may be understaffed or overextended. Are the administrators experienced enough in international adoption to be able to solve all the complex problems that arise?

Does the agency work in more than one country? If a foreign country changes its adoption requirements and you no longer qualify, will they help you to apply in a different country? Does the agency have sufficient financial reserves to cover losses due to major changes in a foreign adoption program and the resultant loss of income?

Other factors to consider are expenses and the extent of service provided. Not surprisingly, the more work an agency does for the adoptive parent, the higher the agency fee is likely to be. For example, some agencies assist the adoptive parents in filing with the INS as well as preparing the dossier of original documents for the foreign court, while other agencies show the adoptive parents how to do it themselves. Either the international agency or its networking agency must be licensed in the state where you reside in order to handle the documentation for you. Generally there is a separate fee for this service that can range from $3,000 to $7,000.

Your choice of an international agency will also be driven by the country or countries you are most interested in adopting from, as well as whether you qualify in terms of age, length of marriage, and so on. No agency has adoption agreements with every country in which it is possible to adopt. However, it's best to have more than one country in mind when selecting an agency. Choose an agency with several foreign programs that interest you.

For example, a lot of potential parents decide to adopt from a particular country because they have met an adoptive family or seen a television show on adopting in that country. This has been particularly true of Russia, and China, where the media has given the orphans a lot of coverage. The couple's next step is to contact an agency with a program in that country. However, if that agency only has one viable program and that country changes its requirements or puts a moratorium on adoptions, the couple may be left without other options.

Step 3
Choose an international adoption agency.

The determination of some couples to adopt from a particular country can some-times get in the way of good sense if they do not fit the age restrictions, length of mar-riage, and so on. If the prospective parents are unusually persistent, they will call every agency in America until they find one that will take them as clients, not fully realizing that they could be turned down at the end of the process by a judge who reviews that country's national adoption law before granting a final adoption decree.

Working with the International Agency

While prospective parents expect to be guided and kept informed, agencies have certain expectations, as well. They expect the potential parents to read their contracts, handbooks, and program packets of directions before calling for help. They also trust that the documents required from the prospective parents will be sent to the agency in a timely fashion. Responsible agencies expect that prospective parents will fully partic-ipate in the agency's training for international adoptive parenting. They also expect that prospective parents will be prepared to take an adoption trip abroad on short notice, if the parents are expected to travel. More importantly, the agencies have the expectation that the adoptive parent has applied to only one foreign child-placing entity.

You may be required to sign a contract that specifies the services performed by the international agency. It should cover the illness or death of a child awaiting adoption, as well as relatives reclaiming the child and adoption disruptions. Waiting pool policies and a postplacement supervisory agreement are usually outlined, as is the addition of a child to the adopting family during the waiting period by pregnancy or adoption through another agency. A reimbursement schedule for international processing and foreign program fees should be included, usually with a disclaimer such as one posted in the International Concerns Committee for Children (ICCC) *Report on Foreign Adoption*:

"Due to circumstances beyond the control of any agency, the possibility exists that the adoption process could be discontinued by foreign nations, governmental action, or judicial decrees beyond the control of the agency. You must further understand that it is necessary to advance funds to accomplish agency objectives and that the portion of those funds already utilized very possibly cannot be recovered in the event of such discontinuance. You need also to understand that in spite of information to the contrary, the child, when received, might have some undiagnosed physical or mental problem or might develop such a problem at a later date. You need to know, finally, that despite agency efforts to work with competent and honest lawyers, their actions are beyond agency control. This is by no means meant to scare you, but to tell you the simple facts about intercountry adoptions."

Table 4-2: Intercountry Adoptions 1999-2001

	1996	1997	1998	1999	2000	2001
All Countries	11,316	13,621	15,774	16,369	18,537	19,137
Europe	3,568	5,176	5,660	6,296	7,028	7,736
Albania	—	—	—	18	22	16
Belarus	36	49	2	32	46	129
Bulgaria	157	148	151	221	216	297
Estonia	—	—	—	3	7	10
Georgia	90	21	6	2	4	16
Hungary	51	72	34	18	25	13
Kazakhstan	3	26	54	113	398	672
Latvia	83	108	76	58	25	27
Lithuania	80	78	72	63	29	30
Moldova	42	43	46	63	79	46
Poland	66	78	77	97	83	86
Romania	554	621	406	895	1,119	782
Russian Federation	2,328	3,816	4,491	4,348	4,269	4,279
Ukraine	10	59	180	323	659	1,246
Other Europe	68	57	65	42	49	87
Asia	6,100	6,483	7,827	8,003	8,901	8,724
Cambodia	30	66	249	249	402	4 0 7
China, total	3,363	3,637	4,263	4,146	5,095	4,750
Mainland	3,313	3,597	4,206	4,101	5,058	4,681
Taiwan	21	19	30	32	28	42
Hong Kong	29	21	27	13	14	27
India	381	349	478	499	503	543
Japan	38	45	39	37	36	39
Korea (South)	1,580	1,654	1,829	2,008	1,794	1,860
Philippines	228	163	200	195	173	219
Thailand	53	63	84	77	88	74
Vietnam	354	425	603	709	724	737
Other Asia	73	81	82	83	86	95
Africa	89	182	172	209	212	234
Ethiopia	39	82	96	103	95	158
Liberia	3	38	9	19	25	20
Kenya	—	—	—	8	17	2
Sierra Leone	—	—	—	28	23	51
Other Africa	47	62	67	51	52	3
Oceania	4	4	4	6	11	19
North America	750	1,228	1,456	315	298	336
Canada	5	1	0	2	0	2
Mexico	89	152	168	137	106	73
Caribbean	135	200	314	12	14	6

	1996	1997	1998	1999	2000	2001
Dominican Republic	15	19	140	16	8	12
Haiti	69	142	121	96	131	192
Jamaica	39	31	38	52	39	51
Other North America	12	8	15	—	—	—
Central America	521	875	976	1,113	1,582	1,655
Belize	7	3	4	5	7	5
Costa Rica	20	22	7	41	17	9
El Salvador	19	5	13	8	9	4
Guatemala	420	788	911	1,002	1,518	1,609
Honduras	28	26	7	14	9	5
Nicaragua	16	13	1,619	19	9	13
Panama	11	18	16	24	13	10
South America	805	548	655	459	445	433
Bolivia	35	77	73	44	60	35
Brazil	101	91	103	64	26	33
Chile	62	41	26	20	10	3
Colombia	258	233	351	231	246	266
Ecuador	52	43	55	61	57	50
Paraguay	261	33	7	6	1	1
Peru	17	14	26	27	38	13
Venezuela	—	—	—	0	2	4
Other South America	19	16	14	6	5	18

CHAPTER 5

Obtaining State Approval: The First Steps

Once you have learned as much as you can about the international adoption experience, attended as many educational seminars as possible, talked to prospective parents and visited with adoptive parents and their children, and thoroughly evaluated the agencies you are interested in working with, you are ready for the next formal step in the adoption process: registering with the licensed agency or certified social worker that will conduct your home study and any postplacement supervision required.

In most states, a home study conducted by an agency is required; however, in some states, such as New York, Iowa, Florida, Louisiana, and Texas, a licensed social worker may conduct the study instead. However, once the Hague Convention is ratified by the United States, any agency or social worker conducting the home study must have an affiliation or contract with the U.S. based international adoption agency.

If the U.S.-based international agency you plan to use to adopt your child is located and licensed in your state, it will be the one to conduct your home study. Even if your international adoption agency is located in another state, it may have a contract or networking agreement with a local adoption agency or social worker who is licensed in your home state. In this case, a local social worker will conduct your home study.

However, if your international adoption agency is not located in your state and does not have a home study agreement with an individual or agency in your state, you will need to find another agency or a certified social worker affiliated with a licensed agency to conduct your home study. Thus, in this case, you will actually need to formally apply with two agencies: a local agency that is close enough to your residence to conduct your home study and the U.S. based, international agency that will connect you with a child overseas.

If you plan to enter into an independent or parent-initiated adoption, you will still need an adoption agency or social worker to conduct a home study in order to comply with INS requirements (see the following section).

Step 4
Choose the agency that will conduct your home study (if different from your international adoption agency).

Fortunately, because most international adoption agencies use a network of local agencies across the United States, finding a local agency to do your home study is usually not difficult. To make certain that the staff is qualified and that the agency is committed to high ethical and legal standards, ask about the agency's compliance with the minimum standards of their licensing body.

The agency conducting your home study must have a countywide or statewide license, but it does not necessarily need to have an office in your city. Many agencies utilize social workers in other cities and counties on a contract basis in order to provide services for a wider area. You will have a long relationship with the agency you choose to conduct the home study, since the agency will follow up to monitor your family's adjustment for six months or more following the child's placement.

The Home Study

The INS mandates that all states require a home study by a licensed adoption agency or a social worker affiliated with such an adoption agency in the adopter's home state before a child is adopted abroad or is brought into the United States for adoption. The home study must follow the requirements of the state licensing department for child-placing agencies. INS requirements must also be included.

A home study usually consists of an orientation meeting, the application, a private interview, a home visit, and group discussions led by a social worker. Data gathered at the study meetings is summarized by the social worker in a document that becomes the official home study. The home study may take anywhere from six weeks to six months depending on individual circumstances.

Home studies deal with the dynamics of the individual adopter, the marriage, the challenges of transracial and cross-cultural adoptions, and the subsequent adjustments of parent and child. Social workers are professionally trained to help prospective adopters explore the many facets of adoption and to help them make the best possible decisions for the family they are planning. The social worker and the prospective adoptive parents must explore and discuss the types of children available and their ability to parent such a child or children. The minimum and maximum age, the number of siblings, gender, race, and possible handicapping conditions must be agreed upon in the social worker's closing recommendation. This study process ends when a mutually agreed upon decision is reached either to proceed toward adoption or to withdraw the application.

Applying to Your Local Agency

Every adoption agency has an application form that must be filled out before the home study begins. If you have a serious disease or disability, a history of mental illness, a history of alcohol or drug abuse, or a criminal record, discuss your problem with the director of the agency before you apply. You may be requested to provide a letter of recommendation from a psychiatrist, counselor, or probation officer before you apply. Many agencies also request that you fill out a form indicating your level of acceptance of certain medical conditions in the child you wish to adopt. (See sample list of handicapping conditions of waiting children at the end of this chapter.) This list ranges from conditions as minor as a lisp or small scar to much more serious health issues. Adopting parents who want a generally healthy child may answer "no" to all listed conditions or may decline to fill out the form.

Step 5
Initiate home study by applying to an appropriate agency.

You may also be required to sign a home study contract, which outlines the agency's responsibilities as well as yours. If, for some reason, your agency or social worker does not offer a home study contract, you might request one. This can clear up any misconceptions at the start. The home study sessions and the conditions necessary for approval are set forth in the contract. Most contracts or agreements will state the conditions under which some or all of the fees you pay will be refunded.

Before you commit to any agency, you should know exactly what services this agency will perform and what its fees will be. Call or contact the agency by e-mail to request literature explaining the agency's requirements for adoptive parents, fees, policies, length of licensure, and accreditation.

Two separate entities are involved in licensing adoption agencies and social workers. Social workers are licensed in their state by the State Board of Social Worker Examiners. The board issues a directory of social workers each year. Adoption agencies are licensed by the licensing division of their state adoption unit. There is a unit in each county. State adoption units go by different names. In Texas, it is the Department of Protective and Regulatory Services. To ensure that you are registering with a qualified adoption agency or social worker, check with the appropriate licensing agency. (See Appendix for contact information.) In addition, before you commit to having an agency conduct your home study, you should know the answers to the following questions:

What does your home study consist of?

Who will conduct it?

How soon will the social worker contact me after I apply?

What credentials does the social worker have and how much experience does he or she have in foreign adoptions?

How long will it take for approval?

Why would someone not be approved?

What happens after the home study?

Obtaining Documents for the Home Study

Once you have registered with an agency to conduct your home study, you should begin to collect the documents needed to meet your home study requirements and the requirements of other federal and foreign agencies that will be involved in your adoption. Many of the documents assembled for your home study will also later be used to prepare a dossier (or collection of documents) for the foreign court or central authority.

You will be collecting a combination of certified and original documents. A certified document is an official document issued by the state or county, as opposed to a document issued by a hospital for a birth or a document issued by a church for a marriage. Original documents are individually generated. Job letters, health certificates, police clearances, letters of reference, and your home study are all considered original documents.

Most of the original documents will need to be notarized. Legally, the individuals who provide the documents or letters of reference — your accountant, employer, friend and so on — must sign their name in the presence of a notary. The medical forms are an exception because your signature will be notarized on those forms, rather than the physician's signature. Try to have your documents notarized at the time that they are produced to save time. (More detailed information on notarizing documents can be found in Chapter 7.)

Each prospective adoptive parent must obtain the following documents before the home study can be approved. (You can initiate the home study before you have all of the documents.)

Step 6
Obtain documents required for home study.

Required Documents

1. Certified birth certificates for each member of the family. Order three for each spouse (one for the foreign dossier, one for the passport, and one for the INS) and one for each child already in your home.

Certified birth certificates can be ordered from the Bureau of Vital Statistics in the state where you were born. If you need help finding this office, contact directory assistance in the capital city of the state where you were born or visit **www.vitalchek.com** for a list of phone numbers of Bureaus of Vital Statistics across the United States. Obtaining certified birth certificates takes about four weeks by mail or two hours in person, unless you use express mail services. In addition, you can order a certified birth certificate from the Internet (see nearby box on Ordering Vital Statistics Records from the Internet or visit **www.vitalchek.com**).

If you are a naturalized citizen, use your naturalization certificate for evidence at the INS office and passport office. Use a certified copy of your birth certificate for the formal adoption dossier. This can be accomplished through the consul of your native country, which will authenticate a photocopy of your original. If you are from a country that does not have a consul here (i.e., Cuba), you may request the consul of the country from which you are adopting to handle this step. If you do not have a birth certificate, ask INS for Form G-342. An alternative is to photocopy your certificate of citizenship and get it notarized.

2. Certified marriage license. Order two (one for the foreign dossier and one for INS).

Certified marriage licenses are available from the County Clerk in the county in which you were married. These usually cost between $3.00 and $10.00. This takes one week by mail or two days if you call ahead and pick it up. Tell them the month, day, and year of the marriage, the names of both parties, and your return address. In addition, you may be able to order a certified copy of your marriage license using the Internet.

Vital Record Services On-line

It's easy to use the Internet to order certified copies of birth, death, marriage, and divorce certificates, and it may be easier, faster and less expensive than using the mail or phone. VitalChek (**www.vitalchek.com**) provides vital records services for 49 of the 50 states (Louisiana is the one exception) as well as the District of Columbia and British Columbia, Canada.

One of the most convenient aspects of VitalChek is that you may be able to order all of the certified copies of vital records documents needed for your adoption at one sitting, rather than tracking down several different Bureau of Vital Statistics offices or county offices. VitalChek also accepts credit card payment, which makes it more convenient for many users.

Not all counties and states issue all four certificates through VitalChek; however, it's still a useful site for collecting the phone numbers, fax numbers and addresses needed to contact the appropriate office for your request.

3. Certified death certificate, if applicable, of former spouses. Order two of each (one for the foreign dossier and one for INS). Certified death certificates are available from the Bureau of Vital Statistics in the state where the death occurred. In addition, you may also order a certified death certificate using the Internet.

4. Divorce decree, if applicable. Order two of each (one for the foreign dossier and one for INS). If both you and your spouse are divorced, you will each need two copies of both divorce decrees. Divorce decrees are available from the Clerk of Court in the county in which the divorce occurred.

5. Job letter from your employer stating your length of employment and annual salary. (You need one letter for each applicant.) If you are self-employed, a public accountant may prepare the statement. In either case, address the letters with "To Whom It May Concern."

6. A statement of net worth written by you or your accountant. (See sample net worth statement at the end of this chapter.)

7. Copies of your health and life insurance policies. You need only the page showing the company name, beneficiary, and amount. A photocopy will usually suffice. (Note: Not all states require this.)

8. Medical examination forms for all household members signed by the family physician. (See sample health form at the end of this chapter.) The date of the exam must be included on the form. The medical examination form is valid for one year from the date of the exam.

9. Photocopies of your federal income tax returns (first and second page only) for the last three years. On the side of the form, type the following statement: "I certify that this is a true copy of the original" and then sign and date the statement in the presence of a notary.

10. For all household members over age 18, a letter from your local police department stating that the individual has no criminal record. You will usually need a separate letter for each applicant. Try to get the signature of the Chief of Police notarized at the same time. Some countries require a state police clearance, usually available from the State Criminal Records Department. If this office doesn't exist in your state, you'll need to get a separate FBI clearance. Call the FBI complex in Clarksburg, WV, (304-625-2000 x3878) for more information.

11. Letters of reference from at least three people (not related) who are acquainted with you and your family. These letters should come from professionals or community leaders if at all possible. (See sample format for letters of reference at the end of this chapter.) Try to obtain letters of reference from people in your locality. Then, the same notary public, secretary of state, and foreign consul can be used to sign, stamp, apostille/verify, and authenticate all or at least most of your documents.

12. Child abuse clearances and criminal clearances for each member of the family over age 18. These documents are obtained by your social worker through your state welfare system while the home study is in progress.

13. Pictures of applicants in front of their home and individual close-ups (or passport pictures). You should also include photos of existing children. You need at least three sets of photos. Pose in business attire. Jeans, shorts, swimsuits, and bare feet will not make a favorable impression, since your dossier should be presented with as much dignity as possible. (See sample photos at the end of this chapter.)

Submit photocopies of your documents to the agency conducting your home study. You must retain the originals for your foreign dossier. Documents not usually required abroad are birth certificates and medical forms on children already in your family and insurance policies.

Documents for the foreign dossier may need notarization or apostilles, verification, and authentication, depending on the country you adopt from. (Some adoptive parents notarize each of the original documents as they are gathered.) Chapter 7 explains the process for ensuring that your documents are appropriately endorsed. Try to get all of your original documents generated in the same state. This way, you may need only one notary public to sign all of your documents. This also makes them easier to verify or apostille.

Sample Guidelines for a Typical Home Study

Most U.S.-based international agencies have a specific guide for social workers conducting the home study as well as addendums, updates, subsequent home studies, and postplacement supervisory reports. Your international agency will inform you if your local agency or social worker needs to follow a specific format.

Since foreign judges and adoption agencies need a translated copy of the home study, adopters should ask their social worker to try to keep the written study no longer than eight to twelve pages. This does not include the required attachment of seven to eight forms and documents.

What follows is an example of a set of home study interview guidelines used by the administering agency or social worker. Prepared by Los Niños International Adoption Center, this particular home study guide incorporates Texas minimum standards, the INS regulations cited in Form I-600A, and the requirements of several of the more active child-sending countries, such as Colombia, China, Russia and the Ukraine. Although the home study guidelines of other agencies may vary somewhat, you can expect that all of these topics will be brought up at some point in the home study process.

In addition, the social worker will also conduct an environmental evaluation and a fire inspection of your house to be sure the home would be safe for a baby or child. (See sample environmental health and fire checklists at the end of this chapter.)

Can't Remember Where You Were Born?

In order to obtain certified birth certificates, you often need to provide information about the county in which you were born. While most people can remember the town or city of their birth, the name of the county is sometimes more difficult to recall. It doesn't help that some larger cities may be broken by more than one county line.

One helpful online resource in narrowing your search may be a geographic database located at **http://www.mit.edu:8001/geo**. Scroll to the bottom of the page and enter the city and state (Dallas, TX) of your birth in the box titled "Place name." Then hit the submit button. Be sure to use a comma to separate the city and state. The counties and zip codes associated with that name will then be displayed.

THIS GUIDE IS FOR THE EXCLUSIVE USE OF LOS NINOS AND NETWORKING AGENCIES

PREPARING THE HOME STUDY

A Guide for Social Workers

© 2002 Los Niños International Adoption Center

A rewrite or addendum will be requested if this guide is not followed.
Please use your agency letterhead

Prospective candidates must be a legally married couple or a single person.

HOME STUDY

Quote: *"This study is approved for the sole use of LNI foreign adoption programs."*

> Name of prospective adoptive parent(s)
> Address (street, city, state and zip)
> Home and work telephone numbers
> E-mail addresses

Quote if accurate: *"Prior to approval, I obtained criminal and child abuse clearances, and a complete set of supporting documents was presented for my review."*

HOME STUDY APPROVED:_____(Date)

Contacts (INS and LNI standards require these separate interviews and date):
- (Date) First consultation or orientation
- (Date) An individual interview with each applicant
- (Date) Interviews with school-age children or other persons living with family
- (Date) At least one visit to the home with all present
- (Date) At least one interview with adult children living at home who are over age 18
- (Date) Interview either by phone or in person with each adult/child no longer residing in the home
- (Date, Place, Method) Interviews by phone, meetings, talks with applicant(s)

China requires a minimum of four documented interviews. These must include discussions, education and preparation as well as face-to-face meetings.

Home Study for Second or Subsequent Adoption
- All contacts listed above, including individual interviews, must be conducted and documented
- Date of the first adoption must be cited
- Approval date of the first home study must be indicated
- All categories must be reviewed

You may write "No Changes" if there have not been any changes since the first home study, providing that they were covered and documented in the first study. However, categories of "Child Desired," "Police Clearance," "Child Abuse Clearance," and "Recommendation" must be covered in the second study.

- Include a section on the child presently in the home and how the parents' life changed when that child arrived
- In regard to studies where "No Changes" are stated, the first study must be attached to the second study

TOPICS TO BE COVERED IN THE HOME STUDY

Child Desired

- Knowledge of types of children available, flexibility, level of acceptance
- Indicate the number of siblings, minimum and maximum ages, gender, health, whether low birth weight or correctable/non-correctable handicaps are acceptable, and the race or ethnicity, such as: Asian, Asian/Anglo, Asian/Hispanic, Asian/Black, Hispanic, Hispanic/Anglo, Hispanic/Black, Caucasian, Black, Caucasian/Black, Caucasian/Gypsy, Caucasian/Turkish or other.

Specify the country from which the child will be adopted. Home studies for China, Russia, and several Latin American countries must state the country.

Motivation and Readiness to Adopt

- Evolution of decision to adopt and reason for choosing international adoption
- Length of time spent considering adoption
- Infertility — diagnosis and attempts at treatment, if applicable
- Efforts to prepare for an adoption
- Summary of worker's preadoption counseling

Quote if accurate: *"I advised and discussed with (Name) the process, expenses, medical risks, difficulties, and delays associated with international adoption; the requirements of the Immigration and Naturalization Service; and the adoption laws of the state. I also explained the need to read the LNI Handbook, the text* How to Adopt Internationally *and the need to complete the International Adoptive Parenting System I, II and III (correspondence courses) in order to be as well prepared as possible."*

- Mention whether they have been previously rejected for adoption or the subject of an unfavorable home study
- Explain whether they are trying to become pregnant or are adopting through another source
- Inform them that if they do become pregnant or they receive a child from another agency before LNI assigns them a child, the adoption plan must be put on hold for six months; when the adoption process is resumed, an update to their home study must be conducted
- Mention whether they will travel abroad for the legal process to adopt and to immigrate their child or children

Knowledge of the Foreign Adoption Process
- Attitude toward the prospect of a child from a different ethnicity, race, culture, and nation
- Understanding of reasons children from foreign countries become available for adoption and willingness to accept an orphaned, abandoned, or relinquished child
- Acceptance of risks and unknowns in foreign adoption

Adoptive Mother
- Worker's description of applicant's appearance, including weight and height
- Date and place of birth (state the word "verified" by birth certificate). Names and address(es) of her parents, their occupation, health, marital status, marital relationship, and each parent's support/nurturing and decision-making abilities
- Siblings' names, sex, order of birth, education, occupation, marital status, children, location, and past and current relationships with each sibling
- Relevant extended family and current contacts, growing-up years, economic circumstances, family lifestyle, and work and play activities
- Type of discipline and/or punishment received and the feelings about it
- How sex education was handled and their plans to educate the child/children.
- Any history as a victim of emotional, physical, and/or sexual abuse or neglect and how this experience was resolved
- Any history of drug or alcohol abuse and the resolution of this experience
- Major family values, friendships and social life, feelings about parents (include information about absent parent, if appropriate), and expectations by parents
- Feelings about childhood including both the happiest and most traumatic memories, what they would change about their parents and their childhood, feelings about themselves, and key factors contributing to sense of self, i.e., significant persons and events, frustrations and successes, ways stress is handled and ways negative feelings are expressed

Adoptive Father
- Same as for adoptive mother

Previous Relationships or Marriages
- History and termination of significant relationships and marriages, reason the relationships ended, how the relationships ended, date and place of divorce(s) (state the word "verified" by divorce decree)
- Children from previous relationships/marriages, parental visitation, and child support

Present Marriage
- Length and nature of courtship, date and place of marriage (state the word "verified" by marriage license)

- Factors that attracted spouses to one another
- Marital lifestyle, roles, and decision-making processes
- Areas of pride in one another and sexual relationship
- Primary areas of stress and/or disagreement
- Effects of adding a child/children to the home.
- Method for resolving differences
- Attitude and satisfaction with the marriage
- Areas that they hope to improve upon
- Separations or threats of divorce
- Participation in marriage counseling — dates, duration, resolutions
- The quality of marital and family relationships in relation to the family's ability to provide an adoptive home

Singles and Couples with Children
- Feelings about themselves as parents
- Their decision-making processes regarding child raising, their agreements and disagreements about parental discipline and how they are resolved, and their support for one another as parents
- Issues of possessiveness or control
- Reasons they decided to adopt when they already have a child
- Understanding adjustment difficulties for the child or children already in the home

Single Parents
- Feelings about being single,
- Significant relationships with both men and women, including sexual relationships. China requires a letter from singles regarding their significant relationships with both men and women, including sexual relationships.)
- Attitude toward marriage in the future.
- If they do marry, feelings they expect from their spouse toward their adopted child/children and the amount of responsibility spouse will have for the child/children.
- Identify their support system

Current Children (This includes adults over age 18. Include those in the home, college age children and children of previous marriages.)
- Name, sex, date of birth, psychological and social adjustment, personality, schooling and academic performance, hobbies, and nature of relationship with each parent
- Child's feeling of how he is disciplined and how he feels about the family's rules.
- Sibling relationship, both strengths and weaknesses
- Attitude toward the adoption of a sibling(s) — include issues relating to birth order and role changes (China requires a documented statement from children 10 and over, regarding their views on their parents' adoption of a child from China)
- Social worker's perception and observations of the child's/children's interactions with parents.

Others in the Home (Include grandparents, exchange students, part and full-time help.)
- Name, age, relation, duration of stay in the home, physical and financial dependency
- Reasons for a single applicant sharing the home with a non-family member
- Interaction with family members
- Attitude toward the adoption
- Indicate whether or not other adults reside in the home. (China requires an affidavit from single applicants who cohabitate with a person of the same sex that neither of them is homosexual. The social worker must make a reasonable, true and responsible assessment.)

Extended Family
- Interaction and relationship with family members, neighbors, church, and community
- Extended family's attitude toward the adoption plan and any opposition

Attitude Toward Discipline and Child-Rearing
- Philosophy
- Understanding child development stages
- Family rules in regards to expectations, responsibilities, division of labor, and privacy
- Methods of disciplining children, including those already in the home
- Discuss LNI Discipline Policy and obtain signatures
- Child care experience if they have no children
- Ability to assess and identify a child's needs to promote self-esteem
- Expectations of their adoptive child
- Capability to prepare an older child to live independently
- Willingness to obtain professional advice

Birth Family Connections
- Understanding the dynamics of child abuse and neglect and how these issues will affect the child/children as well as themselves. Sensitivity and responsiveness to children who may have been subjected to abuse and neglect
- Understanding the dynamics of separation, significant losses, and placement, and the ability to manage a child's behavior associated with separation and loss.
- Ability to help their child/children grieve (Have their own losses equipped them to help?)
- Ability to communicate and help their child with being adopted
- Sensitivity and feelings about the child's birth family and understanding the reasons why the birth mother made an adoption plan
- Acceptance of the adoptive child's feelings about their birth family and their abilities to help the child deal with these feelings

- Capability to help build continuity in the child's life, such as keeping a

memory/life book
- Ability to support a child's search for birth family

Transnational, Interracial, Cross-Cultural Parenting Issues
- Understanding the beliefs, behavior, customs, diet, language, and other practices of the culture from which they wish to adopt a child
- Sensitivity regarding changing the child's name
- Plans for learning about the child's cultural background and cross-cultural parenting
- Strategies for maintaining the child's heritage and identity and incorporating it into their lifestyle. Plan regarding the child's name.
- Commitment to provide the child with positive racial and cultural experiences and information
- Tolerance and ability to deal appropriately with personal questions, ambiguity, or disapproval from others
- Acknowledgment that their foreign-born child may choose friends of every race and nationality and could marry someone from a completely different cultural group and that adopting interracially will make their family interracial forever, impacting all family members

Adopting Siblings or a Child/Children Older than Two
- Level of adoptive applicant's understanding of the increased emotional and social adjustment, language and cultural differences, manifestations of separation trauma, trauma of past experiences, effects of institution-alized care
- Understanding and preparation of the increased responsibility and energy required for more than one child, behavioral problems or medical problems that might occur.
- Ability to manage an older child's behavior, such as aggression, sexual acting out, abusive language, etc.

Child Care Plan
- Immediate plans for an adjustment period following the arrival of a child, taking advantage of the Family Leave Act if both parents are employed, and long range plans

Employment, Education, and Economic Situation
- Current job, title, description, future prospects, job satisfaction, work schedule, salary (state the word "verified" by job letter) and bonuses
- Education
- Other sources of income, including the type and amount of savings, checking, and investments
- Verify policies and insurance coverage (health and life) of all household members including children to be placed
- Stocks and bonds — value
- Outstanding debts — amount and monthly payments, balance between assets and debts.

- Home value, mortgage balance, and monthly payment. Evidence used to verify source and amount of income and financial resources, i.e.1040s, job letter, etc.

The social worker must verify in a statement that the applicants have sufficient money management ability to provide for a child until that child reaches adulthood.

Interests, Hobbies, and Use of Leisure Time
- A statement regarding their philosophy toward society
- Activities they enjoy together and separately
- Social contacts — significant friends of other nationalities, races, religions

Religion
- Formal membership, extent of practice of faith, role of religion in the life of each family member, religious training of current children, plans for religious membership and training of adopted child

Physical and Mental Health
- Significant history of disease, handicaps, illnesses, and general level of current health, prognosis, and life expectancy (cite medical report)
- Method of dealing with health limitations and effect on other family members
- Counseling (A copy of an evaluation or report addressing what transpired, results of treatment, and any restrictions must be attached for our file.)
- Hospitalizations
- Current medications

Quote for each applicant if accurate: *"Name_____is in good health and appears to be able to raise the child to adulthood."*
- A statement must be made regarding each applicant's personality, maturity level, ability to handle stress, logical thinking, and overall judgment

Quote if accurate: *"There is no evidence of psychopathology."*

(For China, the health status of the applicant(s) must be identical with the certificate of General Physical Examination for Adoptive Parent.)

Home Environment and Community
- Description of home — adequacy of space both inside and out (bedrooms must have at least 80' of floor space)
- Discussion of yard area, landscaping, and fencing (if any)
- Rate the housekeeping standards
- Community resources including medical facilities, educational institutions, public services utilities and racial make-up of neighborhood and ethnic attitudes for accepting children from another culture

- Discuss basic care and safety issues with applicant — all medications and poisonous liquids must be kept out of the reach of children or locked in a storage area
- Address any trampoline safety issues, if appropriate
- Discuss firearm safety issues. State whether firearms are or are not present. If they are, be certain that all necessary precautions are taken. LNI requires firearms and ammunition must be kept separate from each other and in locked compartments at all times.
- Discuss water hazards near the property including how to protect the child. LNI requires family swimming pools to have a pool alarm or a lockable fence around the perimeter of the pool.
- Record the number and placement of smoke and fire alarms. All homes must be equipped with at least one working fire extinguisher.
- Inspect the home and property using the LNI Environmental Checklist
- If the home and property pass your inspection, write a statement that the above precautions are taking place and that the physical environment inside and outside the home are safe and appropriate for the care of the child
- If the parents plan to move or if they live abroad but plan to raise the child in the United States, include a description of the house where they will reside, if this is known

Police and Child Abuse Clearances (Must be completed for all household members age 18 and over, including children away at school.)
- Ask each applicant if they have ever been arrested and state their answer
- Write that the letter of clearance from the state or local police verifies that, "(Name) has no criminal record"
- Ask each applicant whether they have ever been accused or charged with child abuse or neglect and state their answer
- Document that the Child Abuse Registry has been checked and state "(Name) does not have a criminal record of child abuse"
- Document if your state does not provide child abuse clearances for prospective adoptive parents registered with private, licensed, nonprofit adoption agencies
- Explain the circumstances of any offenses, the trial and outcome, and the attitude of the offender toward incident
- Ask if there is any history of substance abuse, sexual or child abuse, or domestic violence, even if it did not result in an arrest or conviction and include their response

    Adults must disclose any record of arrest no matter what the disposition, no matter how minor, no matter how long ago, and no matter if they were told that it was expunged. (Failure to do so may result in a denial of the application.) If an applicant does have a record of arrest, ask the applicant if the record of their arrest can be expunged. They may need to consult an attorney for this. If the offense cannot be expunged, LNI may not be able to approve them for adoption.

INS now requires a signed statement submitted from each prospective adoptive parent and household member regarding details, including mitigating circumstances about each incident when there is a criminal history or history of abuse and/or violence. It should be attached to the home study that is submitted to INS.

Will and Guardianship Plan (In event of untimely death of adoptive parents)
- Names, addresses, relationship to adoptive parents, and their commitment to the child (For China, the following information must be documented for the appointed guardian: age, profession, marital status, status of children, health, financial situation, and living situation with a description of the home. The social worker must make an assessment and statement of the suitability of the guardian. The designated guardian for a single applicant must present a statement in writing giving consent to the guardianship of the adopted child.)

References
- State the number of references received and summarize briefly, using direct quotes regarding the applicant's qualities as relating to adoptive parenting
- References from attending physicians — relatives or therapists cannot be accepted

Working with the Agency
- Describe applicant(s)' ability to accept and act on suggestions.
- Describe applicant(s)' participation in training and willingness of continued training
- Discuss applicant(s)' willingness to participate in the required postplacement supervision

Conclusion
- Fitness of couple or single for adoption in general; summarize their strengths
- Adequacy of couple or single for foreign adoption
- Capabilities of couple or single to raise the child/children they requested

  Discuss whether the applicant can accept and can cope with a child whose birth parents' history may show physical or mental illness, alcohol and/or drug abuse/use, a criminal history, or that they may have been accused of neglect or physically and/or sexually abusing the child. (For China, state the strength and mental preparedness of the prospective parent who expresses interest in a child with special needs and /or handicaps, or the emotional and behavioral problems of children two years and older.

  Explain the problems of an abandoned child with no background information
- State what the couple or single can or cannot accept

Approval and Recommendation
- A recommendation of the couple or single for the adoption of child/children. The statement must include age, gender, number of siblings, race, and state of health. The recommendation on this page must match the description in the "Child Desired" section. If the child desired is handicapped or has special needs, a recommendation must include the prospective parent's willingness and ability to provide proper care for such a child. (China requires "China" to be stated in this section.)

Quote if accurate: *"I certify that the family (name) has met all of the preadoption requirements of their state."*

Quote if accurate: *"(Name of agency or social worker's name) agrees to provide postplacement supervision according to the requirements of LNI, the state, and the foreign country, including any required follow-up reports to the child's agency, orphanage, or other source. If necessary, I/we will refer family to outside sources of support and assistance for the well-being of the entire family unit and in particular the adopted child/children."*

Written and Submitted By:

_____

(Include credentials)

Signature of Director:

_____

Notary, (See sample Jurat)
Subscribed and sworn to before me on this_____(day) of_____
(month), _____ (year)
To which witness my hand and seal of office.

Notary Public in and for the State
of_____
County of_____
My Commission Expires_____

Attachments to the Home Study
- Discipline policy
- Environmental checklist
- Service plans (one for child and one for prospective parents)
- Copy of client's child abuse clearance
- Agreement with international adoption requirements
- Copy of license or certification of social worker or copy of license of supervisor of social worker
- Copy of the agency license
- Networking agreement — required by China and Russia

After the Home Study

A social worker with a master's degree (LMSW) reviews and approves the home study. If the adoptive parents work with a separate U.S.-based international adoption agency, the LMSW in that agency will also review the study in view of an appropriate child placement.

Immediately upon the approval of your home study by the supervisor of social work, copies of the home study, supporting documents, and Form I-600A should be filed at INS. Do not forward these documents to the INS until you have formally applied to a U.S.-based international agency. Chapter 6 explains the process for filing Form I-600A.

Updating the Home Study

A home study is valid for six to 18 months depending on state law. A home study update must be written if the home study has expired, or if you have moved or experienced some other major life change. If you move out of state, you must register with an agency in your new state of residence to update your study according to their state requirements. INS fingerprint charts and petitions must also be updated and/or transferred to your new local INS office.

Each home study topic must be covered in the update. If a topic remains the same, "No changes" may be written below the topic heading. Dates on preceding documents 5 through 11 expire according to your state's minimum standards—somewhere between 12 and 18 months. These items must be updated during the time the home study update is in progress.

Handicapping Conditions of Waiting Children

Indicate your level of acceptance of a child who has the following problems:

		Indicate		
NEWBORNS		YES	NO	MAYBE
A.	Low Apgar score, prognosis uncertain	☐	☐	☐
B.	Birth mother on drugs or alcohol, prognosis uncertain	☐	☐	☐

CHILDREN

1. A.	Slight limp	☐	☐	☐
B.	Leg braces	☐	☐	☐
C.	Missing limb	☐	☐	☐
D.	Is in a wheel chair	☐	☐	☐
E.	Is paraplegic	☐	☐	☐
F.	Is quadriplegic	☐	☐	☐
G.	Cerebral Palsy	☐	☐	☐
H.	Cystic Fibrosis	☐	☐	☐
2. A.	Seizure disorder that is controlled by medication	☐	☐	☐
B.	Seizure disorder not controlled but child has infrequent seizures	☐	☐	☐
C.	Seizure disorder not controlled and has frequent seizures	☐	☐	☐
3. A.	A blood disorder that requires blood transfusions every 3 months	☐	☐	☐
B.	Blood disorder that requires hospitalization once a month	☐	☐	☐
C.	Blood disorder resulting in a limited lifespan	☐	☐	☐
4. A.	Heart murmur, activity not curtailed	☐	☐	☐
B.	Heart murmur, vigorous activity curtailed	☐	☐	☐
C.	May require open heart surgery at a later date but at placement needs only to be watched	☐	☐	☐
D.	Definitely will require open heart surgery	☐	☐	☐
E.	Will require more than one open heart surgery	☐	☐	☐
5. A.	Sight in both eyes but vision is limited and special glasses needed	☐	☐	☐
B.	Sight in one eye only	☐	☐	☐
C.	Blind but surgery may give partial sight	☐	☐	☐
D.	Blind and will never have sight	☐	☐	☐
6. A.	Hearing problem with only partial hearing and surgery may help	☐	☐	☐
B.	Hearing problem with partial hearing but surgery will not help	☐	☐	☐
C.	Hearing in only one ear	☐	☐	☐
D.	No hearing, deaf and does not speak	☐	☐	☐
7. A.	Deformed hand	☐	☐	☐
B.	Deformed arm	☐	☐	☐
C.	Deformed leg	☐	☐	☐
D.	Deformed face	☐	☐	☐
E.	Two deformed arms	☐	☐	☐
F.	Two deformed legs	☐	☐	☐

Handicapping Conditions of Waiting Children

			YES	NO	MAYBE
8.	A.	In special education	☐	☐	☐
	B.	In EMR	☐	☐	☐
	C.	In TMR	☐	☐	☐
	D.	Retarded and will always need supervision, such as sheltered home	☐	☐	☐
	E.	Downs syndrome	☐	☐	☐
9.	A.	Hyperactive	☐	☐	☐
	B.	Hyperactive, requires medication but functions relatively normal	☐	☐	☐
	C.	Hyperactive, requires medication and some kind of special classroom setting	☐	☐	☐
10.	A.	Emotionally damaged, very withdrawn and will require therapy for an extensive period of time	☐	☐	☐
	B.	So emotionally damaged he/she is very abusive toward other people; a child who is abusive to animals	☐	☐	☐
	C.	Emotionally damaged; he/she is very abusive toward his/her person, such as pulling out hair, pinching himself/herself	☐	☐	☐
11.	A.	Stutters	☐	☐	☐
	B.	Lisp	☐	☐	☐
	C.	Speech at age 6 is very hard to understand	☐	☐	☐
	D.	Will always have trouble speaking and being understood	☐	☐	☐
12.	A.	Hare lip	☐	☐	☐
	B.	Cleft palate	☐	☐	☐
	C.	Both hare lip and cleft palate	☐	☐	☐
13.	A.	Had one parent who is schizophrenic	☐	☐	☐
	B.	Had two parents who are schizophrenic	☐	☐	☐
	C.	Schizophrenic, but medication helps	☐	☐	☐
14.	A.	Sickle Cell carrier	☐	☐	☐
	B.	Sickle Cell Anemia but relatively controlled	☐	☐	☐
	C.	Sickle Cell Anemia with frequent episodes	☐	☐	☐
15.	A.	Burn scars	☐	☐	☐
	B.	Slight	☐	☐	☐
	C.	Extensive, needing surgery	☐	☐	☐
16.	A.	Birth marks	☐	☐	☐
	B.	Small	☐	☐	☐
	C.	Large or extensive	☐	☐	☐

Statement of Net Worth

NAME(S): _____

ADDRESS: _____

_____

Home Telephone Number: (   )   —

ASSETS

Cash on hand & in banks $ _____

Investments   _____

Savings accounts   _____

Cash surrender value
   of life insurance   _____

Other Stocks & Bonds   _____

Real Estate: _____

1. _____   _____

2. _____   _____

Automobile   _____

Trucks, boats, planes   _____

Personal property   _____

TOTAL ASSETS $ _____

LIABILITIES & NET WORTH

Mortgages & real estate notes $ _____

Notes payable   _____

Credit card (balances):   _____

_____   _____

_____   _____

_____   _____

Loans (balances): _____   _____

_____   _____

_____   _____

_____   _____

_____   _____

TOTAL LIABILITIES $ _____

NET WORTH* $ _____

(*Net Worth is the difference between Assets & Liabilities)

Date _____   Signature _____

Date _____   Signature _____

SUBSCRIBED AND SWORN to before me on the _____

day of 20___. To which witness my hand and seal of office. _____

Notary Public in and for the State of _____ , county of _____

My commission expires:. _____ .

Medical Statement

Medical Statement for Adoptive Applicant
and all Household Members
Page 1 of 2

Name (Last, First, Middle):	Date of Birth:
Address (Street, City, State & Zip):	

1. Have you had treatment for a serious or chronic illness?   ❑ Yes   ❑ No
   Have you been hospitalized in the past five years?   ❑ Yes   ❑ No
   Have you ever received, or been advised to seek, mental health services?   ❑ Yes   ❑ No
   Have you ever received, or been advised to seek, treatment for alcohol/substance abuse?   ❑ Yes   ❑ No
   Have you ever had a communicable disease?   ❑ Yes   ❑ No

   If the answer to any of these questions is yes, please explain:
   _____
   _____
   _____

2. Do you have or have you had any of the following? (Check all that apply.)

   ❑ Arthritis _____   ❑ Heart Disease _____
   ❑ Asthma _____   ❑ Hypertension _____
   ❑ Cancer _____   ❑ Kidney Disease _____
   ❑ Epilepsy _____   ❑ Tuberculosis _____
   ❑ Diabetes _____   ❑ Ulcers _____

   If any are checked, please explain: _____

3. Is there a history of other hereditary disease?   ❑ Yes   ❑ No
   If yes, please explain: _____
   _____

AUTHORIZATION FOR RELEASE OF INFORMATION

I hereby affirm that I have completed this form to the best of my ability, and that the information provided is true and correct. I further authorize the physician completing the reverse side of this form to release any information he/she may have concerning my physical or mental health to:

Name/Address of Agency: _____

Signature of Applicant:	Date:

COMPLETION OF THIS FORM IS REQUIRED FOR THE AGENCY TO PROCEED WITH YOUR APPLICATION.

Subscribed and sworn to before me on the _____ day of _____, 20___ to which witness my hand and seal of office.

Notary Public in and for the State of _____, County of _____.

My Commission Expires: _____

Medical Statement

Medical Statement for Adoptive Applicant
and all Household Members

(This side of form to be completed by a licensed physician.)

Date you last completed a physical examination of this individual:				Date you last treated this individual:	
Do you provide medical services to this individual:	❑ Regularly		❑ Occasionally		❑ First Time

Please respond to each of the following to the best of your knowledge:

1. Does this individual suffer from an illness, including a communicable disease, that would be detrimental to the care of a adoptive child placed in his/her home? ❑ Yes ❑ No

2. Are there any chronic or serious disorders for which this individual has received treatment? ❑ Yes ❑ No

3. Is this individual currently taking medication? ❑ Yes ❑ No

4. Is this individual experiencing any physical, behavioral or emotional problems that would be detrimental to an adoptive child placed in his/her home? ❑ Yes ❑ No

5. Have you ever referred this individual to other medical services , mental health services or treatment for alcohol/substance abuse? ❑ Yes ❑ No

   If the answer to any of the above questions is YES, please explain: _____

   _____

   _____

6. In your opinion, does the individual have the normal life expectancy?_____

7. Physical Examination:

Weight:		Blood Pressure:		Pulse:	
Height:		Temperature:		Lungs:	
Heart:		Abdomen:		Nervous System:	

8. Laboratory Tests:

HIV:		Urinalysis:	
Hep B:		Tine or Mantoux:	
Hep C:		CBC:	

9. Any recommendations for medical care? _____

Please state your professional opinion regarding this individual's suitability as an adoptive parent from the standpoint of health, considering the individual's medical history as given on the reverse side of this form and from knowledge you have of the individual. _____

_____

_____

Physician's Signature:	Date:	Name of Physician (Print or Type):
Physician's Work Address:	Physician's Work Phone Number: ( ) -	Physician's State License Number:

Letter of Reference

Try to obtain letters of reference from people in your locality. Then the same notary public, Secretary of State (verification), and foreign consul (authentication) can be used to stamp and sign all or at least most of your documents.

Photocopy three copies of this form for the persons you have selected to write your letters. Ask them to give you the letter for your formal adoption dossier.

TO: _____

FROM: _____

DATE: _____

RE: Letter of Reference: A letter must be typed and signed before a notary.

We have applied to _____ (agency) for assistance with our adoption plans. We hope that you will be able to write a letter of reference for us, and return it to us by _____ (date). Following are seven categories which the agency wishes you to consider and to include in a letter of reference.

1 How long have you known us and in what capacity?

2 Have you observed us around children? Under what circumstances?

3 Do you believe we can easily handle the problems that could arise when an adopted and/ or foreign child enters our home?

4 Have we discussed our adoption plans with you? How do you feel about our plans?

5 How do you think an adopted and/or foreign child will be accepted in our community?

6 Do you believe we manage our money responsibly?

7 How would you rate our homemaking and property upkeep?
   We will appreciate any additional comments and/or information you would like to include.

Sample Photos for Home Study

Environmental Health Checklist

		YES	NO	N/A
1.	Home is clean and maintained in good repair	☐	☐	☐
2.	Furnishings and equipment used by an ill child are cleaned with soap and water	☐	☐	☐
3.	Sheets and pillowcases are washed before use by another child	☐	☐	☐
4.	Yard is free of hazards to children	☐	☐	☐
5.	Rooms are adequately ventilated and without objectionable odors	☐	☐	☐
6.	Windows and doors used for ventilation are screened	☐	☐	☐
7.	Plumbing appears in good repair. Home is free of water stains or other indications of water leaks	☐	☐	☐
8.	Home has hot and cold water available	☐	☐	☐
9.	Glasses are used by only one child between washings	☐	☐	☐
10.	Outside area is free of indication of sewage overflow or related problems	☐	☐	☐
11.	Home uses a public water supply. NOTE: Where a private well is used, the Texas Department of Health Resources or the local health department may be requested to provide assistance in regard to standards and sampling	☐	☐	☐
12.	Home uses a public sewage disposal system. NOTE: If problems are observed with private sewage disposal systems, assistance may be requested to provide assistance in regard to standards and sampling	☐	☐	☐
13.	Adequate number of garbage containers available	☐	☐	☐
14.	Garbage containers have tight fitting lids	☐	☐	☐
15.	Garbage containers designed for reuse are kept clean	☐	☐	☐
16.	Garbage is collected from the premises at least once a week	☐	☐	☐
17.	Garbage is disposed of in a sanitary manner if collection is not available	☐	☐	☐
18.	Yard is well drained and there is no standing water	☐	☐	☐
19.	Premises are free of garbage and rubbish	☐	☐	☐
20.	Steps have been taken to keep the premises free of insects (flies, mosquitoes, cockroaches) and rodents.	☐	☐	☐
21.	Label instructions on rat and pest poisons are followed	☐	☐	☐
22.	Pesticides and other poisons are kept in areas not accessible to children	☐	☐	☐
23.	Food is prepared, stored, refrigerated, and served under safe and sanitary conditions	☐	☐	☐
24.	Food is obtained from approved sources in labeled containers	☐	☐	☐
25.	Eating and cooking utensils are properly washed	☐	☐	☐
26.	Food preparation area is cleaned after each use	☐	☐	☐
27.	Eating and cooking utensils are stored on clean surfaces	☐	☐	☐
28.	Medication is stored separately from food	☐	☐	☐
29.	Animals are vaccinated for rabies and other diseases as recommended	☐	☐	☐
30.	Bathrooms are located inside home	☐	☐	☐
31.	A minimum of one toilet, lavatory, bathtub, or shower is available	☐	☐	☐
32.	Each child is provided with own clean towel or single use towels are available	☐	☐	☐
33.	Adequate soap and toilet paper are available	☐	☐	☐
34.	Bathroom floors, walls cabinets and work surfaces are clean and easily cleanable	☐	☐	☐
35.	Plumbing facilities are in good working condition	☐	☐	☐

Comments:

_____   _____   _____
Signature   Title   Date

Fire Prevention Checklist

FIRE PREVENTION CHECKLIST

Facility Name	Facility Address	Telephone No.

		Yes	No	N/A
1.	There are at least two unblocked exits to the outside from the home (can include windows)............................	☐	☐	☐
2.	Electrical wiring system appears in good repair..	☐	☐	☐
3.	Electrical outlets in rooms used by children have child-proof covers or are safety outlets................................	☐	☐	☐
4.	Fuses or circuit breakers in fuse box appear in good operating condition.................................	☐	☐	☐
5.	Cords for electrical appliances and lighting fixtures appear in good operating condition..................................	☐	☐	☐
6.	Extension cords are used properly. (Not run under rugs, not hooked over nails, not overloaded.) (Check N/A if extension cords are not in use.)...	☐	☐	☐
7.	Space heaters are enclosed to prevent children from burning themselves................................	☐	☐	☐
8.	Space heaters are vented to the outside. (Check NA if space heaters are not designed to vent to the outside)........	☐	☐	☐
9.	Gas appliances (heaters, water heaters, stoves) have metal tubing and metal connections...........................	☐	☐	☐
10.	Central heating system is periodically inspected by a qualified inspector................................	☐	☐	☐
11.	Woodburning or gas log fireplaces are protected with a spark screen or guard...............................	☐	☐	☐
12.	Combustibles are stored or placed well away from any stove, heater, or fireplace in the home......................	☐	☐	☐
13.	All lighters and matches are kept away from heat and children.................................	☐	☐	☐
14.	Flammable liquids are stored in safety cans and kept away from heat and children....................................	☐	☐	☐
15.	Paint is kept in tightly closed metal containers...................................	☐	☐	☐
16.	The premises are free of rubbish, especially the attic, garage, and basement...............................	☐	☐	☐
17.	Trash is burned in an area away from the children................................	☐	☐	☐
18.	There is an operable #5 pound dry chemical fire extinguisher available for use in the kitchen.......................	☐	☐	☐
19.	Fire extinguisher is serviced after each use and checked for proper weight at least once a year.......................	☐	☐	☐
20.	Family has an evacuation plan for emergencies..................................	☐	☐	☐
21.	Fire drills are practiced regularly.....................................	☐	☐	☐
22.	There is a method available to alert family to a fire (alarm, bell, etc.)................................	☐	☐	☐

COMMENTS:

_____   _____   _____

Signature   Title   Date

LNI FORM B-1

CHAPTER 6
Preliminary INS Approval

Although adoption or readoption procedures are defined by the laws of the county of the state in which you reside, the federal government has an interest in ensuring that your child is entering the United States legally. You will be dealing with two different departments of the U.S. government: the Department of Justice, Immigration and Naturalization Service (INS), which processes orphan visa petitions and applications for citizenship, and the Department of State (U.S. Consular Service office abroad), which issues the orphan's U.S. visa. Keep in mind that the INS is in a constant state of overhaul, especially since the events of September 11, 2001. At the time this edition was written, Congress was in the processing of determining how to split INS into two separate departments, which could affect adoption immigration procedures. Before you proceed with your adoption plan, review the INS website (**www.ins.usdoj.gov**) regarding adoption-related forms, procedures and fees.

Once you are sure you are going to adopt internationally, you should begin advance placement for INS by filing Form I-600A (Application for Advance Processing of Orphan Petition) and supporting documents. With advance filing, the INS processes paperwork on the adoptive parents first, so that later it is only necessary to process the child's paperwork. This helps to keep the approval procedures moving as fast as possible.

A United States citizen who plans to adopt a foreign orphan but does not yet have a specific child in mind can have the immigration paperwork done much faster by advance processing. Even though you may not yet know what child you will adopt or even what country you will adopt from, advance filing will help expedite INS clearance when you are ready to bring your child home. Advance processing can also be applied in the following case: the child is known, the prospective adoptive parents are traveling to a country where there is no INS office, and the petitioners wish to file an orphan petition at a U.S. consulate or embassy in the country where the child resides.

Note: Under the Child Citizenship Act of 2000, which became effective on February 27, 2001, U.S. Citizenship is automatic for children who are adopted abroad and arrive in the United States with an IR-3 visa (indicating that a final adoption decree was issued by the child-placing country). Children who have immigrated to the United States in order to be adopted once here (arriving under an IR-4 visa), automatically become citizens as soon as the adoption is final. (See Chapter 12 for an explanation of IR-3 and IR-4 visas.) If you try to have your child enter the United States under a nonimmigrant student or visitor visa, changing his or her status once you are home from a nonimmigrant or visitor to a U.S. citizen can be difficult, time-consuming, and expensive.

This chapter will cover advance filing of Form I-600A. More detailed information on working with the INS and finalizing the immigration of your adoptive child will be covered in Chapters 9 and 12. Unfortunately, the INS does not have a standard procedure for filing Form I-600A; each INS office has its own procedure. For example, Texas has four district INS offices and each has its own procedure. On the other hand, some states don't have a district INS office at all and residents must file at a designated office in another state.

The following section, however, details the general instructions common to many of the offices. For more specific instructions, contact your district INS office. To find the INS District Office for your area, consult the phone book or visit **www.ins.usdoj.gov** and click on Field Office Addresses and Information from the menu on the left. Then click on List of U.S. Field Offices.

Preparing the Necessary Documentation for Filing

U.S. Immigration and Naturalization Service (INS) forms may be ordered ahead of time by calling your INS District Office or the INS Forms Request Line at 1(800) 870-3676 .

You will need to request the packet of forms to immigrate an orphan as an immediate relative. This package should include Form I-600A (Application for Advance Processing of Orphan Petition); Form I-600 (Petition to Classify Orphan as an Immediate Relative); Form I-864 (Affidavit of Support); and Form I-864A (Contract Between Sponsor and Household Member). The last two forms are not required if both prospective parents (in case of couples) or a single potential parent visit the child prior to the adoption abroad. The I-864 and I-864A are only required in IR-4 cases. (See Chapter 12 for definitions of IR-3 and IR-4.)

You may also want to request at the same time Form DOJ-361 (Certification of Identity). INS requires this form or a written authorization by the prospective adoptive parents and household members allowing INS to release information about your application to the placement agency. Without one of these endorsements, INS district offices will not discuss your case with your adoption agency. Most INS offices do not answer calls from individuals. If you have not received clearance within 90 days, your agency can call INS for you.[1]

You can also download these forms from the Internet by visiting the INS home page at **www.ins.usdoj.gov** and then clicking on INS Forms and Fees from the menu

Step 7
Prepare documentation required for Form I-600A (Application for Advance Processing).

---

[1] If you are adopting independently and have not received clearance in 90 days, send a follow up letter. INS starts a file on your case that it will maintain from the time you file the I-600A to the receipt of your child's foreign adoption documents from a U.S. port of entry.

on the left. The INS actually recommends downloading all forms from its site to ensure that you are using the most up-to-date form available. You can also use this site to verify the fee associated with each form. Keep in mind that the INS makes changes with little advance warning. Fees printed on their forms can be outdated. If you send the wrong fee or form, it may take weeks for INS to return it to you with a form letter telling you how to start over. Keep Form I-600 in your files. You will need it after a child has been assigned to you. (Filing Form I-600 is covered in Chapter 9.)

Required Documents

To begin advance processing, only two items and a cover letter are needed: Form I-600A and the filing fee. However, it is recommended that you also attach Form DOJ-361 (Certification of Identity) or written authorization for the release of information to your adoption agency. The rest of the items listed below can be filed when the home study is completed.

INS does not require notarization of documents.

1. Form I-600A (Application for Advance Processing of Orphan Petition). Both spouses must sign the form. (See sample form at the end of this chapter.)

2. Home study, which covers criteria set forth in Form I-600A. (If your home study is not yet complete, include a statement in your cover letter noting that you will forward the completed home study as soon as final approval is obtained.)

3. Birth certificate, or other proof of birth and citizenship (such as a baptismal certificate), or an original naturalization certificate, or an up-to-date U.S. passport. You need one birth certificate for each applicant, as well as for any other adult or child residing in the home.

4. If applicable, Form I-864 (Affidavit of Support) and Form I-864A (Contract Between Sponsor and Household Member). Copies of your federal tax returns for the past three years must accompany the affidavit. These forms will be filed abroad unless parents are not traveling to complete the adoption, in which case they will be filed in the United States. (Samples of forms I-864 and I-864A can be found at the end of the chapter.)

* The I-864 and I-864A are only required in IR-4 cases (see Chapter 12), in which the adoption is not finalized before the child enters the United States.

5. Marriage certificate, if applicable.

6. Divorce decree and death certificates of former spouses, if applicable.

7. Evidence that your state's preadoption requirements have been met, such as a statement to that effect in the home study, or a Consent and Approval form, if required by your state. (See sample Consent and Approval form at the end of this chapter.) U.S. Consular service offices abroad are usually not aware of the adoption laws in each of the 50 U.S. states. They may require proof that you have met the preadoption requirements of your state and that your home study is valid there. (See first page of home study guide.) Information on how to establish that these requirements have been met may be obtained from public and private adoption agencies.

8. A copy of the license of your local adoption agency (required by some INS offices).

9. A copy of the license or certification of your social worker (required by some INS offices).

Filing Form I-600A

As soon as you initiate your home study, you should file the completed Form I-600A. If you don't know all the details about the proposed adoption, write "unknown at this time" in the appropriate blank. Include a cover letter with your name, daytime telephone number, and address. Most INS offices will let you file Form I-600A and the fee before the home study is approved, in order to save time. The rest of the documents may be forwarded when the home study is complete with another cover letter that indicates your country of choice.

Send the signed, original Form I-600A, plus two copies, and a money order for $460.00 by certified mail or Federal Express. Be sure to request a return receipt. Cash and personal checks are not always accepted. Also remember to include a copy of Form DOJ-361 (Certification of Identity) or written authorization for the release of information to your adoption agency.

Some INS offices will let you send copies of the home study and other required documents. Others will accept copies after they see the originals. Do not leave the original home study with the INS unless you have more than one. You will need the original home study for your dossier (a set of documents you will prepare for the court abroad.)

Be certain to photocopy one full set of documents, including Form I-600A, to hand-carry abroad. In the event that your child is ready to immigrate before the U.S. Consulate receives your file of the above documents sent by diplomatic pouch, you may be able to obtain the visa with your set of copies, in addition to a copy of Form I-171H (Notice of Favorable Determination), which is described later in the chapter.

Instead of sending your file by diplomatic pouch, INS may expedite the process and send "Visa Cable 37" instead. This message indicates that your INS office has issued approval of your Form I-600A and supporting documentation and it also shows that you have met your state's pre-approval requirements (the home study). In emergency situations, INS may fax the information contained in "Visa Cable 37."

Step 8
File Form I-600A
(Application for
Advance Processing).

Fingerprinting

In order to be cleared by the INS, every household member over age 18 and under age 75 must be fingerprinted. At the same time that you submit Form I-600A and the $460.00 money order for the filing fee, submit another separate money order to cover the fees for fingerprinting ($50.00 for each individual to be fingerprinted). If you are mailing Form I-600A, indicate in your cover letter the number of family members who need to be fingerprinted.

The INS has designated Application Support Centers to handle the fingerprint forms for adoption cases. After INS receives your application, the INS will send you an appointment letter with the time and address of your fingerprinting appointment at the nearest Application Support Center. Please read the instructions in the appointment letter and bring it with you when you go to your fingerprinting appointment.

Approval of Form I-600A

INS must decide from the facts listed in the home study whether the prospective adoptive parent is able to take care of one or more orphans properly, depending on the number of children being adopted. Form I-171H (Notice of Favorable Determination Concerning Application for Advance Processing of Orphan Petition) is sent to you if you appear to qualify for further processing.

This notice will also state the date of the determination and the location of the filing of the petition (A sample of Form I-171H is included at the end of this chapter.)

You must send a copy of Form I-171H to your U.S.-based international agency immediately upon receipt. The agency cannot refer an orphan to you without it.

INS does not permit convicted felons to adopt. A misdemeanor that appears on your records must be discussed with the adoption agency if you failed to mention it on your application. Depending upon the nature of the misdemeanor, the agency may request documentation from you and proceed, or they may close your case.

A Notice of Favorable Determination does not guarantee that the orphan petition (Form I-600) will be approved. An orphan petition may still be denied because the child does not qualify as an orphan or for other proper cause.

Filing to approval of Form I-600A takes about 30-60 days and sometimes even longer. INS is required by law to respond to a petition within 120 days. Since they occasionally lose forms and documents, this cushion gives them time to find the items.

Unfavorable Determination

When there is unfavorable information about the prospective adoptive parent(s) and INS concludes that proper care could not be given to a child or children in that case, INS makes an unfavorable determination. You are advised of the reasons for the unfavorable determination and of the right to appeal the decision.

Updating Form I-600A

Form I-600A is valid for 18 months. If an orphan has not immigrated before then, a new application, updated home study and documents, and new fingerprint charts must be filed again, and another $460.00 fee must be paid, as well as an additional $50.00 for each member of the family to be fingerprinted.

Obtaining Your Passport

Step 9
Apply for a passport.

Once your dossier is complete and your child is assigned, you will need to be ready to go abroad on short notice. Check to see that your passport is up to date. (Passports for adults are valid for 10 years; passports for children age 15 and under are valid for 5 years.) Otherwise, you will need to update your passport or apply for a new passport if you do not have one. You should apply for a passport early in the adoption process. It can take three to four weeks to receive your passport in the mail and you will need your passport to apply for a visa or tourist card. This alone can take a number of weeks, depending on the country. In addition, in some countries, a photocopy of your passport is required for the dossier of documents.

Passport numbers are often demanded in foreign courts as another means of identification; each spouse should apply for a passport, even if only one plans to travel.

The passport application form can be picked up at your local post office or other municipal buildings. They can also be downloaded from the State Department web site at **http://travel.state.gov/passport_services.html**. To acquire a passport, you will need this form, two 2" X 2" color photos, and a certified copy of your birth certificate. You can get one-day service on passport photos at many places, such as business centers, photocopy stores, and the American Automobile Association (AAA).

One-day service for passports can also be found in most major cities. You will need to present proof that you have a ticket or a travel itinerary. Call ahead for information about this service and office hours. If you have never had a U.S. passport, you must apply in person at a passport office. To find the passport office nearest you consult your phone book or go on-line to **http://travel.state.gov/passport.services.html** Proof of U.S. citizenship is required, such as a U.S. birth certificate or a certificate of naturalization or citizenship.

Consent and Approval

This letter verifies that prospective adoptive parent(s)_____

of this address: _____

has/have met the preadoption requirements of their state of residence.

A home study, conducted by a certified social worker, which meets the standards of their state of residence, has been completed and approved. Supporting documents provided by the prospective adoptive parents validate the data therein.

I hereby grant consent and approval of an adoptive placement for the aforementioned person(s).

_____   _____
Date   Supervisor of Adoptions (agency name)

SUBSCRIBED AND SWORN to before me on the _____ day of _____ , 20__, to which witness my hand and seal of office.

Form I-600A

Application for Advance Processing of Orphan Petition, Page 1 of 2

OMB No. 1115-0049

U.S. Department of Justice
Immigration and Naturalization Service

Application for Advance Processing of Orphan Petition [8CFR 204.1(b)(3)]

Please do not write in this block.

It has been determined that the

☐ Married   ☐ Unmarried

Fee Stamp

There

☐ are   ☐ are not
preadoptive requirements in the state of the child's
proposed residence.

The following is a description of the preadoption requirements, if
any, of the state of the child's proposed residence:

DATE OF FAVORABLE
DETERMINATION

DD

DISTRICT

The preadoption requirements, if any,
☐ have been met.   ☐ have not been met.

File number of petitioner, if applicable

Please type or print legibly in ink.

Application is made by the named prospective petitioner for advance processing of an orphan petition.

BLOCK I - Information about prospective petitioner	8. If you are now married, give the following information:
1. My name is: (Last) (First) (Middle)	Date and place of present marriage
2. Other names used (including maiden name if appropriate):	Name of present spouse (include maiden name of wife)
3. I reside in the U.S. at: (C/O if appropriate) (Apt. No.)	Date of birth of spouse Place of birth of spouse
(Number and street) (Town or city) (State) (ZIP Code)	Number of prior marriages of spouse
4. Address abroad (if any): (Number and street) (Apt. No.)	My spouse resides ☐ With me ☐ Apart from me (provide address below)
(Town or city) (Province) (Country)	(Apt. No.) (No. and street) (City) (State) (Country)
5. I was born on: (Month) (Day) (Year)	9. I am a citizen of the United States through:
In: (Town or City) (State or Province) (Country)	☐ Birth ☐ Parents ☐ Naturalization
6. My phone number is: (Include Area Code)	If acquired through naturalization, give name under which naturalized, number of naturalization certificate, and date and place of naturalization.
7. My marital status is: ☐ Married ☐ Widowed ☐ Divorced ☐ Single	If not, submit evidence of citizenship. See Instruction 2.a(2).
☐ I have never been married.	If acquired through parentage, have you obtained a certificate in your own name based on that acquisition? ☐ No ☐ Yes
☐ I have been previously married _____ time(s).	Have you or any person through whom you claimed citizenship ever lost United States citizenship? ☐ No ☐ Yes (If yes, attach detailed explanation.)

Continue on reverse.

Received	Trans. In	Ret'd Trans. Out	Completed

Form I-600A

Application for Advance Processing of Orphan Petition, Page 2 of 2

BLOCK II - General information

10. Name and address of organization or individual assisting you in locating or identifying an orphan

   (Name)

   (Address)

11. Do you plan to travel abroad to locate or adopt a child?
   ☐ Yes   ☐ No

12. Does your spouse, if any, plan to travel abroad to locate or adopt a child?
   ☐ Yes   ☐ No

13. If the answer to question 11 or 12 is "yes," give the following information:

   a. Your date of intended departure _____

   b. Your spouse's date of intended departure _____

   c. City, province _____

14. Will the child come to the United States for adoption after compliance with the preadoption requirements, if any, of the state of proposed residence?
   ☐ Yes   ☐ No

15. If the answer to question 14 is "no," will the child be adopted abroad after having been personally seen and observed by you and your spouse, if married?
   ☐ Yes   ☐ No

16. Where do you wish to file your orphan petition?

   The service office located at

   The American Embassy or Consulate at

17. Do you plan to adopt more than one child?
   ☐ Yes   ☐ No

   If "Yes", how many children do you plan to adopt?

Certification of prospective petitioner

I certify, under penalty of perjury under the laws of the United States of America, that the foregoing is true and correct and that I will care for an orphan/orphans properly if admitted to the United States.

(Signature of Prospective Petitioner)

Executed on (Date)

Certification of married prospective petitioner's spouse

I certify, under penalty of perjury under the laws of the United States of America, that the foregoing is true and correct and that my spouse and I will care for an orphan/orphans properly if admitted to the United States.

(Signature of Prospective Petitioner)

Executed on (Date)

Signature of person preparing form, if other than petitioner

I declare that this document was prepared by me at the request of the prospective petitioner and is based on all information of which I have any knowledge.

(Signature)

Address

Executed on (Date)

Form I-864

Affidavit of Support, Page 1 of 3

OMB No. 1115-0214

U.S. Department of Justice
Immigration and Naturalization Service

Affidavit of Support Under Section 213A of the Act

START HERE - Please Type or Print

Part 1. Information on Sponsor (You)

Last Name	First Name	Middle Name

Mailing Address (Street Number and Name)	Apt/Suite Number

City	State or Province

Country	ZIP/Postal Code	Telephone Number

Place of Residence if different from above (Street Number and Name)	Apt/Suite Number

City	State or Province

Country	ZIP/Postal Code	Telephone Number

Date of Birth (Month, Day, Year)	Place of Birth (City, State, Country)	Are you a U.S. Citizen? ☐ Yes ☐ No

Social Security Number	A-Number (If any)

FOR AGENCY USE ONLY

This Affidavit	Receipt
[ ] Meets	
[ ] Does not meet	

Requirements of Section 213A

Officer or I.J. Signature

Location

Date

Part 2. Basis for Filing Affidavit of Support

I am filing this affidavit of support because (check one):

a. ☐ I filed/am filing the alien relative petition.

b. ☐ I filed/am filing an alien worker petition on behalf of the intending immigrant, who is related to me as my _____ .
(relationship)

c. ☐ I have ownership interest of at least 5% _____ .
(name of entity which filed visa petition)
which filed an alien worker petition on behalf of the intending immigrant, who is related to me as my _____ .
(relationship)

d. ☐ I am a joint sponsor willing to accept the legal obligations with any other sponsor(s).

Part 3. Information on the Immigrant(s) You Are Sponsoring

Last Name	First Name	Middle Name

Date of Birth (Month, Day, Year)	Sex ☐ Male ☐ Female	Social Security Number (If any)

Country of Citizenship	A-Number (If any)

Current Address (Street Number and Name)	Apt/Suite Number	City

State/Province	Country	ZIP/Postal Code	Telephone Number

List any spouse and/or children immigrating with the immigrant named above in this Part: _(Use additional sheet of paper if necessary.)_

Name	Relationship to Sponsored Immigrant			Date of Birth			A-Number (If any)	Social Security (If any)
	Spouse	Son	Daughter	Mo.	Day	Yr.		

Form I-864 (Rev. 11/05/01)Y

Form I-864

Affidavit of Support, Page 2 of 3

Part 4.	Eligibility to Sponsor

To be a sponsor you must be a U.S. citizen or national or a lawful permanent resident. If you are not the petitioning relative, you must provide proof of status. To prove status, U.S. citizens or nationals must attach a copy of a document proving status, such as a U.S. passport, birth certificate, or certificate of naturalization, and lawful permanent residents must attach a copy of both sides of their Permanent Resident Card (Form I-551).

The determination of your eligibility to sponsor an immigrant will be based on an evaluation of your demonstrated ability to maintain an annual income at or above 125 percent of the Federal poverty line (100 percent if you are a petitioner sponsoring your spouse or child and you are on active duty in the U.S. Armed Forces). The assessment of your ability to maintain an adequate income will include your current employment, household size, and household income as shown on the Federal income tax returns for the 3 most recent tax years. Assets that are readily converted to cash and that can be made available for the support of sponsored immigrants if necessary, including any such assets of the immigrant(s) you are sponsoring, may also be considered.

The greatest weight in determining eligibility will be placed on current employment and household income. If a petitioner is unable to demonstrate ability to meet the stated income and asset requirements, a joint sponsor who *can* meet the income and asset requirements is needed. Failure to provide adequate evidence of income and/or assets or an affidavit of support completed by a joint sponsor will result in denial of the immigrant's application for an immigrant visa or adjustment to permanent resident status.

A. Sponsor's Employment

I am:
1. ☐ Employed by _____ *(Provide evidence of employment)*

   Annual salary _____ or hourly wage $ _____ *(for _____ hours per week)*

2. ☐ Self employed _____ *(Name of business)*

   Nature of employment or business _____

3. ☐ Unemployed or retired since _____

B. Sponsor's Household Size

Number

1. Number of persons (related to you by birth, marriage, or adoption) living in your residence, including yourself *(Do NOT include persons being sponsored in this affidavit.)* _____

2. Number of immigrants being sponsored in this affidavit *(Include all persons in Part 3.)* _____

3. Number of immigrants **NOT** living in your household whom you are obligated to support under a previously signed Form I-864. _____

4. Number of persons who are otherwise dependent on you, as claimed in your tax return for the most recent tax year. _____

5. Total household size. *(Add lines 1 through 4.)* **Total** _____

List persons below who are included in lines 1 or 3 for whom you previously have submitted INS Form I-864, *if your support obligation has not terminated.*

(If additional space is needed, use additional paper)

Name	A-Number	Date Affidavit of Support Signed	Relationship

Form I-864

Affidavit of Support, Page 3 of 3

Part 4. **Eligibility to Sponsor** *(Continued)*

C. Sponsor's Annual Household Income

Enter total unadjusted income from your Federal income tax return for the most recent tax year below. If you last filed a joint income tax return but are using only your *own* income to qualify, list total earnings from your W-2 Forms, or, *if* necessary to reach the required income for your household size, include income from other sources listed on your tax return. If your *individual* income does not meet the income requirement for your household size, you may also list total income for anyone related to you by birth, marriage, or adoption currently living with you in your residence if they have lived in your residence for the previous 6 months, or any person shown as a dependent on your Federal income tax return for the most recent tax year, even if not living in the household. For their income to be considered, household members or dependents must be willing to make their income available for support of the sponsored immigrant(s) and to complete and sign Form I-864A, Contract Between Sponsor and Household Member. A sponsored immigrant/household member only need complete Form I-864A if his or her income will be used to determine your ability to support a spouse and/or children immigrating with him or her.

You must attach evidence of current employment and copies of income tax returns as filed with the IRS for the most recent 3 tax years for yourself and all persons whose income is listed below. See "Required Evidence" in Instructions. Income from all 3 years will be considered in determining your ability to support the immigrant(s) you are sponsoring.

- [ ] I filed a single/separate tax return for the most recent tax year.
- [ ] I filed a joint return for the most recent tax year which includes only my own income.
- [ ] I filed a joint return for the most recent tax year which includes income for my spouse and myself.
    - [ ] I am submitting documentation of my individual income (Forms W-2 and 1099).
    - [ ] I am qualifying using my spouse's income; my spouse is submitting a Form I-864A.

Indicate most recent tax year _____
(tax year)

Sponsor's individual income $ _____

or

Sponsor and spouse's combined income $ _____
(If spouse's income is to be considered, spouse must submit Form I-864A.)

Income of other qualifying persons.
(List names; include spouse if applicable. Each person must complete Form I-864A.)

_____ $ _____

_____ $ _____

_____ $ _____

Total Household Income $ _____

Explain on separate sheet of paper if you or any of the above listed individuals were not required to file Federal income tax returns for the most recent 3 years, or if other explanation of income, employment, or evidence is necessary.

D. Determination of Eligibility Based on Income

1.   [ ] I am subject to the 125 percent of poverty line requirement for sponsors.
        [ ] I am subject to the 100 percent of poverty line requirement for sponsors on active duty in the U.S. Armed Forces sponsoring their spouse or child.
2.   Sponsor's total household size, from Part 4.B., line 5 _____ .
3.   Minimum income requirement from the Poverty Guidelines chart for the year of _____ is $ _____
      for this household size.   *(year)*

If you are currently employed and your household income for your household size is equal to or greater than the applicable poverty line requirement (from line D.3.), you do not need to list assets (Parts 4.E. and 5) or have a joint sponsor (Part 6) unless you are requested to do so by a Consular or Immigration Officer. You may skip to Part 7, Use of the Affidavit of Support to Overcome Public Charge Ground of Admissibility. **Otherwise, you should continue with Part 4.E.**

Form I-864A

Contract Between Sponsor and Household Member, Page 1 of 2

Part 1. Information on Sponsor's Household Member or Sponsored Immigrant/Household Member

Last Name	First Name	Middle Name

Date of Birth *(Month,Day, Year)*	Social Security Number *(Mandatory for non-citizens; voluntary for U.S. citizens)*	A-Number *(If any)*

Address *(Street Number and Name)* Apt Number	City	State/Province	ZIP/Postal Code

Telephone Number ( )	Relationship to Sponsor: I am: ☐ The sponsor's household member. *(Complete Part 3.)* ☐ The sponsored immigrant/household member. *(Complete Part*	Length of residence with sponsor _____ years, _____ months)

Part 2. Sponsor's Promise

I, THE SPONSOR, _____ *(Print name of sponsor)* , in consideration of the household member's promise to support the sponsored immigrant(s) and to be jointly and severally liable for any obligations I incur under the affidavit of support,

promise to complete and file an affidavit of support on behalf of the following_____ *(Indicate number)* sponsored immigrant(s):

Name of Sponsored Immigrant *(First, Middle, Last)*	Date of Birth *(Month, Day, Year)*	Social Security Number *(If any)*	A-Number *(If any)*
_____	_____	_____	_____
_____	_____	_____	_____
_____	_____	_____	_____
_____	_____	_____	_____
_____	_____	_____	_____

Part 3. Household Member's Promise

I, THE HOUSEHOLD _____ *(Print name of household member)* , in consideration of the sponsor's

promise to complete and file the affidavit of support on behalf of the sponsored immigrant(s):

1) Promise to provide any and all financial support necessary to assist the sponsor in maintaining the sponsored immigrant(s) at or above the minimum income provided for in section 213A(a)(1)(A) of the Act (not less than 125 percent of the Federal Poverty Guidelines) during the period in which the affidavit of support is enforceable;

2) Agree to be jointly and severally liable for payment of any and all obligations owed by the sponsor under the affidavit of support to the sponsored immigrant(s), to any agency of the Federal Government, to any agency of a state or local government, or to any private entity;

3) Agree to submit to the personal jurisdiction of any court of the United States or of any state, territory, or possession of the United States if the court has subject matter jurisdiction of a civil lawsuit to enforce this contract or the affidavit of support; and

4) Certify under penalty of perjury under the laws of the United States that all the information provided on this form is true and correct to the best of my knowledge and belief and that the income tax returns I submitted in support of the sponsor affidavit are true copies of the returns filed with the Internal Revenue Service.

Form I-864A

Contract Between Sponsor and Household Member, Page 2 of 2

Part 4. Sponsored Immigrant/Household Member's Promise

I, THE SPONSORED IMMIGRANT/HOUSEHOLD _____

(Print name o f sponsored immigrant)

in consideration of the sponsor's promise to complete and file the affidavit of support on behalf of the sponsored immigrant(s) accompanying me:

1) Promise to provide any and all financial support necessary to assist the sponsor in maintaining any sponsored immigrant(s) immigrating with me at or above the minimum income provided for in section 213A(a)(1)(A) of the Act (not less than 125 percent of the Federal Poverty Guidelines) during the period in which the affidavit of support is enforceable;

2) Agree to be jointly and severally liable for payment of any and all obligations owed by the sponsor under the affidavit of support to any sponsored immigrant(s) immigrating with me, to any agency of the Federal Government, to any agency of a state or local government, or to any private entity;

3) Agree to submit to the personal jurisdiction of any court of the United States or of any state, territory, or possession of the United States if the court has subject matter jurisdiction of a civil lawsuit to enforce this contract or the affidavit of support; and

4) Certify under penalty of perjury under the laws of the United States that all the information provided on this form is tru and correct to the best of my knowledge and belief and that the income tax returns I submitted in support of the sponsor's affidavit of support are true copies of the returns filed with the Internal Revenue Service.

Part 5. Sponsor's Signature

_____ Date: _____

Sponsor's Signature

Subscribed and sworn to *(or affirmed)* before me this_____ day of _____ , _____

(Month)   *(Year)*

at _____ . My commission expires on_____ .

_____   _____

Signature of Notary Public or Officer Administering Oath   *Title*

Part 6. Household Member's or Sponsored Immigrant/Household Member's Signature

_____ Date: _____

Household Member's or Sponsored Immigrant/Household Member's Signature

Subscribed and sworn to *(or affirmed)* before me this_____ day of _____ , _____

(Month)   *(Year)*

at _____ . My commission expires on_____ .

_____   _____

Signature of Notary Public or Officer Administering Oath   *Title*

Form I-171H

Notice of Approval

U.S. DEPARTMENT OF JUSTICE
Immigration and Naturalization Service
126 Northpoint Drive
Houston, TX 77060

Name and Address of Prospective Petitioner

Prospective Father's Name	
Prospective Mother's Name	
08/21/02	11/04/02

Expires: 05/04/04

**NOTICE OF FAVORABLE DETERMINATION CONCERNING APPLICATION
FOR ADVANCE PROCESSING OF ORPHAN PETITION**

IT HAS BEEN DETERMINED THAT YOU ARE ABLE TO FURNISH PROPER CARE TO AN ORPHAN OR ORPHANS AS DEFINED BY SECTION 101(B)(1)(F) OF THE IMMIGRATION AND NATIONALITY ACT. A SEPARATE ORPHAN PETITION, FORM I-600, MUST BE FILED IN BEHALF OF EACH CHILD WITH DOCUMENTARY EVIDENCE DESCRIBED IN INSTRUCTION 2C, 2D, 2E, 2F, 2G, AND 2H OF THAT FORM. A FORM OR FORMS FOR YOUR USE ARE ENCLOSED. NO FEE WILL BE REQUIRED WITH FORM I-600 IF YOU FILE ONLY ONE FORM I-600 WITHIN EIGHTEEN MONTHS FROM THE DATE OF COMPLETION OF YOUR ADVANCE PROCESSING APPLICATION, YOUR APPLICATION WILL BE CONSIDERED ABANDONED. ANY FURTHER PROCEEDINGS WILL REQUIRE THE FILING OF A NEW ADVANCE PROCESSING APPLICATION OR AN ORPHAN PETITION.

Form I-600 should be filed at the Service office or American consulate or embassy where your advance processing application is being retained or has been forwarded as indicated by an "X" mark below:

1. [ ]   YOUR ADVANCE PROCESSING APPLICATION IS BEING RETAINED AT THIS OFFICE.

2. [ ]   YOUR ADVANCE PROCESSING APPLICATION HAS BEEN FORWARDED TO OUR SERVICE OFFICE
AT _____.

3 [X]   YOUR ADVANCE PROCESSING APPLICATION HAS BEEN FORWARDED TO THE AMERICAN CONSULATE OR EMBASSY AT **MOSCOW, RUSSIA**.

In addition, please note the following:

[ ]   Any original documents submitted in support of your application are returned to you.

[ ]   Your home study is returned to you.

THIS DETERMINATION DOES NOT GUARANTEE THAT THE ORPHAN PETITION WHICH YOU FILE WILL BE APPROVED. AN ORPHAN PETITION MAY BE DENIED BECAUSE THE CHILD DOES NOT QUALIFY FOR CLASSIFICATION AS AN ORPHAN OR FOR OTHER PROPER CAUSE. DENIAL OF AN ORPHAN PETITION HOWEVER, MAY BE APPEALED.

VERY TRULY YOURS,

ACTING DISTRICT DIRECTOR

Form I-171H

M-349, "Notice to Prospective
Adopting Parents", is enclosed.
Please be sure that you read
and understand it before you
accept a foreign born child.

CHAPTER 7

Application to a Foreign Source

I f you have not already done so, now is the time to make a decision on the country from which you would like to adopt. After your home study is approved and you have completed your preliminary INS paperwork, assess the current international adoption situation with your international adoption agency. Requirements for adoptive parents, the age and ethnicity of the children available, the length of wait until the assignment of a child, the number of trips required, the length of your stay abroad, program fees, referral method, and numbers being assigned monthly by each adoption program are all factors you should consider. If you are having difficulty making a decision, consult the agency staff or director, or seek further information from an adoptive parent support group.

Nationality is an important issue for adoptive families. You'll start a long relationship with your child's motherland the day you pick a country. Your future child's self-assurance will be affected by your attitude toward his or her origins. Choose a country that you respect, with a population you admire. Your attitude toward that nation and your child's birth family will be more important than spending time there.

Some parents may also want to consider postplacement requirements of the country of origin in their decision-making process. Many countries require social workers and/or adoptive parents to send them regular progress reports over a period of six months to 18 years. In addition, some countries require that you register your adopted child in its embassy here in the United States. This is not to infringe on your family's privacy, but to assure foreign governments that the children they allowed to immigrate remain in caring, stable families. (For more detailed information on post-placement requirements for individual countries, see Table 14-2.)

Step 10
Select an adoption program in a foreign country.

Methods of Adoption Required by Foreign Countries

A final important factor to consider before choosing a country program is the legal means by which an adoption is facilitated. This is determined by the child's country of origin. One of six different methods may be used to meet the various legal requirements of foreign countries. (See the adoption law summary for each country listed in the Compendium.)

For example, a power of attorney form is used in most countries to initiate adoption procedures prior to the arrival of the adoptive parents. An attorney acts on behalf of the prospective parents. This saves the adopters from spending time abroad at all the appointments with government officials and court hearings and waiting there for legal custody. Power of attorney forms are also used in some countries for a guardianship or a final adoption by proxy. They are also utilized in certain countries for authorized escorts to immigrate children to their new parents. (A sample of a power of attorney form can be found at the end of this chapter.)

Advantages and disadvantages are inherent in each of the six methods. Adoptive parents may choose one country over another simply because they prefer the power of attorney method to avoid a lot of the appointments. Other couples might decide that they prefer to adopt in a country where they can go to see the child immediately after the referral and to be involved in all the adoption proceedings. Adoption by proxy carries more risk for the adoptive parents, since they have not observed the child prior to his or her final adoption and/or immigration. There are more cases of disrupted adoptions in this method, since the families are not always pleased with the child that is delivered. The child does not meet their expectations, and they cannot overcome their disappointment.

Method 1: U.S. parents plan to assign a power of attorney to a foreign adoption agency or attorney who initiates the adoption. The parents present themselves later in the foreign country to complete the remaining adoption procedures. This is the most common method used and is found in both agency-initiated and parent-initiated adoptions.

If you are conducting a parent-initiated adoption and the country you are adopting from uses a power of attorney, request the power of attorney form and custody contract as soon as the adoption source has agreed to place a child with you. Power of attorney procedures can be quite time consuming. From the time you receive the forms, it takes from two to eight weeks for them to be signed, apostilled or authenticated, and returned unless air courier services are used instead of airmail.

Method 2: Proxy adoptions or proxy permanent guardianships are also initiated by a foreign adoption agency or attorney who has been given power of attorney by preadoptive parents. The assigned child is escorted to his or her adoptive family by a person designated by the foreign child-placing entity. INS requires that the adoptive parents must readopt in their state of residence. This is required prior to application for proof of U.S. citizenship.

This method is mainly used in agency-initiated adoptions, especially by countries such as Korea and India. The country, in turn, has child-placing agreements with U.S. adoption agencies. In this case, the child remains under the managing conservatorship of the U.S. adoption agency until the child is legally adopted in the child's new country of residence. Guatemala is one of the few countries that grant a final adoption decree by proxy. The children in these cases are immigrated and escorted by an indi-

Choosing a Country to Adopt From

Choosing a country to adopt from is both an important and personal decision — one that is likely to be shaped by both logic and emotion. Whatever country you choose, keep in mind that you are, in some ways, embarking on a life-long relationship with that country. Some countries may require adoptive parents to send periodic reports updating them on the child's progress. Even if your country doesn't require post-placement reports, parents have the responsibility to expose and educate their child about the country of his or her birth. The country you choose should be one you are excited to travel to and learn about. Here are just a few questions you might want to consider when choosing a country:

How many trips must I make?

How long is each trip?

What are the potential health issues for the babies/children available from this country?

What is the range of age of children available?

What is the condition of orphanages in this country?

What are the age requirements for adoptive parents?

Can a single parent adopt from this country?

How long will it take to complete the adoption and bring the child home?

What in-country support is available to help complete the overseas paperwork?

How many children are adopted from this country each year? (See Table 4-2)

How long has this country been placing children for international adoption?

Does the foreign country require postplacement reports? If so, how many and how often?

Will I have bilingual assistance throughout my trip?

Will I have a choice of accommodations?

vidual authorized by the U.S. adoption agency or the adoptive parents. In addition, India grants final adoption decrees to Hindus who are U.S. citizens and also allows them to adopt independently (without a U.S. adoption agency).

This type of escort service has a down side. The most obvious problem is that the child becomes a part of your family sight unseen. Parents usually have very little idea about the behavior of these children until they are in their new home. Another problem with escorting is that it takes longer to arrange than it would if you traveled there yourself, and it is not substantially cheaper. A final point is that children over two tend to believe that the escort is the new parent. When the escort hands them over to strangers at the airport, their separation from the escort appears to be emotionally shocking.

Method 3: The orphan emigrates the foreign country under a permanent guardianship agreement, usually with the adoptive parents or an authorized escort. Some countries consummate the adoption six to twelve months later. The prospective adoptive parents must promise to adopt the child in their state of residence in order to comply with INS regulations.

Method 4: A formal final adoption decree preceded by a permanent guardianship agreement may be necessary in some countries when the adopters are not old enough or have not been married long enough to meet the adoption requirements.

This method is used in both agency- and parent-initiated adoptions in Chile. The adoptive parents immigrate the child under a permanent guardianship. This is also used in some Muslim countries that do not have adoption laws.

Method 5: Custody transfer, usually with escort service, is used by some international adoption agencies with child-placing agreements in Korea and sometimes in the Philippines. It transfers custody of the child from the foreign institution to a U.S. international agency until the child is adopted in his/her state of residence. This method can only be used by international agencies.

Method 6: A final formal adoption decree, issued at the end of the adoption process.

Preparing Your Foreign Dossier

Once you have decided on a country, your agency or its foreign counterpart will provide you with a packet of materials and instructions for preparing your dossier for the foreign country. Completing the dossier is a big task, but you will have already done much of the work in preparation for your home study.

Cover Letter

Your completed dossier will need to be accompanied by a cover letter. If you are working with an international agency, you typically won't need to write the letter yourself, unless it is specifically requested by the child-placing country. The letter should be translated, but notarization is not usually required.

The cover letter should describe your motive for adoption. In the length of two or three pages, your cover letter must clearly explain why you plan to adopt.

Formally request the child you wish to adopt with a description: State your preference for a boy or girl. Specify the age of the child. Explain your preference, if any, for the child's ethnic background. Indicate the name(s) you have chosen for the child, or if you will consider keeping all or part of the child's original name. (Research indicates that children whose names are retained have an easier adjustment.) Your wait will usually be shorter if you will accept a boy or a girl and if you will accept a child within the age range of one to three years. If you are considering a child with a chronic illness or handicap, state the medical conditions you are willing to accept. Refrain from mentioning the child's or country's social problems or poverty. Don't give the impression that you are trying to rescue an orphan from one of their institutions. Instead, focus on how both you and the child will benefit from your new relationship.

Through the activity of formulating your ideas and communicating your knowledge of international adoption, you will create a letter that will put to rest some of the fears we have heard foreign nationals express concerning international adoptions. (Occasional rumors assert that Americans are adopting children to use as servants or for organ transplants. Nothing of the sort has ever happened.)

Required Documents

Most likely you will have already assembled many of these documents to support the facts you gave the social worker during the home study process. Now is the time to check to make certain you have all of the necessary documents and to move them into a complete dossier for the foreign country. Review Chapter 5 for specific details on requesting this information.

Each foreign country requires different documentation and may change its requirements occasionally. However, the country will inform you or your agency of the current procedures. They will also state which documents need notarization, verification, authentication, and translation. (A section at the end of this chapter describes this process.)

Consider ordering and generating two sets of originals to protect against loss, or in case you have to switch countries later on. Keep these original documents and a set of copies for your agency in protective folders with plastic sleeves. Just be sure not to punch holes in the documents.

Documents generally required for your dossier will include:

1. Application form of the child-placing entity. Government authorities in charge of adoption in many countries have their own application forms. These forms are also used by their adoption committees for preapproval in some countries.

2. Certified birth certificates for each member of the family.

3. Certified marriage license, if applicable.

4. Certified divorce decrees, if applicable.

5. Certified death certificates of former spouses, if applicable.

6. Job letter (one for each applicant) from your employer, stating your length of employment and annual salary. If you are self-employed, a public accountant can provide this.

7. A statement of net worth written by you or your accountant.

8. The first two pages of your federal income tax returns for the last three years.

9. Current medical examination forms for all household members. (Good for one year from the date of the exam.)

10. Letters of reference from at least three people who are acquainted with the family unit. These letters should come from professionals or community leaders, if at all possible.

11. Letter(s) from your local police, stating that you have no criminal record. Some countries now ask for a state police clearance.

12. Pictures of you in front of your home and individual close-ups (or passport pictures). You will need three of each. Pose in business attire for all photos.

Step 11
Obtain documents required for your foreign dossier.

13. Specific forms particular to the foreign child-placing entity.

14. International processing contract. This document explains the agency's responsibilities and yours in locating a child for you and arranging your legal custody of the child.

15. Photocopies of the first two pages of your passports.

16. Photocopy of your completed Form I-600A.

Changes to Countries or Adoption Programs

If you switch adoption programs after evidence of your INS clearance (Form I-171H) was sent to the U.S. Consulate in the original country you selected, you will need to transfer your file to the U.S. Consulate in the new country you have chosen. To do this, request Form I-824 (Application for Action on an Approved Application or Petition) from the INS, fill it out, and mail it in with a money order for $140.00.

Translating Services

Your international agency or foreign liaison will advise which documents need translating and at what point this should take place. Most translations of dossiers are accomplished abroad by official translators. If translations must be accomplished in the United States, most U.S.-based international agencies can recommend a skilled translator who can produce legal documents for review by a foreign court. In addition, skilled translators can be found through international institutes. About 40 international institutes are located around the nation in the larger cities. Consult the telephone book to find the institute nearest you. In addition, you may be able to find translation services on the web. One such organization, the American Translators Association (**www.atanet.org**) can help you find an accredited translator. In addition, many individuals and organizations offering translation services host individual sites on the web. Before submitting your letter to a translator, agree on a price. Twenty-two dollars or more per typewritten page is typical. Some translators charge by the word.

Step 12
Obtain translations for documents in your foreign dossier.

A cover letter certifying the translator's competency must be attached to the translated document. One letter will suffice for all documents translated by the same person. Notarize and verify this letter. Some countries also require an apostille or authentication of this letter. (A sample for the translator's statement of competency appears at the end of this chapter.) On the other hand, some countries require that translations be accomplished in their Department of Foreign Ministry. In this case, your U.S.-based international agency will air courier your documents there. Whether you work with an independent translator or a Department of Foreign Ministry, you should supply the translator with a photocopy rather than the original document in order to keep the originals pristine.

Notarization, Verification or Apostille, and Authentication

All documents must go through the process of notarization and verification before they can be authenticated by the consul of the country from which you are adopting. To make sure that the information you provide is reliable, the consulates require that the papers sent to them for authentication be notarized by a notary public and verified by your county clerk or secretary of state.

Check with your international agency or foreign source to find out exactly what documents need to be notarized, verified/apostilled and/or authenticated. Differences occur even among the courts in a foreign country. Any supporting documents that you choose to submit, such as a cover letter or a tax return, need not be notarized.

Step 13
Obtain notarization, verification (or apostille), and authentication of documents in your dossier.

Obtaining Notarization

A notary public verifies that the signatures on your documents are valid by affixing his or her seal.

You can find a notary public in the phone book. Fees may range from free to $10.00 per document. Legally, the persons who provide the documents or letters of reference — your doctor, banker, employer, friends, and so on — must sign their name in the presence of the notary public. If a doctor, police chief, or so on, cannot leave the office to sign before a notary, the alternative is for you to also sign the form as a release of information and have your signature notarized. Ask your notary to use a jurat form similar to the one found at the end of this chapter.

If you must notarize documents for which you can't provide the originals (for example, your past tax returns), you may type or neatly print the following statement in the margin:

"I certify that this is a true copy of the original."

You can then sign and date that statement in the presence of the notary.

Sending for Verification or Apostilles

Verification or apostille is the process by which the state or county verifies the validity of the notary's signature. (Mexico, Colombia, Bolivia and some Eastern European countries like Russia and Kazakhstan request apostilles rather than verifications.) Verification and apostille sheets are available from the county clerk or the secretary of state who verifies that the notary's signature and seal are valid. Fees for verification or apostille vary from state to state. Do not verify documents until you have chosen an adoption source. Not every country requires this step. (Samples of verification and apostille forms for the state of Texas can be found at the end of this chapter.)

Send a typewritten sheet with the name, county, and expiration date of your notary's commission, along with the fee for each signature, to obtain apostille or verification sheets with state seals to the secretary of the state in which the document was issued. Check with the appropriate office before sending in your fees and sheets. In some other states, you may be able to send a photocopy rather than the original document, if they need to see the document. Check before sending. Remember that even if one notary signs six documents, you will need six verifications, not just one.

Birth and marriage certificates are certified documents; in most cases they do not require additional verification before they are accepted by the consul. Honduras is one of the few exceptions here.

A county clerk can legally verify the seals of only those notary publics who reside in his or her county and register with his or her office. All notaries, however, must register with the Secretary of State.

All documents must be verified in the states where they originated; for this reason, it is advisable that all of your documents be prepared by persons living in your present state of residence. Out-of-state documents will require verification out of state, which just creates one more hassle.

Obtaining Authentication

After notarization and verification, most countries require that certain documents be authenticated by a consul representing the country from which you wish to adopt that has jurisdiction in your locality. (Authentications are not needed when apostilles are accepted.) Consuls attest to the authenticity of the document or the signer of it by their seal, stamp, and signature. U.S.-based international agencies will provide a list of documents requiring authentication by the country from which you plan to adopt. Check with your international agency or foreign liaison to ensure that you follow the correct steps, especially if you are adopting from a country not mentioned here.

To locate the nearest consul, look in the phone book under U.S. Government Offices, Federal Information Center. These centers have consulate addresses and phone numbers. The U.S. Department of State maintains a list of foreign consulate locations on its web site (**www.state.gov/s/cpr/rls/fco/**). The INS also has the addresses and phone numbers of various consulate offices.

The process with foreign consulates is as follows: Send your notarized and verified documents, with translations if required, to the foreign consulate for authentication. Enclose a check or money order for the total amount and a stamped, self-addressed envelope when you send your documents. Obviously, you will have to call the consulate first to inquire about the fees per document. Fees for authentication range from as low as $10.00 per document for Guatemala to $60.00 per document for the Ukraine. Most consulates will double the charge for rush services. China triples its fee for rush services.

If the consulate is located in your city, you may be able to handle this much more quickly in person. Be certain to dress in business attire since the cooperation of the consul is essential. Treat the consul with the dignity to which he or she is accustomed. However, if the consul is not cooperative, call the embassy of the country from which you are adopting for help. All of the foreign embassies are located in Washington, D.C. Ask your telephone operator for the number. You can also find a list of contact information for all foreign embassies in Washington by visiting the web site **www.embassy.org/embassies**. This web site provides the address, telephone and fax numbers, email address, and URL (if the embassy maintains a web site) for all foreign embassies located in Washington.

Some states near the Washington, D.C. area and some foreign countries without consulates outside of Washington, D.C. require that the U.S. Department of State certify the notarized and verified documents before they will authenticate them. This is always required if you deal with a consulate attached to a foreign embassy. For instance, Russia has only three consulates in the United States, one of which is attached to its embassy. Vietnam has only two, one of which is at its embassy. Romania has no consulates outside the D.C. area. At present there is a $5.00 charge per document for this service. Call or e-mail them for instructions before sending your money order or certified cashier's check made payable to the U.S. Department of State. The address and telephone numbers are as follows:

Supervisor, Authentication Office
U.S. Department of State
518 23rd Street N.W.
State Annex 1
Washington, D.C. 20520

Tel: (202) 647-5002
Toll-free: (800) 688-9889

Fax: (202) 663-3636
E-mail: AOPRGSMAUTH@STATE.GOV

The office's website (**http://www.state.gov/m/a/auth/**) presents information on a variety of subjects from adoption information and information on authentication to travel warnings.

A Word of Caution: Documents and Fees

Safeguard your documents. After your documents have been notarized, apostilled or verified, and authenticated, make one photocopy of each before they are sent abroad. This is your proof in case of loss in the mail or elsewhere. Hand carry these copies with you on your adoption trip abroad.

Do not give your dossier of original documents to anyone in the United States except a licensed adoption agency or licensed social worker. Be suspicious of unlicensed individuals who for any reason keep their sources secret, insist upon handling your dossier, or expect payments, whether these payments are to be made in advance or at a later date to a for-profit corporation or individual.

International Communication

If you are working with a U.S.-based international agency, your agency will send your dossier to its representative abroad and handle the communications for you. If you are not using an agency, you should send this information to your lawyer or foreign representative. Several methods of international communication are available.

1. E-mail. Your adoption agency, as well as its representatives or agencies abroad, communicate by e-mail on a frequent basis.

2. Telegrams. Many foreign businesses and institutions have short, registered cable addresses, usually acronyms. A return voucher is sent along with the message if a reply is expected.

3. Fax. Faxes are quite common around the world. (See the information below on telephone communication for specifics.)

4. Telephone. Long-distance phone calls range from $4.00 to $12.00 per minute, person-to-person. Keep the time difference in mind! An international operator can advise you of the time in a specific country. When dialing most countries from the United States, you must dial 011, followed by the country code, the city code, and then the number you are trying to reach. For some countries, especially some Caribbean countries, it is only necessary to dial 1, rather than 011. Numerous web sites provide a comprehensive list of country and city codes. Try **http://globaltele-com.org/telecom.htm** or use your favorite search engine to search for the term "country code telephone."

5. Courier Service. International air courier services, such as Federal Express and DHL, guarantee service from pickup in a foreign country to personal delivery here and vice versa. The cost varies. U.S. Postal EMS (Express Mail Service) is the least expensive and now goes to most foreign capital cities. Unfortunately, it is not as reliable as Federal Express or DHL.

Power of Attorney

TO WHOM IT MAY CONCERN:

This is to certify that we, the undersigned _____

presently living at _____

are herewith granting full power of attorney to _____

presently living at _____

to carry through and complete on our behalf any and all formalities required for the process of

the adoption of a _____ born child.

This is also to confirm that we herewith grant full power of attorney to _____

to carry through and complete on our behalf any and all formalities required by the American

Consulate in _____ in this matter.

Name _____   Date _____

Name _____   Date _____

Subscribed and sworn to before me on the _____ day of _____ 20 __ to which

_____

Notary Public

My commission expires: _____

Statement of Competency

I, _____ , hereby certify that I am competent to translate from the _____

language to the _____ language and that the above translation is accurate.

Date: _____   _____   (name printed or typed)

                         _____   (address)

                         _____

Jurat

Subscribed and sworn to before me on the _____ day of _____ , 20 _____
to which witness my hand and seal of office.

_____

Notary Public in and for the State of _____ , County of _____

My Commission Expires _____.

Verification

The State of Texas
Secretary of State

I, _____ , Secretary of State of the State of Texas, DO HEREBY CERTIFY that according to the records of this office,

(name of notary)

qualified as a Notary Public for the State of Texas on July 27, 2002. for a term ending on July 27, 2003.

Date Issued: November 13, 2002

_____
Secretary of State   sai

Apostille

STATE OF TEXAS

APOSTILLE
(Convention de La Haye du 5 Octobre 1961)

1. **Country:**   **United States of America**
   This Public document

2. **has been signed by**   (name of notary)

3. **acting in the capacity of Notary Public, State of Texas**

4. **bears the seal/stamp of**   **, Notary Public, State of Texas, Commission Expires: 07-27-03**

CERTIFIED

5. **at Austin, Texas**   6. **on December 3, 2002**

7. **by the Deputy Assistant Secretary of State of Texas**

8. **Certificate No. N-118607**

9. **Seal**   10. **Signature:**

Deputy Assistant Secretary of State
LSW/NO/ sai

CHAPTER 8

Preparing for the Referral

Once your completed, apostilled and authenticated dossier has been sent, you are ready for a referral for your child. For some people, the wait for a child to be assigned is the most difficult part of the process. Make good use of the time by volunteering to baby-sit for friends, taking child care classes (see the section below), finding a good pediatrician or family doctor (consider looking for a foreign-born pediatrician, one who specializes in health conditions in developing countries, or one who has experience treating children adopted from your country of choice), attending adoptive parent support group functions, subscribing to their newsletters (see Bibliography) or Internet news groups or list serves, and researching the culture, customs and geography of your child's native land. Buy a book on child care that explains the signs and symptoms of childhood illnesses. Study the language. Assemble what you will need to pack, using our tips in Chapter 10.

Step 14
Prepare for the
referral of your child.

Most reputable agencies offer courses on international adoption, travel, and parenting. (See nearby box.) Check with your agency for a copy. Completion of such courses is sometimes a state requirement for adoption. In addition, the Joint Council on International Children's Services also publishes a booklet called "The Adoptive Parent Preparation System." The booklet is available for free through adoption agencies and organizations that are members of the Joint Council. Check with your international adoption or home study agency to see if it can provide you with a copy. Otherwise you can order a copy for $30.00 by telephone at 202-429-0040 or by email at **jcics@jcics.org**. The JCICS web site is at **www.jcics.org**.

Preadoptive Resources

The American Red Cross, local hospitals, and some adoption agencies offer courses on infant care. While these courses are essential for every inexperienced new mother and father, the courses do not cover problems typical of orphans from developing countries and malnourished babies with infectious diarrhea. (See Chapter 13 for more information on health issues of babies and children from developing countries.)

Also contact adoptive parent groups and child development centers for information. See Chapter 15 for more information on parenting adopted children and refer to the Bibliography for additional resources.

Referral Methods

Since child-placing countries may change their referral methods as well as their laws and procedures, check the State Department web site (**http://travel.state.gov**) for the most current information. Countries refer orphans in at least three different ways: A formal referral with complete information; an information referral with brief information; or an invitation to visit an orphanage with no information, but the chance to meet children and choose one. When the Hague Convention is finally enforced, every country will be required to refer adoptable children by providing complete social and medical histories as well as a photo or video prior to meeting the child.

Your international adoption agency's representative abroad, in conference with an orphanage director, knows which child or children are suitable for you, based on your home study and application form. With few exceptions, Asian and Latin American children are formally referred. Countries that were once part of the Union of Soviet Socialist Republics tend to refer children informally or extend an invitation to the prospective parents. At this time, some regions in Russian countries send formal referrals and other regions send informal referrals.

Formal referrals are sent to international adoption agencies. Basing their decisions on the home study, China and Colombia are leaders in selecting a family for the child and providing full referral information to them. In any case, good adoption practice requires that the prospective parents are given all the time they need to make a decision, knowing that the child is waiting. Once parents have accepted the referral, some countries like Guatemala initiate the adoption with a power of attorney form signed by the adoptive parents prior to their adoption trip. Samples of referral information from China, Colombia and Russia are shown at the end of this chapter. (These children have all been placed in loving families.)

Informal referrals, indicating only the age and gender of the child are telephoned to the adoptive parents waiting for such a child. Invitations from a foreign government to visit and select an institutionalized child from a small group are also relayed by telephone to potential parents. In both types of referrals, prospective adopters travel to meet the child and review a translated summary of the child's social and medical history while they are there. Prospective parents can ask their interpreter to help them consult with the orphanage pediatrician and orphanage director regarding the child's history. Although it takes more time, some families need reassurance from an international pediatric specialist (see nearby box on Preadoptive Medical Consultations). In this case, the family can take photos or videos and send them, along with the translated information, to one of the pediatricians or international adoption clinics listed in Chapter 13. If the family decides to adopt that particular child, they return home to wait for a court date. These referral methods often require that the parents make two trips due to lengthy court proceedings. The selection of a child and the initiation of the adoption are handled on the first trip and the adoption and immigration of the child are handled on the second trip.

Such varied methods of assigning children will change after these countries sign and ratify the Hague Convention. The Hague Convention requires that full information is shared with an adoptive parent prior to the adoption trip.

The Referral Call

When the call comes with the formal referral of your child, the suggestion of a child or an invitation to travel to select a child, panic may render you nearly witless and speechless. Make a list of questions in advance and keep it by your phone. If this is a baby, you might ask whether the child needs a special formula or special bottles and nipples. Other questions you might ask, include:

Who is taking care of the child?

What is the child's general state of health?

Was the child orphaned, abandoned, or relinquished?

How long has he or she been in the orphanage?

In the event that you are assigned an abandoned child, the authorities abroad will have already drawn up a birth certificate with a birth date estimated by a pediatrician and names generated by the orphanage director.

Don't hang up without asking for the name and the phone number of the person who is calling you. Write it down. You will need to contact that person again. Good social work practice dictates that you are given as much time as you need to make a decision. Unfortunately, if you are traveling without a formal referral, once you are abroad, you may feel pressured into making a quick decision.

Depending upon the policies of the child-sending country, the referral or assignment information you receive will include a photograph or possibly a video, health, educational, social, and genetic information, possibly a power of attorney form, and a custody contract.

Medical information and tests are not always accurate, and record keeping is poor in many countries. Information for some children may be almost nonexistent beyond their approximate age and weight. In other cases, the medical information may be overwhelming. In former Union of Soviet Socialist Republics, infants and children are often overdiagnosed or misdiagnosed. If you're referred a child who looks fine, but has an ominous-sounding medical evaluation, take matters into your own hands. While you are abroad, take an interpreter along to consult with the orphanage pediatrician. If you're still worried, send a video tape and and the written information to an international pediatric specialist in the United States. Follow up with an international phone consultation.

The same type of information will be provided for the referral of older children; however, the social worker at the orphanage will also include observations about the child's personality and behavior. However, keep in mind that the child's behavior may be different for a while when the child is interacting in a family. (See Chapter 15 for more information on adoptive adjustments for older children and their new families.)

Adoption Parenting Courses

If your adoption agency doesn't offer parenting courses, but you are required to take one or you are simply interested in the additional experience, you can use the book you are reading now as a first step.

How to Adopt Internationally is the text for a non-graded international adoption parent training system available through Erichsen Consultations. The system was authored by Jean Erichsen, LSW-MA, one of the authors of this book.

The first of three six-week courses helps prospective parents understand the physical and emotional needs of institutionalized children. The second helps potential parents prepare and pack for their adoption trip and expands on child care in developing countries. The third requires that the prospective parent review appropriate books and films to become intimately acquainted with their child's homeland.

The total for all three courses is $100. The system can be ordered by e-mailing Erichsen Consultations at jerichsen@losninos.org.

Most people are quite happy with the babies and children they are assigned, unless they object to the skin color, the age, or there is a serious health problem they are worried about. If you are concerned about the child referred, you can take the translated information, photos, and videos to discuss with a pediatrician. In addition, you can contact an international adoption clinic (see Chapter 13 for names and contact information) and send them the information for an opinion. Developmental delays in orphanage children are common. Your child may lag far behind infants and children of the same age level in your neighborhood. Generally, the children overcome developmental delays fairly quickly.

If you choose to accept a referral, telephone your acceptance to your adoption agency and then follow this up formally by mail or fax. Most adoption agencies, however, send along an approval form for you to sign. The child-placing entity will send copies or fax the child's documents to your agency or you if required by INS and possibly the Department of Public Welfare in your state. The originals are retained for their court.

However, if the child's medical information indicates problems you cannot or do not wish to handle, or if the child does not fit the guidelines you originally specified, then by all means, turn down the referral. You will eventually be given another. If you are in a foreign country when you make a decision not to adopt a particular child, it is extremely important that you cooperate with the authorities abroad and also with your child-placing agency in the United States if you wish to try again.

The referral of a child is a nerve-wracking time for everyone. The new parents start worrying about who is taking care of the child, his or her state of health, and possible legal hitches. The agency starts worrying about getting the adoptive parent's approval in order to begin coordinating the travel itinerary with the adoption hearing. This can get complicated. Sometimes the adoptive parents or their doctor request an updated medical evaluation, which can take a month or two for the physician, lab, and translator to complete. An aggravating problem at this point can be the rescheduling of the adoption hearing, which may mean changing your travel plans one or more times.

Consider the referral of a child tentative until you have left your child's native land and crossed a U.S. port of entry — with the child in your arms. Refrain from telling everyone about your child right away and don't pass out copies of his or her photo. Wait until you're ready to leave the country — the adoption situation could change.

You can help prepare a child over age two for adoption. Mail the following items to the authorities in charge of your child: pictures of yourselves, your home, your parents, and, if applicable, the child's future siblings. Also include pictures of the local playground, pets, and/or a fabulous toy like a tricycle. And, include translations of short letters from new family members that can be read to him or her.

Obtaining a Visa or Tourist Card

American citizens do not usually need visas except in formerly or presently communist countries with the exception of Colombia. If you are adopting from Africa, China, Vietnam, Russia, or other countries formerly part of the Union of Soviet Socialist Republics, your international agency or the consulate of that country will advise you regarding the type of visa needed. They will also tell you how to use special expediting services in order to get the visa in a day or two. If not, visa expediting services can be found on the Internet. Simply go to your favorite search engine and type in "visa expediting services."

Once the authorities abroad know that you plan to visit and adopt an orphan, they will send you an invitation to travel to their country. When you have this letter and

Step 15
Obtain visa or tourist card (if necessary) for travel to your child's country.

Preadoptive Medical Consultations

Over the past few years, a new pediatric specialty has evolved that assists adoptive singles and couples with their decision regarding the acceptance of the child they were referred. Adoptive parents forward any information they receive with a referral (video, photos, and medical and social history) to an international pediatric specialist for review. (See Chapter 13 for a list of clinics that may offer preadoptive medical consultations).

After the doctor reviews the information, a consultation takes place by phone or in person for a summary of medical problems, congenital anomalies, possibilities of other problems, and a discussion of services and treatment that might be required. If the information is inadequate or worrisome, the pediatrician will request updated information, typically new growth and developmental parameters or family or social history. A wait of several weeks for updated, translated information is not unusual. And some of the information, such as social or family history may not be available.

If parents are traveling in advance of referral information on a specific child (Eastern European countries, for example), once abroad, they can take videos or photographs of the child and forward it along with any written information and their own personal observations to the pediatric specialist. If parents are planning on using a pediatric specialist, they should be sure to make arrangements before they travel.

Since pediatricians do not have the child before them, there's a limit to how much they can really tell a parent. However, they can be of great help in some situations. For example, most medical evaluations from Russia contain archaic terms and diagnoses not easily understood in the United States.

Pediatricians will not make adoption decisions for potential parents. Parents, not pediatricians, must take the responsibility for the adoption decision. They need to trust their ability to use their hearts as well as their heads to make an informed decision. Ultimately the decision must be based on the best interest of the child and the adoptive family (i.e. What are the child's needs, the family's expectations and resources, and do these two areas match?)

your travel itinerary, you will fill out their visa application forms. If you are adopting from an international agency, they will furnish these forms. Otherwise, they can be obtained at the consulate of that country. The length of stay will depend on the length of the adoption process in the foreign country. Some countries require two short trips of about one to two weeks each. Otherwise, they let one or both adoptive parents break up a potentially long stay with two short trips. The question regarding the object of the journey should be answered. "To conclude business and carry out humanitarian aid." In Russia, you can write in "adoption." Be certain to sign and date the form.

Send copies of the letter and itinerary along with the visa application to the consulate. Obtaining a visa can take a week or two unless you use special expediting services.

Most tourist cards or visas are issued in duplicate. The original is surrendered upon entry. The copy is turned in at the time of departure. The other documents required to enter a country are needed again to leave it.

Sample Referral Information for Colombia

MEDICAL REPORT

January 21, 2002

PERSONAL INFORMATION
Name of child: Jorge

Jorge is three months old. He was born on October 3, 2001, at 6:15 a.m. He was admitted to the Institution on October 3, 2001, by referral from Casa de Madre. He was born spontaneously, in a vertex presentation. His Apgar was 10 at one and five minutes. He was born from his mother's first pregnancy.

Weight at Birth:	4 pounds 13 ounces
Length at Birth:	18 inches
Weight at Admission:	5 pounds
Length at Admission:	17.5 inches
Head Circumference at Admission:	13 inches

GENERAL PHYSICAL EXAMINATION
Head:	Normal, patent anterior fontanelle
Eyes:	PERLA, sclerae normal
Ears:	Normal otoscopy bilaterally
Nose:	Normal anterior rhinoscopy
Mouth:	Normal
Neck:	No lymph node enlargement
Heart:	Rhythmic heart sounds, no murmurs
Lungs:	Well-ventilated, no adventitious sounds
Abdomen:	Soft, no organ enlargement
Genitals:	Testicles have descended
Extremities:	No hip click
Skin:	Normal
Neurological System:	Reflexes present and normal

DIAGNOSIS
Jorge was born with a low birth weight. He was premature. His weight was appropriate for his gestational age. Immunizations have been begun. He has shown good growth and weight gain.

LABORATORY TESTING
Neonatal TSH testing done on October 6, 2001:	Normal
Serological testing done on October 6, 2001:	Non-reactive
Antigen for Hepatitis B testing done on October 6, 2001:	Negative
Blood Type:	O(-)

CURRENT GROWTH INFORMATION
Weight:	12 pounds, 2 ounces
Length:	22 inches
Head Circumference:	14 inches

Sample Referral Information for Russia

ANASTASIA AND TATIANA

Information on biological parents:
Mother: Russian, born in 1972, healthy, beautiful, blonde hair, unemployed.
Father: Tartar, born in 1962, professional school graduate, healthy, unemployed.
The marriage is not officially registered, but the father has officially recognized his fatherhood. Biological parents were deprived of their parental rights in April 2000. They often use alcohol. They reside in the town of St. Petersburg. The mother has two other children who are parented by their father (previous husband of the mother). Legal aspects of the adoption: no obstacles for the adoption.

Information on the children:

Anastasia (DOB February 21, 1999)
Place of birth: St. Petersburg. The girl was a full-term baby and was born in a maternity hospital, birth weight – 2.600 kg. At present, her weight is 10.300 kg, height – 64 cm. Health as of July 4, 2001 — residual consequences of rickets, she is often ill with respiratory infections. Had varicella. Physical development is harmonic, health group 3. No delays in development, the girl is smart, agile and active. Speech is at the level of separate words. No physical defects, the girl has well-proportioned body and is well-built. The walk is normal and sure. She eats very well and sleeps well. The child is beautiful, nice, not capricious, sociable, does not allow others to treat her badly and has a mind of her own. She has brown soft hair, dark brown eyes, clean white skin, oriental type of face and straight legs. The child resides in the orphanage.

Tatiana (DOB April 17, 1998)
Place of birth: St. Petersburg. The girl was born in a maternity hospital.
Health as of July 17, 2001:
  - consequences of perinatal CNS damage
  - delay in psychic and motor development
  - kyphoscoliosis (the scoliosis is very grave. Possibly, there is a congenital pathology of T9. The nature of this pathology is not yet clarified. The girl is to be treated in Chelyabinsk for 2 months and after that examined once again.
  - rickets 2
The heart is normal. The girl has no mental weakness. RW test result is negative. She is not HIV or hepatitis carrier. At present, her weight is 11.500 kg, height 79 cm., head circumference – 48 cm, chest circumference – 51 cm.
According to her doctor, she has a good potential and should respond well to medical treatment. The scoliosis is not too conspicuous. The child is socially neglected. She needs good food and massage, speech therapy and psychotherapy. With the right treatment all visible defects (one shoulder is higher than the other, incorrect walk etc.) are correctable. The girl is very nice, eats and sleeps well. On July 03, 2001, the girl was placed in the Diagnostic ward of Chelyabinsk Regional Hospital for a thorough examination.
Personal impressions: the child is very sociable, well-behaved, affectionate, independent (dresses and eats without assistance and prefers to do most things herself), not capricious and is patient. She is agile, active, inquisitive and talkative. She likes to obtain new information and talk about it. She easily adapts to new environment. Her walk is somewhat waddling. Feet are turned outside. The girl can run. She and her sister Kristina look very much alike. She is beautiful and charming. She has brown, soft and straight hair and dark-brown eyes. She is not thin. Her skin is white and clean (although with a lot of mosquito bites on the face and body). No negative personal qualities are noticed. The child lives in the orphanage.

Sample Referral Update for China

GROWTH REPORT — MEI LI

Mei Li, Female, was found abandoned in the morning about 6:10 AM on June 10, 2001, in front of the gate of Old People's House in Shanghai city by a staff of the said House. She was put inside of a bamboo basket, with some clothes, diapers, formula, a bottle, and a paper note in which it says that Born June 5, 2001. The said House reported to the Civil Office; a Civil Officer and the Police Station of Shanghai Police Bureau sent her to our Social Welfare Institute on the same day. Up to this day, we couldn't find her biological parents and other relatives.

When Mei Li was sent to our Institute, she was healthy, growing well, hands and feet normal. Height 51 CM, Weight 3.5 KG, Head Circle Size: 34.2 CM, Chest Circle Size: 34.2 CM. As she is very smart and lovely, we gave her the name Mei Li. Li means beautiful and pretty.

Since she entered our Institute, she has been healthy, eating and sleeping well, with regular immunization. In 2001-09-06, she had the first time of DTP and Poliomyelitis. In 2001-10-16 she had the 2nd time of DTP and Poliomyelitis, in 2001-11-15 she had the 3rd time of DTP and Poliomyelitis. We have a pediatrician to see the children every day. Now she is healthy. When she was about 4 months old, because of weather changing, she had some diarrhea, but with the caring of the nannies and pediatrician, she recovered very soon. We haven't found she has any allergy.

1. Routine:

She has a very good routine. Every day she wakes up about 7:00AM, 7:30AM has breakfast which is formula plus congee, she can drink a bottle of 230 ml a time. The formula is made in Guangzhou with the brand of Jinding. 9:00AM bathing. The have some sunshine or play in the room. 9:30 has some water plus vitamins 11:00AM has formula, 12:00 AM-14:30PM nap time. 15:00PM has formula. 16:00PM has water. Then enjoys music or plays with little friends. 19:00PM formula. 20:30 sleep. 23:00PM and 03:00AM has some formula again. She eats well.

2. Body and mental development:

She has been living in our Institute since her finding day. When she was about 2 months old her eyes could gaze the moving objects. When 3 months old, she could grasp objects by hands. When 4 months, she could put toys into her mouth, would like to sit in the waving chair and push her feet to make the chair waiving. When 5 months, she could roll over in bed. When 6 months old, she could smile when nanny hold her. Now she can sit by herself, and even can stand for a moment. She likes to sit in the walking-car for activity, turn her head back when nanny calls her name, and enjoys music peacefully.

3. Personality:

Mei Li is an active, happy, out-going, group-able girl. Her skin is fair, beautiful and very pretty. She likes to sit in the waving chair, or in the walking-car. She doesn't like to sit in the bed. She enjoys music, plays with toys, and games. She is a very healthy, active, smart, and pretty girl.

Descriptor: Shanghai Social Welfare Institute (With seal) Date: 2001-Dec. 3

CHAPTER 9

Filing the Orphan Petition

Eligibility to File for an Orphan Petition

In order to be able to file a petition, parents must meet INS eligibility requirements.

A Petition to Classify an Orphan as an Immediate Relative (Form I-600) for issuance of a visa may be filed by a married or unmarried United States citizen. (If married, they must adopt jointly; if unmarried, the citizen must be at least twenty-five years of age.) The spouse need not be a United States citizen. It must be established that both the married petitioner and spouse, or the unmarried petitioner, will care for the orphan properly if the orphan is admitted to the United States. If the orphan was adopted abroad, it must be established that both the married petitioner and spouse, or the unmarried petitioner, personally saw and observed the child prior to, or during the adoption proceedings. If both the petitioner and spouse, or unmarried petitioner, did not personally see and observe the child during the adoption proceedings abroad, they must establish that the child will be adopted in the United States and that any preadoption requirements of the state of the orphan's proposed residence have been met. This generally means an approved home study. The petitioner must submit, if requested, a statement by an appropriate official in the state in which the child will reside that the prospective parents are approved to adopt in that state. If the orphan has not been adopted abroad, the petitioner and spouse, or the unmarried petitioner, must establish that the child will be adopted in the United States by the petitioner and spouse jointly, or by the unmarried petitioner, and that the preadoption requirements, if any, of the state of the orphan's proposed residence have been met. Again, this means an approved home study.

To download Form I-600 or to gather other up-to-date information on INS forms and fees, visit its website at **www.ins.usdoj.gov** and then click on Forms and Fees. You can also request Form I-600 by calling the INS Forms Request Line at 1(800) 870-3676 .

Documentation of Orphans

In addition, in order for approval of Form I-600, it is crucial that the child you are adopting meets the INS definition of an orphan and that proper supporting documentation of the child's status be available.

In the first paragraph of the application and the petition, the INS definition of an orphan is provided:

> *"The term orphan under the immigration laws means a foreign child who is under the age of 16 years at the time the visa petition in his behalf is filed and who is an orphan because both parents have died or disappeared, or abandoned or deserted the orphan, or the orphan has become separated or lost from both parents."*[1]
>
> *"If the orphan has only one parent, that parent must be incapable of providing for the orphan's care and must have in writing irrevocably released the orphan for emigration and adoption. An illegitimate child whose father acknowledges paternity and signs a relinquishment along with the mother is also considered an orphan. In addition, the orphan either must have been adopted abroad or must be coming to the United States for adoption by a United States citizen and spouse jointly or by an unmarried United States citizen at least 25 years of age. [Section 101] (b)(i)(F) of the Immigration and Nationality Act."*

A child who is abandoned to a government institution by both parents may qualify for classification as an orphan under immigration law, but immigration law does not define the term abandonment, and the subject is only discussed once in INS regulations.

According to the regulations, a child who has been unconditionally abandoned to an orphanage is considered to have no parents. A child is not considered to be abandoned, however, when he or she has been placed temporarily in an orphanage, if the parent or parents are contributing or trying to contribute to the child's support or the parent or parents otherwise show that they have not ended their parental obligations to the child.

Difficult Issues in Orphan Cases

Under U.S. immigration law, the child of a sole or surviving parent may be considered an orphan if that parent is unable to care for the child properly and has forever or irrevocably released him or her for emigration and adoption. The child of an unwed mother normally may be considered to be an orphan as long as the mother does not marry. The child of a surviving parent may also be considered to be an orphan if it is proven that one of the child's parents died and the surviving parent has not since married. However, a marriage results in the child's having a stepfather or stepmother under immigration law.

Legitimate versus Illegitimate Designations

Most countries have legal procedures for the acknowledgment of children by their natural fathers. Therefore, adoptive and prospective adoptive parents of children who were born out of wedlock in any country should find out whether the children have been legitimized. Legitimized children from any country have two legal parents and cannot qualify as orphans (until the passing of the proposed Hague amendments). This

---

[1] INS makes exceptions for children over age 16, who are the oldest in a sibling group adopted at the same time.

does not apply to institutionalized children relinquished to adoptive parents, but to children relinquished by their birthmothers to adoptive parents, as is the case in many private or independent Guatemalan adoptions.

Some countries have passed laws that eliminate all legal distinctions between legitimate and illegitimate children. In those countries, all children are considered to be legitimate or legitimized children of their natural fathers as of the effective date of the laws in question. Of course, paternity must be established. A child born out of wedlock and living in a country that has such a law and whose paternity has been legally established has two parents even though the parents never married and may not be living together.

Adoptive and prospective adoptive parents of children who were born out of wedlock should become familiar with the legitimacy laws in the countries where the children are born and reside. If a child born out of wedlock is from a country that has eliminated all legal distinctions between legitimate and illegitimate children, the child could still qualify for classification as an orphan under immigration law.

Refugee Children

Every year the world experiences significant natural disasters. Earthquakes, hurricanes, and epidemics create hundreds of orphans. "Ethnic cleansing," war, and famine create even more. Media coverage of such traumatic events and the children left orphaned by them often motivates individuals to seek information on adopting these children.

Unfortunately, adopting children orphaned by these sudden and extreme circumstances is much more difficult than adopting a child already relinquished by a parent to an institution. Documented evidence must prove that the child has no living relatives, and investigating a child's social history and creating identifying documents is a slow process, particularly in an area that has been destroyed by nature or man. American consulates may be overwhelmed and unable to issue orphan visas, and the INS does not have a special category for refugee orphans. In exceptional cases, the INS might be able to issue a humanitarian visa, but again, such an occurrence is rare.

Many people remember all too well the painful lessons learned during the Vietnam War when American agencies placed refugee children in U.S. homes. Many parents of the "orphans" actually survived the fall of Saigon and eventually made their way to America to find their children. In such cases, the courts returned the children to their biological parents. This is the only instance in which an international adoption has resulted in a custody suit.

Filing the I-600 Orphan Petition

Where you file the I-600 Orphan Petition depends upon the country and the kind of adoption you are planning, such as an agency-initiated adoption requiring one or both spouses to travel abroad; an agency-initiated adoption with escort for the child to the United States; or a parent-initiated adoption. Your U.S.-based international adoption agency or INS will advise you whether to file the Orphan Petition with your local INS office or the U.S. Consulate in the child's native country. For most foreign adoptions, Form I-600 is filed at the U.S. Consulate abroad. However, if you are advised to file the form in the United States, you will file it at the same INS office where the Application for Advance Processing (Form I-600A) was filed. If the petition is filed in the United States, a cable of approval of Form I-600 will be forwarded at your request to the appropriate U.S. visa-issuing post abroad. Ask your INS office to send abroad to the U.S. Consulate a "Visa Cable 39." This message indicates that your INS office has issued approval of your Form I-600 and supporting documentation.

Step 16
File Form I-600 (Orphan Petition) if this is to be filed in the United States. (This is usually filed abroad if the adoption is finalized in the child's country and both parents travel to meet the child.)

U.S. Citizens Residing Abroad

Transferred business employees of international companies, military personnel and U.S. government employees, missionaries, students, Peace Corps volunteers, and other U.S. citizens who are not expatriates (residing abroad voluntarily without a contract or military orders) and who will be residing abroad should follow these procedures for the following situations:

U.S. citizen departing for a foreign post.
Filing Form I-600A, Application for Advance Processing, will be easier if your move is still in the planning stages. Ask an adoption agency to give you top priority if you are planning to leave the United States in the near future. You must get advance processing before you leave if you wish to avoid future delays.

U.S. citizens residing abroad who have been living with an adopted orphan for less than two years.
At least three to six months before you plan to return home, you must process Form I-600, Petition to Classify an Orphan as an Immediate Relative. Contact the nearest U.S. Embassy or Consulate for the names of social workers who conduct home studies and for the appropriate INS service office in order to file Form I-600. Allow enough time before your departure to obtain a home study that meets the legal requirements of your state of residence. If the country only places children through U.S. agencies they have licensed, you will need to contact the U.S. Consulate in that country for a list of approved agencies.

U.S. citizens who have adopted abroad or had legal custody and have been living abroad for two years with the foreign orphan.
You may file Form I-130, Petition to Classify an Alien as an Immediate Relative. Form I-130 is for aliens of any age who can be classified as immediate relatives. The U.S. Embassy located in the country where you reside will provide you with Form I-130 and the list of supporting documents that you will need in order to file for the child's IR-2 visa. If you can prove that the child has lived with you for two years, you do not need a home study or an FBI clearance.

If you have been living abroad, you may not be able to satisfy the U.S. domicile requirement. Your child's visa application may be denied unless you can provide the following.

- Proof that you are re-establishing residency in the United States with one of the following documents: acceptance of a job offer in the United States; purchase of a residence in the United States; or a signed lease for a personal residence in the United States.

- American citizens posted abroad as missionaries, members of the U.S. Armed Forces, or employees of a U.S.-based company are not subject to the re-establishing residency requirement.

- If you cannot satisfy the residency requirement, Section 322(s)(4) of the Immigration and Nationality Act permits the parents of an adopted child to apply for a B-2 tourist visa to enable them to travel to the United States in order to expedite a U.S. passport as proof of citizenship. To obtain a B-2 visa, the adoptive parents must prove that they have made all the necessary arrangements with the INS office in their home state or the state where their adoption agency is located, by presenting a G-56 Form to the officer issuing the B-2 visa.

Proof of U.S. citizenship for adopted children of military and other personnel under SOFA (an armed forces agreement in Germany, Italy, Japan and Korea) is as follows:

If a family stationed in Germany adopts from Eastern Europe and wants to return first to their home base before traveling to the United States to obtain proof of U.S. citizenship for their child, they must get a letter from their Judge Advocate General (JAG). JAG requires that the adoption is final and that an IR-3 visa is issued. With this, they should not have any problems entering their "host country."

Families stationed in Japan and Korea who adopt in Asia may travel directly to the INS office in Hawaii to obtain the child's U.S. passport.

Filing in Absence of Form I-600A

If no Application for Advance Processing (Form I-600A) has been filed because you located a child who meets INS criteria before you knew and understood their requirements, file Form I-600A and Form I-600, and then register with an adoption agency and follow the remaining steps, beginning in Chapter 3.

Required Documents

1. Form I-600, Orphan Petition. Both spouses must sign the form. (See sample form at the end of this chapter.)

2. Birth certificate of orphan. If the birth certificate cannot be obtained, the prospective adoptive parent should submit an explanation together with the best available evidence of birth.

3. Death certificate(s) of the orphan's parent(s), if applicable.

4. Form of relinquishment, if applicable, which shows evidence that the orphan's sole or surviving parent cannot provide for the orphan's care and has in writing forever or irrevocably released the orphan for emigration and adoption. If the orphan has two unmarried parents, both must sign relinquishments. However, a child with two parents must be relinquished to a government agency prior to the adoption.

5. Certificate of abandonment, if the orphan is institutionalized, which shows evidence that the orphan has been unconditionally abandoned to an orphanage.

6. A final or initial decree of adoption or permanent guardianship.

7. Evidence that the preadoption home study requirements, if any, of the state of the orphan's proposed residence have been met, if the child is to be adopted in the

United States. A statement to this effect is often included in the home study. If, under the laws of the state of the child's proposed residence, it is not possible to submit this evidence when the petition is first filed, it may be submitted later. The petition, however, will not be approved without it.

8. The home study and supporting documents previously listed with Form I-600A, Application for Advance Processing, unless this evidence was already submitted with a pending Form I-600A application or it is within one year of a favorable determination (Form I-171H) in a completed advance processing case.

Documents 2-6 are obtained by the foreign lawyer or foreign child-placing entity, who also arranges for the translation of these documents. Two sets of certified copies are needed to complete the legal immigration and readoption in your home state. The adoptive parent, or international agency in the case of an escort, is responsible for submitting a complete set of these translated originals to the American Consulate abroad. If you are traveling to meet your child, be sure to take the originals on your adoption trip unless, of course, your agency has already sent them.

Exceptions to the Process

If documentary evidence relating to the child or the home study is not yet available, the I-600 Orphan Petition and fee may be filed without that evidence.

If the necessary evidence relating to the child or the home study is not submitted within one year from the date of submission of the petition, the petition is considered abandoned and the fee is not refunded. If the petitioner later decides that he or she wants to petition for the same child or a different child, it will be necessary to file a new Application for Advance Processing (Form I-600A) or a new Orphan Petition (Form I-600) and pay a new fee.

Updating the I-600 Orphan Petition

As with Form I-600A, Form I-600 is valid for 18 months. If an orphan has not immigrated before then, a new application, updated home study and documents, and new fingerprint charts must be filed.

Overseas Orphan Investigation

When an I-600 Orphan Petition is sent to a U.S. Consulate or Embassy for possible issuance of a visa to the child or when an Orphan Petition is filed there, a consular officer conducts an overseas orphan investigation as part of the normal processing. This is usually done quickly, and the adopting parent need not do anything to initiate, expedite, or finalize this process. The purpose of the investigation is to make certain that the child is an orphan as defined in immigration law, and the child does not have a significant illness or disability not described in the Orphan Petition. A sample of Form I-604, Request for and Report on Overseas Orphan Investigation, can be found at the end of this chapter. Note: The I-604 is generated by the INS and is not submitted by parents.

If a child is not eligible for classification as an orphan under immigration law, INS notifies the petitioner and spouse, if married, and gives them the choice of withdrawing the petition or having the question considered in revocation proceedings. Revocation proceedings give the petitioner a chance to submit evidence to overrule the stated grounds for revoking the approval of the petition.

Form I-600

Orphan Petition, Page 1 of 2

OMB No. 1115-0049

Petition to Classify Orphan as an Immediate Relative

[Section 101 (b)(1)(F) of the Immigration and Nationality Act, as amended.]

U.S. Department of Justice
Immigration and Naturalization Service

Please do not write in this block.

TO THE SECRETARY OF STATE;
The petition was filed by:
☐ Married petitioner   ☐ Unmarried petitioner

The petition is approved for orphan:
☐ Adopted abroad   ☐ Coming to U.S. for adoption. Preadoption requirements have been met.

Remarks:

Fee Stamp

File number

DATE OF ACTION
DD
DISTRICT

Please type or print legibly in ink. Use a separate petition for each child.

Petition is being made to classify the named orphan as an immediate relative.

BLOCK I - Information about prospective

1. My name is: (Last)   (First)   (Middle name of notary)

8. If you are now married, give the following information:
(Date and place of present marriage)

2. Other names used (including maiden name if appropriate):

Name of present spouse (include maiden name of wife)

3. I reside in the U.S.   (C/O if appropriate)   (Apt. No.)

Date of birth of spouse   Place of birth of spouse

(Number and street)   (Town or city)   (State)   (Zip Code)

Number of prior marriages of spouse

4. Address abroad (if any): (Number and street)   (Apt. No.)

My spouse resides ☐ With me   ☐ Apart from me (provide address below)

(Town or city)   (Province)   (Country)

(Apt. No.)   (No. and street)   (City)   (State)   (Country)

5. I was born on: (Month)   (Day)   (Year)

9. I am a citizen of the United States through:
☐ Birth   ☐ Parents   ☐ Naturalization

In: (Town or City)   (State or Province)   (Country)

If acquired through naturalization, give name under which naturalized, number of naturalization certificate, and date and place of naturalization:

6. My phone number is: (Include Area Code)

If not, submit evidence of citizenship. See Instruction 2.a(2).

7. My marital status is:
☐ Married
☐ Widowed
☐ Divorced
☐ Single
    ☐ I have never been married.
    ☐ I have been previously married _____ time(s).

If acquired through parentage, have you obtained a certificate in your own name based on that acquisition?
☐ No   ☐ Yes

Have you or any person through whom you claimed citizenship ever lost United States citizenship?
☐ No   ☐ Yes (If yes, attach detailed explanation.)

Continue on reverse.

Received	Trans. In	Ret'd Trans. Out	Completed

Form I-600 (Rev. 11/28/01)Y Page 1

Form I-600

Orphan Petition, Page 2 of 2

BLOCK II - Information about orphan beneficiary

10. Name at birth　(First)　(Middle)　(Last)

11. Name at present　(First)　(Middle)　(Last)

12. Any other names by which orphan is or was known.

13. Sex　☐ Male　☐ Female

14. Date of birth (Month/Day/Year)

15. Place of birth (City)　(State or Province)　(Country)

16. The beneficiary is an orphan because (check　One)
    - ☐ He/she has no parents.
    - ☐ He/she has only one parent who is the sole or surviving

17. If the orphan has only one parent, answer the　following
    a. State what has become of the other parent:

    b. Is the remaining parent capable of providing for the orphan's support?　☐ Yes　☐ No
    c. Has the remaining parent, in writing, irrevocably released orphan for emigration and adoption?　☐ Yes　☐ No

18. Has the orphan been adopted abroad by the petitioner and jointly or the unmarried petitioner?　☐ Yes　☐ No

    If yes, did the petitioner and spouse or unmarried petitioner personally see and observe the child prior to or during the adoption proceedings?　☐ Yes　☐ No

    Date of adoption

    Place of adoption

19. If either answer in question 18 is "No", answer the following:
    a. Do petitioner and spouse jointly or does the unmarried intend to adopt the orphan in the United States?　☐ Yes　☐ No
    b. Have the preadoption requirements, if any, of the orphan's proposed state of residence been met?　☐ Yes　☐ No
    c. If b. is answered "No", will they be met later?　☐ Yes　☐ No

20. To petitioner's knowledge, does the orphan have any physical or affliction?　☐ Yes　☐ No
    If "Yes", name the affliction.

21. Who has legal custody of the child?

22. Name of child welfare agency, if any, assisting in this case:

23. Name of attorney abroad, if any, representing petitioner in this

    Address of above.

24. Address in the United States where orphan will reside.

25. Present address of orphan.

25. If orphan is residing in an institution, give full name of institution.

26. If orphan is not residing in an institution, give full name of person whom orphan is residing.

(name of notary)
27. Give any additional information necessary to locate orphan such as name of district, section, zone or locality in which orphan resides.

28. Location of American Consulate where application for visa will be made.
    (City in Foreign Country)　(Foreign Country)

Certification of prospective petitioner
I certify under penalty of perjury under the laws of the United States of America that the foregoing is true and correct and that I will care for an orphan/orphans properly if admitted to the United States.

(Signature of Prospective Petitioner)

Executed on (Date)

Certification of married prospective petitioner's spouse
I certify under penalty of perjury under the laws of the United States of America that the foregoing is true and correct and that my spouse and I will care for an orphan/orphans properly if admitted to the United States.

(Signature of Prospective Petitioner)

Executed on (Date)

Signature of person preparing form, if other than petitioner
I declare that this document was prepared by me at the request of the prospective petitioner and is based on all information of which I have any knowledge.

(Signature)

Address

Executed on (Date)

CHAPTER 10

The Adoption Trip

This is the moment you've been waiting for. If you're feeling happy and frightened at the same time, it's to be expected. You're about to become a parent in the midst of a whirlwind of activity.

Your adoption trip will be planned down to the last detail if you are adopting through an international agency. They will make certain that you are in the right place at the right time for all of your appointments. If this is a parent-initiated adoption, you will plan the trip yourself, scheduling your travel around the adoption-related appointments.

Depending upon the country you are adopting from, you might be told to travel anywhere from a few days to a few months after you receive a referral or an invitation. If you have chosen a country that provides a complete, formal referral and you sign a power of attorney form, the foreign attorney acts on your behalf so that you do not need to leave immediately.

Your adoption experience in a foreign country is uniquely your own. If you have never spent much time in a foreign country before, the food, customs, and language can give you a first-rate case of culture shock. The average stay for adopters is two to four weeks, just long enough to reach a peak in jubilation and exasperation, triumph and frustration, as well as culture shock. No one has ever died of it, but recovery requires several months. After a year back home, almost everyone has fully recovered and wants to make the trip again — either to adopt more children or to visit.

Unfortunately, as described in Chapter 8, some adopters will have to make a trip first to meet the child and then, depending on the country and the laws, return a second time for the adoption. However, some parents who travel twice find that it makes packing and caring for your adopted child much easier and less stressful, since you can scout out stores and services and have a much better idea of what to expect for your second trip. Parents who travel twice have also appreciated the opportunity for sightseeing and shopping on their first trip; something they're often too busy to do on the second trip.

Step 17
Prepare for your adoption trip.

International Travel

Adopters traveling to foreign countries become unofficial ambassadors for the United States, especially for the U.S. adopters who come after them. Adopters who wish to make and leave a favorable impression do their homework first — a study of the host country's language, culture, and etiquette. While orphans are usually from the lower classes, social workers, directors, lawyers, and liaisons are from the privileged classes. Proper social form and behavior are important to them. Most North Americans are in a hurry to return home. This is understandable. What is not understandable is rude and pushy behavior, which, incidentally, does not get the family home any faster. Most delays occur during the court procedure. The court cannot be rushed, no matter what part of the world you are in. Be accessible, responsive, and cooperative to avoid further delays.

Several excellent travel books explain how we should behave in foreign countries as well as 1,001 things every traveler should know. New editions are published each year. The language barrier appears to present the greatest obstacle to bridging the gap between the two cultures. Books, tapes, records, and hand-held computers are available to assist or help you learn most of the major languages. In most cases, a representative associated with your U.S. agency will meet you abroad and stay with your group, but the more you know, the more independent you will be when you arrive at your destination. Consult the Internet for more information.

As you prepare for your adoption trip, learn the travel requirements and procedures in the foreign country, too. After sending your dossier, gather your travel documents together; then you will be ready to travel when your referral comes. While the average adoption stay is two to four weeks, your stay could last up to eight weeks, depending upon your foreign source and other variables.

Following Entry and Exit Requirements

Foreign immigration authorities only permit travelers with proper documents to enter their countries. Be aware that many foreign governments change their entry and exit requirements frequently. For up-to-date information on entry and exit regulations, contact your airline or the consulate of the foreign country you wish to visit.

If you are working with an international agency, they will advise you about your travel documents. Otherwise, you will need to consult a travel agent.

Generally the following documents are required:

1. A passport. Married couples should obtain separate passports since one spouse may need to return home ahead of the other spouse.

2. A tourist card or visa (if required). See Chapter 8 for more detailed information on obtaining your visa.

3. A round-trip ticket. Non-penalty tickets are more expensive, yet they are the best way to purchase airline tickets for an adoption. That way, if the hearings are rescheduled or other problems occur overseas, you won't lose any money. You can exchange the tickets.

4. Identifying photos. A passport photo will be sufficient.

If for some reason you were not able to get your passport earlier, keep in mind that one-day service for passports can be found in most major cities. You may need to present evidence that you must leave the country within forty-eight hours. Call ahead about this as well as their office hours. (See Chapter 6 for more information on obtaining passports.)

Most tourist cards or visas are issued in duplicate. The original is surrendered upon entry. The copy is turned in at the time of departure. The other documents required to enter a country are needed again to leave it.

Making Travel Arrangements

You can make your travel plans by phone or on the Internet. U.S.-based international agencies as well as some travel agencies are aware of adopters' needs and will advise you about fares and nonpenalty tickets. Be certain to buy nonpenalty, changeable tickets, or you'll lose money if the orphanage is quarantined, your court date is rescheduled, or some other delay pops up. In addition, some travel agents specialize in adoption travel. Ask other adoptive parents or your adoption agency for a recommendation. Do not make reservations until the INS sends a cable of clearance and the court hearing is scheduled. Remember to arrive at the airport three to four hours before any international flight and two hours before a domestic flight.

Since different excursion rates are offered from time to time by various airlines and since airfares are subject to sudden changes, you should check the fares of several airlines before your adoption trip is scheduled. You will also need to purchase a one-way ticket back to the United States for your child. Infants and small children who won't need a separate seat are only charged a small percentage of the overall cost of an adult ticket.

In most circumstances, your international agency will arrange for your lodgings. If you are traveling individually to adopt, the agency representative abroad will help you find lodgings according to your taste and budget. If you are traveling in a group, your lodgings will be arranged ahead of departure.

Prior to leaving, try to find a doctor knowledgeable about health problems in developing countries. Arrange for a consultation with the doctor before you leave. The most commonly recommended vaccines are for hepatitis A and B with updating of your tetanus and polio series. Other vaccines are not generally indicated. You can reference the Centers for Disease Control and Prevention (CDC) web site (**http://www.cdc.gov/travel/**) for the most up-to-date recommendations for travelers.

Health Precautions for Travelers

Your adoption trip will be one of the peak experiences in your life. It's definitely not the time to get sick. Taking some simple precautions listed below should minimize your risk of becoming ill while overseas.

Travelers to developing countries must be extremely careful about what they eat and drink if they want to avoid spending a substantial portion of their trip in search of a bathroom. Rule number one is to eat only in first-class restaurants or to dine in the homes of the upper-class nationals. However, this is not always guaranteed safe or even possible.

Even then, do not eat raw salads. And, don't eat raw vegetables or fruits unless you disinfect them with iodine before peeling them yourself. The tried and true mantra "Boil it, peel it, wash it, or forget it," still holds true.

Do not eat raw meat or raw fish. Don't eat or drink milk products unless you know they are pasteurized. And avoid foods, including condiments, that have been sitting around at room temperature for long periods of time.

So what do you do if you are far from an AAA-rated restaurant and hungry? Find a bakery and buy some just-out-of-the-oven rolls or the equivalent staff of life for that country, such as steaming hot rice or boiled or roasted potatoes. Hot noodle soup or hot tea or coffee should also be safe. Clean your hands before you eat with the packaged, pre-moistened towelettes you brought from home. Or, stash some U.S. breakfast bars or other high protein bars in your pockets.

What should you drink? Bottled mineral water, with seal intact, with or without carbonation, or other carbonated beverages, preferably drunk from the bottle through a straw. You should purify water for hygienic use. The easiest method is to purchase a pint-sized water purifier from a camping outfitter to take along. Otherwise, you can purify water by boiling it for twenty minutes. (Take a hot pot and, if necessary, an electrical current adapter, if you plan to boil water.) If boiling is not possible, treat water with Halazone tablets or mix in 10 drops of 2% tincture of iodine to one quart of water and let stand for 30 minutes. (Keep in mind that Halazone only treats bacterial agents, not viruses. Use this method only as a last resort.) If the water is cloudy, filter it through a cotton cloth.

In Latin American countries, U.S. adoptive parents who stay in better hotels will have little to worry about regarding food and water. Luxury hotels post notices in each room explaining the purity of the water supply. However, if you stay in lower rate hotels, bottled water can be ordered. Check to make certain that the seal isn't broken. For all of the former Soviet Union, Eastern Europe, and all of Asia, except Japan, you must use bottled water at all times. This includes water for rinsing your toothbrush as well as for brushing. With the frequency of international travel, most hotels will provide boiled and filtered water.

Should you be unlucky enough to ingest contaminated food or water, the vomiting and/or diarrhea are more of a threat to your health than the particular pathogen, whether it be a virus, bacterium, or parasite. Mild diarrhea in adults can be managed with Imodium (available over-the-counter) or Lomotil (available by prescription). However, diarrhea drains salts and fluids from the body, causing the dehydration that accounts for the deaths of babies worldwide. While an adult's diarrhea is not usually life threatening, grown-ups should replace the salts and fluids they are losing with almost any fluid. If diarrhea is severe (more than one stool every two hours), adults should use an oral rehydration solution (ORS) such as Pedialyte. An ORS powder to be mixed with boiled water is available over the counter at pharmacies around the world.

Should you or your child feel ill the first year after your trip, alert your doctor as to which country you visited. The doctor will then order the appropriate series of stool examination kits. Most diarrhea-producing parasites such as crypotosporidium or giardia are transmitted by contaminated water. Even if the diarrhea abates, you may still be harboring the parasite. Get rechecked at home if you are not completely back to normal.

Other parasites, such as tapeworms and flukes, are transmitted by contaminated foods and, occasionally, by water. Some, like hookworms and schistosomes, which cause schistosomiasis, are acquired through the skin by walking barefoot outside or swimming in contaminated water. Most of these parasites require an intermediate animal host and are not contagious from person to person. These parasites typically do not give diarrhea and may be detected only months or years after travel.

Since most parasites are transmitted in a food-fecal chain, consider each diaper a transmitter. Make certain that all members of your family keep up a scrupulous hand-washing ritual. All orphans and their new parents with symptoms should be tested for parasites after their arrival home. Some worms and parasites have dormant periods and will not show up in every stool sample. You or your child should be rechecked if symptoms persist. (Chapter 13 provides a more detailed overview of the potential health problems of children from developing countries.)

Most bacterial pathogens, such as salmonella and shigella resolve on their own. There is no need to recheck after arrival unless symptoms persist or new problems develop. A few viral pathogens may be spread by travelers after arrival home, especially hepatitis A and hepatitis B. Of course, strict hand washing should be practiced even after arrival back home. An ill person should not prepare food for the family, nor share food or utensils with anyone.

Now is also a good time to talk to your current insurance company about benefits and reimbursements for overseas health emergencies, accidents, and illnesses. Examine your policy to make certain that your child is covered when placed with you, not when you adopt, which could be months later. If coverage is not provided at the time of placement, take out a short-term policy. Military personnel will find extensive coverage in their Champus policies.

You might consider getting travel insurance, which can protect you in case of an emergency evacuation and assist you through many possible emergencies, even an emergency transfer of funds. One such company, Medex (**www.medexassist.com**), offers a host of benefits. Another good source is International SOS (**www.internationalsos.com**).

Vaccinations and Immunizations

Adopters planning international travel may phone the Centers for Disease Control and Prevention (CDC) hotline in Atlanta at (404) 639-3311 or log on to the Center's web site at **www.cdc.gov/travel** for information on epidemics, diseases, and precautions as well as the inoculations necessary for travel to each country. Bear in mind that you usually will be in urban, not rural areas. A short stay in a foreign city requires fewer inoculations than a stay in a rural area or a long stay abroad. If you will be staying in an orphanage or living in a remote area for several weeks, you may need more extensive health precautions.

Many state and local health departments throughout the United States provide travel immunizations and information about health precautions for travelers. If they do not have travel clinics, they usually know who in the area provides vaccines for travelers. If you don't want to visit your health department or public travel clinic, private travel clinics are located in many cities. If you are interested in visiting a private clinic, consult your phone book or visit one of the two web sites that provide directories of private travel clinics throughout the United States. The first is maintained by the International Society of Travel Medicine and can be found at **www.istm.org/**. The second is maintained by the American Society of Tropical Medicine and Hygiene and can be found at **www.astmh.org**.

At the minimum, individuals traveling abroad should update their tetanus and polio vaccinations and should receive the vaccination series for hepatitis A and B. The vaccination for hepatitis B requires a series of three inoculations given over several months, so you may need to begin your inoculations even before you receive a referral. In addition, you might consider immunizing all household members (even those not traveling) for hepatitis A and B.

Most travelers should consider immunization against influenza between November and April. Adults traveling to Asia, Eastern Europe, or any part of the former Soviet Union should also receive the one-time adult polio booster. If you have never had chicken pox or received the vaccine before, consider an inoculation before you leave. Although generally a mild disease, chicken pox may be severe in adults. Adults are more likely to contract a serious case and have a higher rate of complications from the virus. Some doctors also recommend an MMR vaccine (measles, mumps, and rubella) if the prospective parents were born after 1957, have not had the diseases, or had only one shot.

Malaria

Malaria is carried by certain kinds of mosquitoes in coastal and jungle areas, including parts of Mexico, Central America, some Caribbean Islands, and the northeastern half of South America. The disease is also present in parts of Asia, including China. Since most adoption programs are in large cities where malaria outbreaks are rare, antimalarial drugs are not usually necessary, but check the CDC's web site before you travel. The site is updated daily as needed and carries the most current recommendations for each country, region, and season of travel. Do not depend on your travel agent or the consulate of the country you are traveling to for accurate advice. Finally, if you plan on bringing your other children with you on the adoption trip, read carefully the CDC's advice for child travelers as many of the recommendations differ by age, weight of the child, etc. Health precautions for traveling with children can be found at **www.cdc.gov/travel/child_travel.htm**. In addition, **comeunity.com** features advice for adoption travel from parents who have already made their adoption trip. Their adoption travel section features articles on traveling with children and traveling alone, in addition to other related subjects.

Packing for Health and Convenience

Practice packing two weeks before you leave. Take any necessary pharmaceuticals along as well as a mix and match wardrobe that doesn't wrinkle or show stains. You should be able to pack everything you need for yourself in one large piece of rolling luggage and a medium-sized piece that fits on top. In addition, pack one medium-sized bag on wheels for your baby or child. Put the baby's diaper bag or the child's carry-on inside the bag for the trip abroad. A small backpack that can double as a diaper bag will keep your hands free for other items. This pared down set of luggage will make transfers from one mode of transportation to another much easier. By the time you get your child, your hands will be full. Porters and skycaps are not available in many Asian and Eastern European countries. Jetways are not common either. Passengers often board the plane by climbing a metal stairway pushed up against the airplane while it's parked on the tarmac.

The Essentials

Suitcases and Bags: For checked luggage, two pieces per passenger is the limit. One suitcase can be no larger than sixty-two inches; the other, no larger than fifty-five inches. In order to compute the size allowed by airlines, measure the height, length, and width and add them together. Each suitcase can weigh no more than 70 pounds. You will be charged for overweight and oversized luggage. (Luggage restrictions may vary according to country. Also, the luggage requirements for plane trips within your country of destination (from one city to another, for example) may be different than for international travel. Some countries apply a 44 pound rule (total weight of luggage). Check with your travel agent or air carrier for the exact requirements for your particular trip.

In addition, each passenger is allowed one carry-on bag, forty-five inches wide, plus a purse or camera. If your bag is stowed overhead, it cannot weigh more than fifty pounds; if stowed beneath the seat, it can weigh no more than seventy pounds. Be sure that your carry-on luggage does not contain any sharp instruments like knives or scissors.

Be certain to get all of the documents for the adoption in your carry-on luggage. You may reach your destination, but your checked luggage may not arrive for another day or two (or ever)! Plan for this emergency by placing nightwear and clothes for the next day in a soft-sided bag or folding garment bag that will fit under the seat ahead of you. Items for the child can be purchased abroad. In most cities, you'll be able to find wonderful handmade toys, national costumes, unique children's clothing, children's books and music tapes, fancy mosquito nets or bedspreads for beds and cribs, weavings, pictures, hats, baskets, and native jewelry. You can also buy an inexpensive bag to bring them all home in.

Clothing for adults: Plan a coordinated wardrobe to cut down on the number of clothes and shoes you will need. Check the Internet or a travel book for climate and customs. Most of the time you will be dressed in casual clothes. However, for business appointments, you should dress like the attorneys and social workers. Suits for men and a suit or modest dress for women are the acceptable clothing for appointments with government officials and lawyers. This will help make a favorable impression and will look good on the pictures you show your child when he or she is older.

Because of security considerations with terrorist threats against Americans, it is suggested to avoid outside showing of national symbols, flags, T-shirts displaying American slogans, etc.

Dress conservatively but comfortably for your flight. Low heels for women — you never know how much running you may have to do when you change planes, especially if your flight schedule is changed at the last minute.

Foreign money: Take only American Express, Cook's, or Citibank traveler's checks. Check with your bank to see if ATM machines in the country to which you are traveling will accept your bankcard. When using an ATM overseas, it's important that you know the approximate rate of exchange as the money will be dispensed in local currency. However, some countries do not use ATMs and do not routinely accept traveler's checks. Check with your agency for recommendations on how much cash to bring.

Have some foreign money handy for the first taxi and probable expenses for your first day. You can obtain it at exchange houses in most international airports. It is helpful to inquire about the rate of exchange a day or two before traveling, and to make up your own rate-of-exchange chart in a notebook for $1, $2, $5, $10, etc. Pay attention to when your flight is arriving overseas to be sure that you will have access to a bank the following day. If you are arriving on a weekend or national holiday, you may need to take more foreign currency with you. Be certain to get small change for tips. We take $20 or $30, in $1 bills, for tips. American dollars are prized in most foreign countries. Request newly printed U.S. bills without any marks or tears. Damaged U.S. currency is not accepted in most foreign countries.

What to Take – Packing for You

If your trip will only be for a few days, you won't need to take most of these items. For a trip of two weeks or more, you will need most of these items. However, if you stay with families most of the time, you won't need the hot pot or food items.

Camera: If you have a digital camera, practice with it before you leave and take extra batteries. If you have a new 35mm or other camera, shoot a roll of practice film and use all of the camera's features before you leave. Make certain that you know how to use the camera or you may end up with nothing. If your camera takes 35mm film, extra rolls can be purchased abroad. Other film is difficult to find. Don't forget extra batteries. You may also want to take an x-ray safe film bag; your film may go through 20 or 30 security checks before you get home! Heightened security means that even checked luggage will be x-rayed.

Polaroid, with film: Good for making friends with children.

Video camera: As light in weight as possible. Again, practice with it and be certain the charger and batteries are working.

Electrical current adapter: Ask your travel agent or consult a travel book to see if your hotel has outlets for A/C current. If not, you need the adapter for U.S. electrical appliances. You may also need special plug adapters as well.

Water supply: Ask if the hotel has its own potable water supply. Water for the baby's formula must be boiled twenty minutes, regardless. Bottled water is available in most countries. Buy a supply as soon as you arrive overseas or order it at your hotel. Asian hotels usually give you a thermos of boiled, hot water every day — more if you ask for it.

Remember that you can buy almost anything in most large, international cities. However, depending on the country, your accommodations, and the length of time abroad, you might also need:

A hot pot: Easily packed and handy for boiling water. Take a thermos to store the boiled water in. A water purifier is also a good idea. Pint-sized purifiers are available through camping outfitters.

Travel alarm: To make sure you make it to those early morning appointments.

Flashlight with extra batteries: Most countries have blackouts. Hotels provide candles, but a flashlight is better.

Instant foods: Many couples bring packets of foods — cocoa, instant coffee, cup-of-soup, Tang, crackers and peanut butter, etc., for their own use, making some meals convenient and less expensive than eating out or depending upon room service. Take a supply of drinking straws for carbonated beverages.

Entertainment: In countries where the wait is more than a week, you will have time to read, play board games, and do handiwork. Pack your favorites. Include a travel dictionary, phrase book of the native language, or a hand-held computer translator.

Small notebook: A small, bound notebook will provide a convenient place to write down names and addresses of people you meet, notes about your rolls of film, and brief notes about your trip. You may think you'll never forget the details of this important trip, but you will!

Laundry aids: Try to be as self-sufficient as possible and also be prepared to do the baby's wash in the sink. Hotels in Asia will launder your clothes overnight. Hotels in other countries may also have laundry service, but your child may be using clothes faster than the hotel can wash them. A portable clothesline is helpful. Dryer sheets or other lightweight forms of fabric softeners are great in the rinse water; they make line-dried clothes softer. Also, bring a small bottle of liquid detergent (or use shampoo) and plastic bags with closures of assorted sizes.

Insect repellent: Mosquito and insect body lotion and room spray. You may also want to bring roach spray if you will have a kitchenette.

Sewing kit: Tiny size, with basics: threads, shirt buttons, needles, and several sizes of safety pins. (Pack sharp objects like scissors and pins in your checked baggage.)

Wash cloths: Some foreign countries use natural or synthetic sponges. Thus, few hotels furnish wash cloths. Take some with you.

Stationery supplies: Writing pad, Post-it notes, folder, pens, paper clips, and tape.

Roll of nylon tape: To repair suitcases or close bottles, etc. Carry a roll in your pocket or purse.

Tape or CD player (small): Also bring children's music tapes and batteries.

What to Take – Packing for Your Child

You'll need to be as self-sufficient as possible in caring for your baby while at the hotel and on the plane ride home. Items you'll need to care for your new child are listed below.

Baby bottles: We suggest you buy the old-fashioned baby bottles with the large nipples as close as possible to what the orphanage is using abroad. If you are in touch with others who adopted from the same orphanage, ask them what kind to buy. Otherwise, buy an assortment. Babies often refuse to suck from unfamiliar nipples. You may need to try different kinds. Babies over five months of age usually reject the bottles with small nipples and plastic inserts. If your child is very young or of low weight, take "preemie" nipples, which are available at larger drug stores — it makes nursing much easier for the little ones. Special nipples are also manufactured for babies with cleft palates. Also, remember to bring tongs for removing nipples from the boiling water.

Baby carrier: Cloth baby carriers, such as a Snuggly or Bjorn, in which the baby is carried in front of you, can be purchased for babies under a year. Larger, older babies can be carried behind you where the weight is better distributed.

Baby stroller: Find one that folds down for sleeping and folds up for storage in the overhead rack of the plane. Buy stroller netting to keep insects off the child.

Booties, socks, and shoes: In developing countries, people without shoes are the poorest of the poor. Never take your baby outdoors without something on his or her feet.

Caps and bonnets: Summer caps and bonnets should have visors or brims. For winter, hats should cover the ears.

Baby clothing: A few changes, prewashed for softness.

Baby soap and lotions: Bring mild baby soap for the baby's bath. Babies react to changes in temperature. By lining the hotel basin with a towel and filling it with water, the bath should be accomplished fairly peacefully. Test the water with your wrist or elbow first before easing the baby in. For a sponge bath, uncover the baby slowly, one body part at a time. Start with the feet and work up. Wash and dry the first part before uncovering another part of the body. Most children are used to showers, usually cold ones in most countries. Many have learned to hate water and may need to be gently coaxed into a warm bubble bath by floating some toys in it first. This might take several days.

Baby food: Canned baby food and instant baby cereal are readily available overseas. Some restaurants will make it for you. Buy just a small supply to take along. Be sure to bring a can opener for food and formula.

Formula: Continue using the same formula and baby bottle as used by the orphanage while you are abroad. We recommend that you pack one or two cans of powdered formula in case you don't have time to buy it when you receive the baby. Ask your agency or others who have adopted from the same orphanage what kind of formula to purchase. Generally, the switch from one formula to another should be made gradually, since many babies suffer stomach upsets from drastic changes in food. You may wish to take soy-based formula along in case the infant is lactose intolerant. When traveling, put the prescribed amount of dry formula in as many bottles as you will need. Take about six extra preparations. Add sterile water to a bottle when the baby needs it.

Diapers: Be certain to take an adequate supply of disposable diapers — estimate ten per day. Diarrhea warrants an extra supply. If you bring too many, excess diapers are welcome gifts at the foster home as you leave and lifesavers for other American couples you will meet who may have not brought enough. Take a good supply of pre-moistened towelettes. Be sure to bring plastic bags for soiled diapers.

Diaper changing pads: Waterproof pads to put under the child, especially for messy jobs.

Pacifiers: Bring several kinds of pacifiers and clips to attach on a short ribbon to the baby's clothes.

First aid kit: A good first aid kit is essential. See the nearby boxed insert for a list of basic supplies you'll need to carry.

Hand puppets: (For children over one year). Bring enough for the whole family. Actions speak louder than words, and puppets can help you break the language barrier. Also bring picture books of your state, pictures of your home, relatives, and pets, as well as a small, musical, stuffed toy animal to sleep with.

First-Aid Kit for International Adoption

The items listed below will cover most needs. It is better to keep a few standard items than have a large mixed collection that can confuse. Anything you use should be replaced with new items as soon as possible. Replace sterile items any time you open their sealed contents. If you plan to pack the first-aid kit in your carry-on luggage, be sure to take out any sharp instruments such as knives or scissors and stash them in your checked luggage.

Instruments:
- Infant/child medicine dropper marked in ml or cc
- Syringes (3, with a needle attachment) in case you or your child need an injection due to accident or illness
- Thermometer (To take a baby's temperature, put the thermometer under the armpit for three minutes. Add one degree to the final reading.)
- Tweezers and scissors (used only for this purpose)
- Safety pins
- Small scissors

Bandages:
White gauze; absorbent cotton; paper tissues; 2-inch and 3-inch wide plain bandages; ready-to-apply sterile dressings, each packed individually in its protective covering (these are obtainable in various sizes); 2-inch and 3-inch wide adherent dressing strips that can be cut to size for covering simple wounds; 1-inch wide adhesive tape.

Medicines/Salves:
The following pharmaceutical preparations should help you deal with most common infant/childhood ailments. The ones marked with an asterisk are most important and useful. The others are nice, but you can usually buy them if necessary.

*Analgesics
- Tylenol or Motrin (Infant or children's. Have your pediatrician advise you on dosage before you leave.)

Antibiotics
- Amoxicillin (prescription — do not add bottled water until ready to use)
- Bacitracin Ointment— for cuts, burns, rashes
- Tobrex—Used to treat pink eye or conjunctivitis

Coughs, colds and allergies
- Saline nose drops (Ocean, Nasal, Ayr)
- Bulb aspirator
- Benadryl or Dimetapp (Infant or children's. Have your pediatrician advise you on dosage before you leave.)

*Diaper Rashes (Apply with each diaper change)
- Baby wipes (unscented and without alcohol)
- Desitin, A & D Ointment, Balmex (any of these)
- Nystatin cream 1% for diaper rash (prescription)

*Diarrhea and Vomiting
- KAO Lectrolyte packets to mix with 8 oz. of bottled water (plain, bubble gum, and grape)
- ORS powder for adults

Skin Problems
- Aquaphor or Cetaphil cream for eczema
- Hydrocortisone 1% cream or ointment
- T-gel shampoo (Neutrogena)
- Soap — unscented
- Elimite cream 5% for treating scabies (prescription)
- Eucerin, also for treating scabies

Lice
- Nix cream rinse shampoo
- Fine-tooth comb

Water Purification Tablets (if necessary)
- Halazone tablets

U.S. Embassy and Consulate Services

In addition to issuing visas, embassies and consulates perform many other functions. The responsibility of the Department of State, as well as U.S. consular offices overseas, is to do everything possible to protect the rights of U.S. citizens abroad while, at the same time, alerting the U.S. traveler to his or her responsibilities and obligations. Few of us know exactly what services consular offices can provide. For example:

> If you lose your passport, you can get an on-the-spot free temporary passport from the nearest U.S. Consulate. Keep a record of your passport number, some extra photos, and a photocopy of your original passport.

> If you become seriously ill, destitute, are arrested, or experience a similar emergency, a consular official can provide assistance.

> If there is political turmoil in the country where you are headed, check for travel advisories and warnings from the State Department or call the U.S. Consulate there for an on-the-spot analysis of the situation before you leave. The U.S. State Department web site (**www.travel.state.gov**) offers an up-to-date list of travel warnings and consular information sheets.

> If you register at the U.S. Consulate upon arrival in a country of political unrest, you will be notified of an emergency evacuation. If you get into difficulties, the Consulate will be aware of it.

The U.S. State Department also maintains an Overseas Citizens Hotline (888-407-4747), which answers calls on travel advisories and emergencies involving U.S. citizens abroad.

The Office of Special Consular Services offers these recommendations for worry-free travel:

1. Provide family and friends with complete itinerary.

2. Take twice as many dollars and half as many clothes as you originally planned. Take a combination of cash, personal checks, credit cards, ATM card, and worldwide brands of traveler's checks. Always take traveler's checks that can be cashed, or replaced if stolen, in the country of your destination.

3. Keep your documents and some of your money in the hotel safe. Or, split up money with your spouse. It is better to lose half rather than all of it.

4. In a separate inner pocket, carry each other's passport numbers and the names and phone numbers of people to contact in an emergency. The next piece of advice is extremely important, but is often overlooked by traveling spouses and friends. Write down the name, address, and phone numbers of the places you will be staying and the dates you will be there. Should you and your traveling companion get separated in a crowd, on a bus, or a train, you will know how to get back to your hotel or apartment. There is nothing quite as scary as being stranded in a strange city where you don't speak the language and you don't have money, a passport, or even your temporary address. You can easily imagine how an abandoned child feels.

CHAPTER 11

Meeting Your Child

Step 18
Meet your child.

Adoptive parents with high expectations are more likely to experience some initial disappointment with their child than new parents who have few expectations. The happiest parents have disengaged the dream child they carried around in their minds for so long. They have considered the fact that this child not only descends from different ancestors, but has survived in conditions that they have never experienced. They have opened their hearts and minds to let this real child enter their lives at a time and in a place they could never have imagined when they first thought of having children.

In most Asian and Latin American countries, you will usually be given custody of your child the first or second day after your arrival. In most Eastern European countries, on the other hand, you will visit the child every day but you will not be given custody until the final adoption decree is issued and the waiting period is waived or completed. When you receive your child, you will be expected to provide his or her going-home clothes and shoes, just as you would for a newborn birth-child. You must also be prepared to feed the child according to the directions given you. You may see your child for the first time at the adoption agency abroad, an orphanage, a foster home, or a hotel.

Placements are joyous occasions. After so much longing, work, and struggle, the placement is climactic. But we express emotions differently. We look at the child with awe. Can this really be our child? Your joy is superimposed upon the birth parents' grief. I remember shedding a few tears. "They look just like I thought they would," I said. (We had not been sent pictures.) Heino said in a voice quavering with emotion, "They are lovely girls."

Your first moments together are cinematically recorded in your memory. Even newborns lock eyes with their new parents. A few months later, they focus on faces and in response to your voice, will babble and coo. This is where differences in language and ways in which various cultures talk to babies begin to make a difference. For example, the Chinese clap their hands before they pick up a baby. Babies are distressed by extremely loud noises and soothed by quiet sounds. Unfortunately a quiet place is difficult to find in the frenzy and clamor of most cities.

Wear something soft the day you first meet your baby or child. Holding and rocking becomes an even more enjoyable experience when you feel soft and cuddly. Studies confirm that infants are more sensitive to developing attachment behaviors between four months and six months. Hard plastic baby carriers and infant seats should be used as little as possible. The child needs holding to promote bonding.

Between six and nine months, relinquished and abandoned children may not be fearful of strangers. Most likely, they have been cared for by many people and try to keep a mother figure nearby with smiles and coos, since the urge for attachment is extremely strong. Adoptive parents at this stage must interact warmly with the baby, showing approval for this behavior and must not reject clingy and whiny behavior. To reject this negative behavior will only intensify it. Your goal here is to promote attachment, which in turn will help them relax. Then they can play and learn.

Children between eighteen months and three years of age are able to recognize that they are separate individuals. Institutionalized babies spend most of their lives cooped up in a box or crib, simply observing. When they finally climb out, they seek out adults, watching them work, and imitating their motions. They have learned there is no one to go to for comfort if they are hurt or afraid. One of your tasks is to win the child's trust and to prove that you are now there to give aid and comfort. Children are now able to talk and to understand most of what is being said in their native language. Suddenly they must learn a new language and a new routine in a new environment.

School-age children have all of these challenges and, in addition, must submit to the discipline required for a formal education in a new country and culture. Formidable! Addressing all of the adjustments that children of different ages and their new families go through in an adoption requires a book in and of itself. Fortunately, many excellent resources are available to provide a more detailed discussion of adjustment issues in children of all ages. Please see the Bibliography at the end of the book for a few recommendations.

Caring for Your Child Overseas

You will be caring for your child in his or her native country for two weeks or several months, depending on the country you are adopting from and the length of wait for the final adoption decree. This is a stressful period for most people. It takes a lot of fortitude to focus on the adoption proceedings, to get to know your child, and to begin to win his or her trust.

Babies eight months and up usually enjoy playing peek-a-boo. You can make up other simple games with a few small toys. (See nearby box for suggestions on interacting with institutionalized orphans). For children over one, use a hand puppet. The puppet can act out ideas for both of you as well as provide some comic relief. If your child is too large to be carried and held a lot, giving the child smiles, pats, and light back massages when he or she is sitting or standing near you is an excellent way to give the child a feeling of closeness.

New children are fearful, but they may cover it up. Since they were rejected once, they may be again, or so they may reason. Boys and girls who begged on the streets and lived in orphanages have learned survival techniques, some of which will probably stay with them forever.

Older children need to believe that you will be there for support when they have problems — when something good happens or something bad happens. Be creative these first few days to start winning their trust. Attachment begins when you acknowledge their feelings and share their experiences. Shared laughter and shared tears are the glue of parent-child relationships.

We tend to treat orphans as First World kids, overwhelming them with toys, furniture, and clothes. However, they have never even had the luxury of making personal choices regarding style and color. And, if they had the leisure to play, they probably made their own toys from stones, sticks, and paper. Your carefully chosen educational or trendy toys will probably be played with for five minutes and then carefully put back in the toy box. That was our experience with Omar, and countless other adoptive parents have reported similar behavior. Most psychologists agree that parents should separate a child's rights from a child's rewards. After you provide the basics, teach your child that rewards and privileges must be earned.

Your child has likely been eating the cheapest food available with little variety and no second helpings. Each child responds to this situation differently. They may eat the crumbs off the floor and hoard food. At home, your refrigerator and pantry will become a source of wonder and pride. The child may eat twice as much as you do, creating worries about obesity. Such concerns are usually unfounded. Let the child overeat for several months. You can control the calories by carefully shopping for meals and snacks. Children are no different than adults when it comes to seeing food as a comforter. Since their emotional needs have not been met, food soothes the soul, as well as the stomach. As children become more secure, food will lose its importance. Other children may eat very little and be suspicious of new foods. Introduce new foods a tablespoon at a time. Don't worry or fuss about it. In a few months, things will change. Concentrate on meal time as a happy family time. Turn off the TV and get to know your child. Struggles over food can hurt your relationship.

Many parents also report incidents of bedwetting. If you discover your child is a bedwetter (nocturnal enuresis), do not despair. Most children from developing countries are beaten for this problem, thus they will probably try to hide the evidence. Help is available as soon as you get home in the form of behavior modification, bed alarms available from Sears, or large size disposable diapers for nighttime for a while. See a doctor; the condition often responds to treatment within a few weeks.

Are Your Expectations Fulfilled?
What to Do if They Are Not

Many people feel rather let down when they first see the child they were assigned. Orphanage children often look too small for their ages; they may have a runny nose, flu symptoms, and a bad skin rash. On top of that, they are usually dressed in worn out, ill-fitting orphanage clothes, and often have shaved heads to treat insect bites or lice. Babies may have bald spots on heads that are flattened on the back or one side from spending too much time lying down. Disappointing. After all the work and all the waiting, the child does not match the dream child parents have been carrying around in their heads for so long. Some of this is normal. Mothers and fathers report similar let downs with biological children.

What this tells you is that you don't have to fall in love with the child immediately. You put your best efforts into nurturing the child and hope for the best. Suddenly, you feel more needed than you ever have in your life! Bonding, that much overused word, is a two-way feeling. A good adjustment takes place when the parents are able to overcome their initial disappointment and let their feelings and the child's feelings of love gradually develop.

If you can't stop emotionally rejecting the child, or the child seems to be rejecting you, what do you do? This depends on the kind of person or people you are. Mothers usually take the lead at a time like this, and fathers support them. Parents who do not have high expectations fare the best. If they believe they are good for the child and that the child has a lot of potential, they will show their admiration for the child and make him or her feel special. The parents will put a great deal of effort into building a loving relationship with the child. They realize that it may take years for the child to trust them completely and to believe that they won't go away.

Prior to the adoption, most parents worry about the child's health; however, the major reason children are rejected is due to behavior. Orphanage children have learned to survive in what could be best described as a 24-hour big city public school. They have found ways to protect themselves. Children on the extreme ends of coping behavior worry parents the most — whether it be the depressed, withdrawn child or the child who cries a lot and rejects them. If children have become attached to a caretaker or another child, they are confused as to why they have to leave their "home." They may not be able to trust this new relationship enough to show genuine affection or to depend on you for a long time. They have no concept of what you can do to make them happier, more comfortable, and secure.

The greatest difficulty in making a decision about adopting a child is that you have to make it so fast; usually, you are only given a few days before you must make up your mind about going ahead with the adoption. No one can really advise a parent caught in such a quandary. You can talk to doctors and psychologists abroad, or even by long distance here, but in the end, only you know whether you have the patience and tolerance to raise this child. Think about it as long as possible before making a decision that will affect both you and the child for a very long time.

If you are flooded with feelings that adoption is wrong for you or that this is not the right child for you, stop the legal proceedings. But be gracious. You may still want to adopt someday. Cooperate with all the authorities involved, to assure that the child gets another chance for an adoptive home. Depending upon whether or not you have a final decree, you will need to communicate with your foreign agency or attorney, the U.S. Consulate, the INS, and your local adoption agency to cancel the placement.

Other Child-Placement Issues

Unfortunately, the U.S.-based adoption agency does not have as much control as they would like over the referral information sent by the child-placing entity abroad, especially countries of the former Soviet Union.

Once in a while, the child you were assigned is not the one placed with you abroad. This occasionally happens in China and Bolivia. If the authorities make a substitution, you can be assured it was for a good reason. Serious health concerns or a death would be the usual reason for making the switch. Adopters who have had this happen have had to make some quick adjustments. In China, because of time constraints, the child you receive will probably have the documents of the child you were assigned. You can change the child's name during the readoption in the United States.

How to Play and Interact with Institutionalized Orphans
Donna Barlow, MA, Child Development

You can relax and interact with children between the ages of one and three when you take a "bag of tricks" along on your visits. The toys can be small enough to carry in your purse or you can put them in a little bag.

Praise your child for her efforts in working with these toys. Some orphans have never had the opportunity for play. If possible, play with the child outdoors, where the interaction is better.

Huge developmental differences exist between one year olds and three year olds. Even within the same age group, children are at different stages of ability.

Please note that some children may need to see your toys several times before they are ready to touch them.

If you are visiting the orphanage, be certain to take the toys back when you leave. On future visits, the child will probably get excited when she sees that you have the toys. Best of all, you'll have something to play with together.

Interaction
Call the child by name. Repeat the child's name when you start a new activity. If you plan to change the child's name, use the names interchangeably. Notice if the child squeals, laughs, babbles or vocalizes words. This is a good sign.

Handkerchief or scarf.
This game is universal. You go first. Put the cloth over your head to hide your face, say "peek-a-boo" and pull the cloth off to show your face. After a few times, put the cloth over the child's head and say "peek-a-boo." She'll pull it off. Pretty soon, she'll put the cloth over your head. Babies and children love this game.

Keys
Jingle your keys behind the child's head on each side. See if he hears and turns to find them. Let him jingle the keys. (Then try to get them back!)

Pencil or crayon and spiral pad
You go first. Draw a line and a circle. Does the child hold the implement in her fist or in her fingers? Does she scribble or draw lines?

Small rubber ball
Roll the ball to the child. Does he try to pick it up? Does he roll it back?

Small blocks
You go first. Stack them, arrange them in patterns or colors. See what the child does with the blocks.

Little doll, preferably with bottle
Touch the nose on the doll and then on yourself. See if the child will mimic you. Touch your ears, hair and so on to encourage the child to mimic you. This can also teach them English words for body parts. Does the child hold the doll in a nurturing way? Does she feed or talk to the doll?

Little truck
Zoom it around on the ground. Make truck noises. Give it to the child to play with on the ground. Does he mimic you?

Tiny box of raisons
Put three to five raisins down in a clean place. Can the child pick one up at a time? The reward is a sweet treat!

CHAPTER 12

Preparing for the Trip Home: Adoption, Emigration and Immigration

Guardianship and Final Adoption Decrees

In some countries, you will be granted a final adoption decree the same day the child is placed with you, while in other countries, you will be given a temporary custody agreement when your child is placed with you. Placement usually occurs the first or second day after your arrival. Most countries of the former Soviet Union usually do not allow you to have custody until the child is adopted in their country, although you may visit the child in the orphanage. Other countries let you take the child away from the orphanage during the day, but you will be required to return the child to the orphanage at night. Orphanage directors in other countries may also ask that you return older children at night in order to make the transition easier. Once you are granted a final adoption decree, the temporary custody agreement is no longer in effect.

While lawyers handle adoptions in some countries, government welfare officials or private, licensed institutions handle adoption in others. If you are working through an adoption agency, the agency will engage a lawyer in countries where adoptions are handled by the courts. If you are adopting independently, you will need to contact your own foreign attorney or the national authority in charge of adoptions.

Step 19
Obtain the guardianship or final adoption decree.

Required Documents

The foreign attorney or other designated official obtains the birth documents (items 1-3 in the following list). After the court hearing and definitely before applying for the orphan visa, adoptive parents should make sure they have the originals and two sets of certified copies with translations attached of the following documents. The U.S. Consular Service abroad has the authority to certify copies and to notarize documents.

1. Child's birth certificate, showing date and place of birth. Some countries record the child's original name and birth parents, if known. Other countries amend the certificate to show the child's new name and the names of the adoptive parents.

2. A release form signed by the birth mother, birth parents, court, or government welfare office (or if applicable, the death certificates of one or both parents). The release must state the reason for relinquishing the child. The name of the biological father should be stated if known. A release by two parents must be made to an institution.

3. Certificate of abandonment issued by the court after publishing for the child's relatives prior to the court hearing. The certificate grants custody to a legal child-placing entity or to the adoptive parents.

4. Decree issued in that particular country, such as the initial adoption decree, final adoption decree, guardianship, or custody transfer, previously explained.

5. The child's passport photos and passport. You will either receive these from the representative, or you will be instructed and assisted in obtaining them. No copy of this is required.

6. A "Permission to Leave the Country" form signed by a judge or other appropriate official, if required. In some countries, this is included in the decree or guardianship. Additional documents are required in Eastern European countries, such as Russia and those countries of the former Soviet Union.

7. Documents confirming that the child has been registered with the Central Data Bank of orphans at the Ministry of Education and relatives did not attempt to claim the child and nationals have not applied to adopt the child.

8. A statement from local child welfare authorities that the adoption is in the child's best interest.

9. If the child is older than 10, a statement of his or her consent to the adoption.

10. A statement of consent from the director of the institution where the child lives.

11. DNA test results to prove the biological relationship between birth mother and child, if required by the child-placing country. This is required in Guatemala and may be required in other countries in the future as positive identification.

General Adoption Proceedings

The following sections provide a very general overview of what you might expect during the adoption proceedings in your country of choice. Keep in mind that each summary includes several different countries that are similar in process; however, the specific laws and procedures for each country may vary. In addition, procedures and laws change frequently. For the most up-to-date information, contact your international adoption agency, the U.S. Consulate abroad or the State Department web site at **www.travel.state.gov**. (Scroll down and click on the heading for International Adoption.)

General Adoption Proceedings for Russia and Eastern Europe

Adoption cases are heard by judges in special, closed proceedings. The prospective parents, a state prosecutor, and a representative from the local child welfare organization must attend the hearing. At its discretion, the court may also contact the biological parent(s), other relatives or other interested persons, including the child, if over 10 years of age. Ordinarily a representative of the parents' adoption agency is allowed to attend. The hearing is held in the language of the country and the court is responsible for providing interpreters and for the accuracy and quality of the translation. You may wish to consider offering to pay for your own certified interpreter, to spare the court this expense and to guarantee the quality of the interpreting.

The court's decision is issued on the day of the hearing, and, in Russia, it takes effect ten calendar days later unless the judge waives the waiting period. During the ten-day interval, the decision can be appealed. Once it takes effect, the new parents are granted parental rights and full responsibility for the child. In some regions in the Ukraine, the judge can impose a wait of 30 days. Kazakhstan and Romania require a "bonding" period (up to three weeks for Kazakhstan and about a week for Romania).

Up until the time of the hearing in these countries, only a summary of the child's social and medical history has been available to the adopters. By the time of the hearing, the full history has been reviewed and translated. You may hear about hospitalizations and surgeries for the first time, or siblings, or parental neglect and abuse of the child.

After the decision takes effect, a copy of the court decree must be sent within three days to the local registry office. When the adoption has been officially registered, the new parents can apply for the adoption certificate, a new birth certificate (issued in the child's new name and showing the adoptive parents as the child's parents), and a passport. In some Eastern European passports, the name appears in Cyrillic and in Latin letters. The Latin version of the name is spelled phonetically, not the way you spell it (for example, Murphy will be "Merfi"). The spelling of the child's name in the passport does not have to agree with the way it is spelled on the visa or other documents. After you're back in the United States, you can change the spelling of the name through readoption or reaffirmation in your country of residence.

The time needed to complete the adoption abroad in Eastern Europe varies from country to country. Because of the length of time between agreeing to adopt the child and the finalization of the adoption (six to eight months in Bulgaria) most adopters take two trips rather than stay abroad for such a long period. Bulgaria only requires a trip of one week when the adoption is finalized. Yet before they become the legal parents, most adopters prefer to spend a week in Bulgaria to get to know the child first.

In vast Russia, procedures change frequently and are not consistent between regions. Two to four weeks are needed to complete the formalities. Some regions require one trip; others require two.

Presently, adopters can spend a week or more just finding an institutionalized child in countries like Kazakhstan and the Ukraine. The finalization process takes about two weeks prior to obtaining the U.S. orphan visa in Moscow. On the other hand, in the Ukraine, the adoption process takes only 10 days.

General Adoption Proceedings for Asia

The time needed to complete an adoption in Asia varies from country to country. In China, the China Center for Adoption Affairs (the central authority located in Beijing) efficiently matches officially abandoned children in all provinces with adoptive families in America and Western Europe. It takes about two weeks to complete the adoption and immigration formalities. The adoption process is simple, since the rights of relinquishing birth relatives do not have to be formally dealt with as they do in Vietnam, Korea, and most other countries.

Vietnam is in the process of changing its laws and organizing a central authority similar to the Chinese model. The central authority will license or approve adoption agencies abroad. In addition, they will match orphans to prospective parents, apply a standard adoption procedure to the entire country, and supervise adoptions within the provinces to maintain compliance with national standards.

The time needed to complete an adoption in Korea is quite different. After a child is legally freed for adoption, Korea arranges custody transfers with international adoption agencies in the United States in order to place them with specific families. Children are brought to the United States by designated Korean escorts, or adoptive parents can travel to immigrate the children themselves. The children are adopted in the Untied States three to six months after their immigration.

At this writing, Cambodia was in the process of changing its adoption laws and procedures. No detailed information was available at the time the book went to press.

General Adoption Proceedings for Latin America

Although the process may vary slightly depending on the country, in most cases, the foreign attorney will prepare a presentation letter to the Family Welfare Department or the family court of the child's country, if one exists.

The presentation letter states the adoptive parents' identity according to the documents you have prepared; the parents' motives for adoption (that the only intention is to make the orphan a legal child and heir); that the adoptive parents will honor the adoption laws of the child's native country; that the adopted child will emigrate to your home address; and that you will notify the Family Welfare Department of any change of address that might occur before you receive the final adoption decree. Adopters who travel abroad may be required to sign this document in the presence of a family welfare official.

Next, the attorney presents the case for preliminary review to the Civil Court for Minors, or a similarly named court. The attorney delivers your dossier of translated, notarized, verified, and authenticated documents to the court for legal consideration and secures a date on the court calendar. When the attorney presents the case, the court verifies that the documentation is legal and complete. Then, it either issues an initial adoption decree and a permanent custody agreement (which is effective until a final adoption decree is issued), or a final decree, or a permanent guardianship agreement (which is effective until the child is adopted in the country of the adoptive parents). Possibly, a Family Welfare Department official may hold the adoption decree for one day to several weeks while he or she reviews the case. This person represents the orphan in court.

After this review, the attorney may direct the adopters to the judge's chambers. The judge may ask for a personal interview with the adoptive parents to study their dossier with them. Depending upon local procedures, the court may issue the final adoption decree anywhere from one week to one month after the case has been presented in court by your attorney. The law office will obtain notary seals for the final decree and present the decree to you in person. The attorney also obtains the child's documents and organizes and helps present them for the child's U.S. visa.

The time needed to complete the adoption varies among countries. For example, in Central America, it takes Guatemala six months or more. At that point, the court permits the child to be escorted to the new parents or they can take a three day trip to immigrate their child themselves. Most adopters want to visit their children first and get to know them before the judge decrees that they're legal parents. In Mexico, the majority of adoptions are private and can take weeks or months depending upon the adoption procedures in that state. In Honduras, it can take six months to a year to complete an adoption.

In South America, Colombia and Ecuador are the best organized. Depending upon the department (state), the adoption is completed in two weeks to two months. When the process is long, the adoptive parents may make two trips of a few days each, the first to initiate the adoption and the second to return to immigrate the child. Ecuador is similarly organized, with a wait between initiation and finalization of about six to eight weeks. On the other hand, adoptive parents are expected to take custody of their child in Peru and at least one spouse must stay for proceedings that can take a month or more.

No matter where you adopt your child remember that your child is still a foreign citizen, traveling on a foreign passport. If you plan to transit a third country (e.g. England, Germany, Holland) on your way back to the United States, check with that country's embassy in Washington, D.C. before your adoption trip to find out whether your child will need a visa. Most embassies abroad do not offer same-day visa service.

Meeting and Communicating with Birth Mothers

In Guatemala it is possible that you may meet the birth mother around the time of the court appearance in order to transfer custody. Naturally, this is an emotionally stressful time for everyone concerned. However, you must remember that the decision was made in the best interest of the child by the birth mother. Such meetings are unlikely in most adoptions. They are illegal in most countries, as well as prohibited by the Hague Convention.

It is important that you keep your last name and address confidential. Some families have received letters from their child's birth mother or relatives requesting money. These are impoverished people who have real needs; however, experience tells us that these requests for money will continue for the rest of your life. Your obligation to the child does not extend to the child's birth mother and her other children and relatives. We strongly recommend that you do not send gifts or money to the birth mother, during or after your trip. Your generosity could be interpreted as buying the baby. If you wish to correspond with the birth mother or family, let the orphanage or your international agency act as your post office.

Obtaining the Orphan Visa

After the child's adoption or guardianship has been granted, the adoptive parents must obtain an orphan visa before the child can enter the United States. An orphan's U.S. visa is obtained at the U.S. Embassy or consular section that has jurisdiction over the country in which the child resides. U.S. embassies are usually located in the capital city of foreign countries. Your adoption agency will take the lead in coordinating most of this. If not, make an appointment at the visa section of the U.S. Embassy or, in some cases, the U.S. Consulate abroad. Since some consuls require additional documents, ask what is required, as well as which INS forms. Before you appear, fill them out. Usually, visas are issued the same day as the interview or the day after.

INS requires that the orphan's documents are originals or certified copies. INS also requires English translations of documents in foreign languages.

Step 20

Apply for the orphan visa and file Form I-600 (Orphan Petition) if this was not filed earlier.

For most adoptions, either the foreign child-placing entity or the U.S.-based adoption agency will arrange for translations. If not, contact the American Consulate for names of translators. The translation must be attached to the original or certified copy. To certify the competency of the translation, a brief statement signed by the translator must accompany the orphan's documents. Typically, this letter must be notarized and/or authenticated for INS. (A sample of a statement of competency letter can be found at the end of Chapter 7.)

Present the original set of documents to the U.S. Consulate abroad and keep the certified copies and copies of the translations. You will need your certified copies when you reaffirm the foreign adoption or readopt, as well as when you apply for the child's social security number and for proof of U.S. citizenship.

Required Documents

You'll need documents 1-11 listed in the discussion of the Guardianship and Final Adoption Decree at the beginning of this chapter. In addition, you'll need the following required documents, which are available at the visa section of the U.S. Consulate.

With the exception of the orphan visa application, you can download these forms and get updated information on required fees before your trip by visiting the INS website. Go to **www.ins.usdoj.gov** and then choose Forms and Fees from the menu.

12. Form I-600, Petition to Classify an Orphan as an Immediate Relative. Depending on the country from which you are adopting, you will file Form I-600 either in the United States or while you are abroad. If you are supposed to file while in the United States, you will be sent a full set of the child's documents prior to your adoption trip. (See Chapter 9 for more detailed instructions.) If you are supposed to file while abroad, the orphan's original documents will be given to you or your agency's representative. The completion of Form I-600 and Form OF-230 (the orphan's visa application) is usually done at the same time, at the end of the adoption process. (A sample of Form I-600 can be found at the end of Chapter 9.) If filing abroad, you will need to be prepared to pay the fee of $460.00 in cash (either U.S. dollars or the local foreign currency). Query the consulate before your appointment just to be certain about the method of payment and to ask about any recent fee changes.

13. Form OF-230, Application for Immigrant Visa and Alien Registration, and a $335.00 filing fee. These forms are available at the U.S. Embassy or Consulate. You will need two copies. (A sample of Form OF-230 can be found at the end of this chapter.)

14. Affidavit by Adoptive Parent or Prospective Adoptive Parent. This form certifies that the new parents will take responsibility to obtain medically appropriate vaccinations for the child in 30 days. (A sample of this form can be found at the end of this chapter.)

15. Medical examination report form for the child issued by a U.S. Embassy-approved doctor. This form is available at the U.S. Consulate. Your agency representative may be able to help you get the form, exam, and vaccination record from the orphanage or the doctor. (A sample of the medical examination report can be found at the end of this chapter.)

16. Three color photographs of the child for the U.S. visa application. Your agency representative may be able to help you obtain the correct visa photos. (Photo specifications for a U.S. visa are included at the end of this chapter.)

You will also need the following documents, which are generated in the United States. Note: If you file Form I-600 at your local INS office in the United States, INS cables your clearance to the U.S. Consular Office abroad. You will need to take a set of documents 17-21 with you on your trip. You will obtain documents 1-11 from your representative or agency abroad.

17. Copy of your home study. The original is filed in court.

18. Copies of your federal income tax forms for the last three years (most recent) complete with W-2s and schedules — signed and notarized as "true copies of the original."

19. A recent letter from your employer with an original signature.

20. INS Form I-864, Affidavit of Support, and Form I-864A, Contract Between Sponsor and Household Member. Note: These forms are needed if only one parent (of a married couple) travels or if both parents have not observed the child prior to the completion of the adoption process.

21. INS Form I-171H, Notice of Favorable Determination Concerning Application for Advance Processing. The U.S. Consular office must receive this form. In most states, this clearance is either sent by diplomatic pouch or cable, via Washington, D.C. Bring a copy of your I-171H in case the copy at the U.S. Consular office is missing.

Early Return of One Spouse

If one of the parents plans to return to the United States before the end of the adoption process, the following documents must be provided for the spouse attending the interview. Items 1-3 must be signed by the returning spouse and notarized at the consulate.

1. Power of attorney form.

2. Form I-600, Petition to Classify an Orphan as an Immediate Relative.

3. Form I-864, Affidavit of Support, and Form I-864A, Contract Between Sponsor and Household Member (only for IR-4 visas, see item 20 above).

4. A statement from the parent who is returning to the United States confirming that he or she saw the child and reviewed the medical report.

5. Photo of both parents with the child.

6. Copy of the passport of the returning spouse.

Photography for the Orphan Visa

Three photographs of the child in color with a white background must be presented for the orphan visa.

The U.S. Consulate will advise you regarding their approved photographers. INS forms M-370 and M-378, Color Photograph Specifications, detail the requirements (see sample at the end of this chapter).

Size of photograph: 4cm x 4cm (1 1/2 inch square).
Head size: 2.54 cm (about 1 inch) from chin to top of hair.
Subject should be shown in 3/4 frontal view showing right side of face with right ear visible.

Lightly print name on the back of each photograph and sign your name on the front left side of two photographs using pencil or felt pen.

Arranging a Medical Evaluation for the Orphan Visa

Every foreign child must have a physical exam conducted by a U.S. Embassy-approved doctor before departing for the United States. In some countries, adoptive parents can also request that the child be taken to a pediatrician for a more thorough evaluation before they obtain custody.

Waivers must be signed by U.S. citizens who adopt foreign orphans with certain disabilities, which is the reason a medical report from the U.S. Embassy-approved doctor or clinic is required. Before approving the visa, the U.S. Consular service needs to know that the parents are aware of a child's disability and will take full responsibility for the child's care. Waivers must be applied for, but are not necessarily granted for, children diagnosed as Class A and Class B. No waiver is needed for those diagnosed as Class C.

The U.S. Embassy will direct you to an approved physician or clinic that will fill out a medical form. (See sample form at the end of this chapter.) Screening for diseases such as tuberculosis and HIV are not necessarily required in children and is left to the discretion of the physician based on the history and condition of the child.

According to an article in the *American Journal of Diseases of Children*, March 1989, "International Adoption," by Margaret Hostetter, M.D. and Dana E. Johnson, M.D.:

"The quality of this visa medical evaluation is so extraordinarily variable that an assurance of health should be viewed by parents and their physician as confirming only that the child is alive rather than free of unsuspected medical problems. Parents may ask their physician to interpret the classification system (A, B, or C) used by the federal government in the examination. Class A includes psychiatric disorders, mental retardation, and dangerous contagious diseases, including chancroid (venereal ulcer), gonorrhea, granuloma inguinale (inflamed lesion of the groin), infectious leprosy, lymphogranuloma venereum (inflamed lymph nodes of the groin), infectious syphilis, active (untreated) tuberculosis, and as of December 1, 1987, human immunodeficiency virus (HIV) infection."

"Parenthetically, testing for HIV-seropositivity is not required in children younger than 15 years unless they have a history (hemophilia or an HIV-positive parent) or signs and symptoms suggestive of the disease. Therefore, few children will actually be screened for acquired immunodeficiency syndrome (AIDS) before their arrival in the United States.[1] Class B is defined as physical defect, disease, or disability serious in degree or permanent in nature amounting to a substantial departure from normal physical well-being. Although this category sounds ominous, minor cosmetic defects, such as occipital hemangiomas or dark red birthmarks (stork bites), are often placed in Class B. Class C is defined as minor conditions. If the overseas investigation is successfully concluded, the child is issued a permanent resident's visa and can then be admitted to the United States."

---

[1] Although some potential parents insist on testing, the test may do more harm than good. Re-used needles expose children to these diseases and due to the lack of sanitary laboratories and trained technicians, false positive and false negative readings are common.

When an orphan is so ill that he or she must travel to the United States immediately, adopters who have fulfilled their state and federal requirements may apply for a visitor's visa for their child that is specifically issued for medical emergencies. Before attempting to have the child emigrate for emergency medical reasons, adoptive parents should discuss the procedures with the appropriate U.S. consular service office. They must present a statement from a doctor that describes the medical emergency and explains the need for that child to undergo medical treatment at once in the United States. Once in the United States, adopters must apply for permanent resident status for the child.

When an orphan is not only critically ill but resides in a war-torn country, the potential adopters may apply for a humanitarian parole, with as much documented evidence as possible. The help of a member of Congress is essential, but does not guarantee success.

Orphan Visas IR-2, IR-3 and IR-4

Upon completion and submission of all of the required paperwork, your child will be issued one of the three types of U.S. visas listed below. The visa number is stamped in your child's passport. Check the visa number stamped in the passport; immigration officials can make mistakes and record the wrong type of visa or fail to stamp it at all.

- **Visa IR-4.** Orphan to be adopted in the United States by a citizen and spouse (or single parent). IR-4 is used in countries where the adoption process is not completed before the visa is filed. The court issues a guardianship agreement or an initial adoption decree. This visa is also issued if both adoptive parents have not observed the child prior to final adoption, since the child must be readopted in the United States.

- **Visa IR-3.** Orphan adopted abroad by a U.S. citizen and spouse (or single parent). IR-3 is used for orphan visas in countries where the adoption decree can be presented to the U.S. Consulate before the visa is issued. Both adoptive parents must observe the orphan prior to adoption in the foreign country to receive this visa.

- **Visa IR-2.** Applies to orphans who have lived abroad with their adoptive parents for at least two years. Documented proof that the orphan has lived with the parents for two years must be provided.

It should be noted here that you do not need a U.S. lawyer until three to six months after the child has immigrated with an IR-4 visa under a guardianship or initial adoption decree. Then you will need to consummate the adoption in your state of residence. If the child immigrates with an IR-3 visa, under a final adoption decree, your state may recognize this final decree and you will only need to reaffirm or certify the adoption in court. If you were unable to change the child's name abroad, you will need to change it at the readoption or reaffirmation, unless a simpler means of a name change is available in your county. The name change is important for the child's social security number and to obtain proof of U.S. citizenship.

U.S. State Requirements and Importation Laws

Since each of our 50 states has its own set of laws concerning adoptions, every adopter must take the responsibility for knowing and understanding his or her state's requirements concerning the importation of a foreign child into that state. In some countries, a permanent guardianship decree is issued rather than a final adoption decree. This document permits a child to leave the country based on the adopter's promise of a future adoption at home. In all cases, adopters must have completed their home study, their state's preadoption requirements, and INS requirements. To discover which countries issue permanent guardianships or final decrees, see the adoption law summaries in the Compendium. Once the United States has ratified the Hague Convention, every state will have to accept foreign adoption decrees issued under the convention.

The Trip Home

Once you have your child's visa, you are ready for the trip home. Book your return trip before leaving the United States. Request bulkhead seats where there is more room. Also request a baby bed on your return flight. It cannot be reserved ahead of time, as they are given on a first-come, first-serve basis.

Confirm your international return flight 72 hours before departure so as not to get bumped. Be at the airport at least three hours early. If you have a baby, be prepared to have enough bottles and formula accessible to get you through your flight, transits, and any delays you might experience. Some parents use disposable bottle liners and bring plenty of clean nipples, others wash the bottles and nipples on route, and others simply bring a hefty supply of clean bottles on the plane. Premeasure the formula in small plastic bags or bottle liners before traveling. Some manufacturers provide formula in premeasured packages for traveling. Ask the cabin attendants to add water for one bottle at feeding time. Include premoistened towelettes to clean the child, since washing on board is difficult.

On the airplane during takeoff and landing, be certain the baby is sucking on a bottle or pacifier. This will prevent painful pressure on the delicate eardrum. Older children can be given candy to suck or gum to chew. You may consider taking children's Dramamine along, in case the child has motion sickness. Some kids fight being buckled in. Bring toys and activities for the flight.

The flight home is symbolic, recalled almost as a rebirth to children age two and up. Make it as pleasant as possible — the memory will be with them forever.

The Airport Tax

Have foreign cash ready at the airport to pay a departure tax for yourself and your child. People leaving foreign countries, regardless of whether they are citizens, adopted children, or travelers, usually have to pay the foreign governments this kind of tax. In some European countries, the tax is included in your ticket. If it's not included, find out how much it is when you buy your airline tickets. The tax must be paid in foreign currency. You will need to have this amount with you when checking in for your trip home.

U.S. Immigration upon Arrival

At the same time that the child's temporary U.S. visa is presented to you, the visa-issuing office will also give you a sealed envelope containing the original supporting documents you filed for the child's visa. A list of the contained documents appears on the outside of the envelopes. (Officials in some countries must see this when you exit.)

When your flight arrives in the United States, the child's foreign passport will be stamped by INS with a temporary visa, valid for several months. When your child arrives in America with an IR-3 Visa, the child is automatically a U.S. citizen. Unfortunately, there have not been any provisions to issue citizenship papers upon entry. Proof of your child's U.S. citizenship is needed for school, travel abroad, and of course, state and federal programs and college loans. The quickest, least expensive way to obtain proof of citizenship is to apply for a U.S. passport by presenting all of the adoption-related documents. The passport application fee is currently $70.00 for a child and the passport issued is valid for five years. (See Chapter 6 for additional information on applying for a passport.) The other way to obtain proof of citizenship is to file an N-643 Application for Certification of Citizenship on Behalf of an Adopted Child. The fee is $145. (A sample of Form N-643 can be found at the end of Chapter 14.) INS cannot estimate how long it will take them to review the adoption documents and issue the certificate.

An alien card is mailed to you for both IR-3 and IR-4 cases. If the card does not appear within 120 days, request Form G-731 (Inquiry about Status of I-155 Alien Registration Card). You'll need the alien card in order to apply for the certificate of U.S. citizenship. During your appointment with INS, you'll turn in the alien card in order to receive the certificate of citizenship.

In IR-4 visa cases, the old process remains. Present the envelope to the INS officer; it will then be forwarded to the INS District Office where you filed the I-600A. Prior to applying for U.S. citizenship, you will need to arrange for the adoption or a re-adoption in your county of residence to adopt the child under your state laws. If you do not have a set of originals or certified copies, you can obtain these once the file arrives at the INS District Office. To receive a set of the documents you presented in the sealed envelope when you arrived in the United States, request Form G-884 Request for Return of Original Documents.

Form OF-230

U.S. Visa Application, Page 1 of 4

OMB APPROVAL NO. 1405-0015   *ESTIMATED BURDEN: 1 HOUR

APPLICATION FOR IMMIGRANT VISA AND ALIEN REGISTRATION

PART 1 - BIOGRAPHIC DATA

INSTRUCTIONS: Complete one copy of this form for yourself and each member of your family, regardless of age, who will immigrate with you. Please print or type your answer to all questions. Questions that are not applicable should be so marked. If there is insufficient room on the form, answer on a separate sheet using the same numbers as appear on the form. Attach the sheet to this form.

WARNING: Any false statement or concealment of a material fact may result in your permanent expulsion from the United States.

This form is Part I of two parts which, together with Optional Form OF-230 PART II, constitute the complete Application for Immigrant Visa and Alien Registration.

1. FAMILY NAME   FIRST NAME   MIDDLE NAME

2. OTHER NAMES USED OR BY WHICH KNOWN (If married woman, give maiden name)

3. FULL NAME IN NATIVE ALPHABET (If Roman letters not used)

4. DATE OF BIRTH
(Day)   (Month)   (Year)

5. AGE

6. PLACE OF BIRTH
(City or town)   (Province)   (Country)

7. NATIONALITY (If dual national, give both)

8. SEX
☐ Male
☐ Female

9. MARITAL STATUS
☐ Single (Never married)   ☐ Married   ☐ Widowed   ☐ Divorced   ☐ Separated

Including my present marriage, I have been married _____ times.

10. PERSONAL DESCRIPTION

a. Color of hair _____
b. Color of eyes _____
c. Height _____
d. Complexion _____

11. OCCUPATION

12. MARKS OF IDENTIFICATION

13. PRESENT ADDRESS

Telephone number: Home   Office

14. NAME OF SPOUSE (Maiden or family name)   (First name)   (Middle name)

Date and place of birth of spouse:

Address of spouse (if different from your own):

15. LIST NAME, DATE AND PLACE OF BIRTH, AND ADDRESSES OF ALL CHILDREN

NAME	DATE AND PLACE OF BIRTH	ADDRESS (If different from your own)

THIS FORM MAY BE OBTAINED GRATIS AT CONSULAR OFFICES OF THE UNITED STATES OF AMERICA

NSN 7540-00-149-0919
50230-106

OPTIONAL FORM 230 I (English)
REVISED 4-91
DEPT. OF STATE

Form OF-230

U.S. Visa Application, Page 2 of 4

16. PERSONS NAMED IN 14 AND 15 WHO WILL ACCOMPANY OR FOLLOW ME TO THE UNITED STATES.

17. NAME OF FATHER, DATE AND PLACE OF BIRTH, AND ADDRESS (If deceased, so state, giving year of death)

18. MAIDEN NAME OF MOTHER, DATE AND PLACE OF BIRTH, AND ADDRESS (If deceased, so state, giving year of death)

19. IF NEITHER PARENT IS LIVING PROVIDE NAME AND ADDRESS OF NEXT OF KIN (nearest relative) IN YOUR HOME COUNTRY.

20. LIST ALL LANGUAGES YOU CAN SPEAK, READ, AND WRITE

NAME	SPEAK	READ	WRITE

21. LIST BELOW ALL PLACES YOU HAVE LIVED FOR SIX MONTHS OR LONGER SINCE REACHING THE AGE OF 16.

CITY OR TOWN	PROVINCE	COUNTRY	OCCUPATION	DATES (FROM - TO)

22. LIST ANY POLITICAL, PROFESSIONAL, OR SOCIAL ORGANIZATIONS AFFILIATED WITH COMMUNIST, TOTALITARIAN, TERRORIST OR NAZI ORGANIZATIONS WHICH YOU ARE NOW OR HAVE BEEN A MEMBER OF OR AFFILIATED WITH SINCE YOUR 16TH BIRTHDAY.

NAME AND ADDRESS	FROM/TO	TYPE OF MEMBERSHIP

23. LIST DATES OF ALL PREVIOUS RESIDENCE IN OR VISITS TO THE UNITED STATES. (If never, so state) GIVE TYPE OF VISA STATUS IF ANY. GIVE I.N.S. "A" NUMBER IF ANY.

LOCATION	FROM/TO	VISA	I.N.S. FILE NO. (If known)

SIGNATURE OF APPLICANT

DATE

NOTE: Return this completed form immediately to the consular office address on the covering letter. This form will become part of your immigrant visa and your visa application cannot be processed until this form is complete.

*Public reporting burden for this collection of information is estimated to average 24 hrs per response, including time required for searching existing data sources, gathering necessary data, providing the information required, and reviewing final collection. Send comments on the accuracy of this estimate of the burden and recommendations for reducing it to: Department of State (OIS/RA/DR) Washington, D.C. 20520-0264, and to the Office of information and Regulatory Affairs. Office of Management and Budget, Paperwork Reduction Project (1405-0015), Washington, D.C. 20503

Form OF-230

U.S. Visa Application, Page 3 of 4

EXPIRES 00-00-00
*ESTIMATED BURDEN: 24 HOURS

APPLICATION FOR IMMIGRANT VISA AND ALIEN REGISTRATION

PART II - SWORN STATEMENT

INSTRUCTIONS: Complete one copy of this form for yourself and each member of your family, regardless of age, who will immigrate with you. Please print or type your answer to all questions. Questions that are not applicable should be so marked. If there is insufficient room on the form, answer on a separate sheet using the same numbers as appear on the form. Attach the sheet to this form. DO NOT sign this form until instructed to do so by the consular officer. The fee for filing this application is listed under tariff item No. 20. The fee should be paid in United States dollars or local currency equivalent, or by bank draft, when you appear before the consular officer.

WARNING: Any false statement or concealment of a material fact may result in your permanent expulsion from the United States. Even though you should be admitted to the United States, a fraudulent entry could be grounds for your prosecution and/or deportation.

This form is a continuation of Form OF-230 Part I, which together, constitute the complete Application for Immigrant Visa and Alien Registration.

24. FAMILY NAME | FIRST NAME | MIDDLE NAME

25. ADDRESS (Local)

Telephone No.

26. FINAL ADDRESS TO WHICH YOU WILL TRAVEL IN THE UNITED STATES (Street Address including ZIP code)

Telephone No.

27. PERSON YOU INTEND TO JOIN (Name, address, and relationship)

28. NAME AND ADDRESS OF SPONSORING PERSON AND EMPLOYER

29. PURPOSE IN GOING TO THE UNITED STATES

30. LENGTH OF INTENDED STAY (If permanently, so state)

31. INTENDED PORT OF ENTRY

32. DO YOU HAVE A TICKET TO FINAL DESTINATION? ☐ No ☐ Yes

33. United States laws governing the issuance of visas require each applicant to state whether or not he or she is member of an class individuals excluded from admission into the United States. The excludable classes are described below in general terms. You should read carefully the following list and answer YES or NO to each category. The answers you give will assist the consular officer to reach a decision on your eligibility to receive a visa.

EXCEPT AS OTHERWISE PROVIDED BY LAW, ALIENS WITHIN THE FOLLOWING CLASSIFICATIONS ARE INELIGIBLE TO RECIEVE A VISA. DO ANY OF THE FOLLOWING CLASSES APPLY TO YOU?

a. An alien who has a communicable disease of public health significance, or has or has had a physical or mental disorder that poses, or is likely to pose a threat to the safety or welfare of the alien or others; an alien who is a drug abuser or addict. [212(a)(1)]   YES ☐   NO ☐

b. An alien convicted of, or who admits committing a crime involving moral turpitude, or violation of any law relating to a controlled substance; an alien convicted of 2 or more offenses of which the aggregate sentences were 5 years or more; an alien coming to the United States to engage in prostitution or commercialized vice, or has engaged in prostitution or procuring within the past 10 years; an alien who is or has been an illicit trafficker in any controlled substance; an alien who has committed a serious criminal offense in the United States and who has asserted immunity from prosecution. [212(a)(2)]   YES ☐   NO ☐

c. An alien who seeks to enter the United States in espionage, sabotage, export control violations, overthrow of the Government of the United States, or other unlawful activity; an alien who seeks to enter the United States to engage an terrorist activities; an alien who has been a member or affiliated with the Communist or any other totalitarian party; an alien who under the direction of the Nazi government of Germany, or any are occupied by, or allied with the Nazi government of Germany, ordered, incited, assisted, or otherwise participated in the persecution of any person because of race, religion, national origin, or political opinion; an alien who has engaged in genocide. [212(a)(3)]   YES ☐   NO ☐

d. An alien who has become a public charge. [212 (a)(4)]   YES ☐   NO ☐

e. An alien who seeks to enter for the purpose of performing skilled or unskilled labor who has not been certified by the Secretary of Labor; an alien graduate of a foreign medical school seeking to perform medical services who has not passed the NMBE exam or its equivalent. [212(a)(5)]   YES ☐   NO ☐   Not Applicable ☐

f. An alien previously deported within one year, or arrested and deported within 5 years; an alien who seeks or has sought a visa, entry into the United States, or any U.S. Immigration benefit by fraud or misrepresentation; an alien who knowingly assisted any other alien to enter or try to enter into the United States in violation of the law; an alien who is in violation of Section 274C of the Immigration Act. [212(a)(6)]   YES ☐   NO ☐

THIS FORM MAY BE OBTAINED GRATIS AT CONSULAR OFFICES OF THE UNITED STATES OF AMERICA

Previous editions obsolete

OPTIONAL FORM 230 II (English)
REVISED 4-91
DEPT. OF STATE

Form OF-230

U.S. Visa Application, Page 4 of 4

g. An alien who is permanently ineligible to U.S. citizenship; a person who has departed the United States to evade military service in time of war. [212(a)(8)]   Yes ☐   No ☐

h. An alien who is coming to the United States to practice polygamy; an alien is to a guardian required to accompany an excluded alien; an alien who withholds custody of a child outside the United States from a United States citizen granted legal custody. [212(a)(9)]   Yes ☐   No ☐

An alien who is a former exchange visitor who has not fulfilled the 2-year foreign residence requirement. [212(e)]   Yes ☐   No ☐

If the answer to any of the foregoing questions is YES or if unsure, explain in the following space on a separate piece of paper.

34. Have you ever been arrested, convicted, or ever been in a prison or jailhouse; have you ever been the beneficiary of a pardon or an amnesty; have you ever been treated in an institution or hospital or other place for insanity or other mental disease? [222(a)]   Yes ☐   No ☐

35. I am unlikely to become a public charge because of the following:
☐ Personal financial resources (describe)   ☐ Employment (attach)   ☐ Affidavit of Support (attach)

36. Have you ever applied for a visa to enter the United States?   Yes ☐   No ☐
(If answer is yes, state where and when, whether you applied for a nonimmigrant or an immigrant visa, and whether the visa was issued or refused)

37. Have you ever been refused admission to the United States?   Yes ☐   No ☐
(If answer is yes, explain)

38. Were you assisted in completing this application?   Yes ☐   No ☐
(If the answer is yes, give name and address of person assisting you, indicating whether relative, friend, travel agent, attorney, or other)
Name   Address   Relationship

39. The following documents are submitted in support of this application:

☐ Passport	☐ Military record	☐ Evidence of own assets
☐ Birth certificate	☐ Police certificate	☐ Affidavit of support
☐ Marriage certificate	☐ Medical records	☐ Offer of employment
☐ Death certificate	☐ Photographs	☐ Other (describe)
☐ Divorce decree	☐ Birth certificate of all children who will not be immigrating at this time. (List those for whom birth certificate is not available.)	

DO NOT WRITE BELOW THIS LINE
The consular officer will assist you in answering items 40 and 41.

40. I claim to be exempt from ineligibility to receive a visa an exclusion under item _____ in part 33 for the following reasons:

212(a)(5)   Beneficiary of a waiver under:

☐ Not applicable	☐ 212(a)(3)(D)(ii)	☐ 212(e)	☐ 212(h)
☐ Not required	☐ 212(a)(3)(D)(iii)	☐ 212(g)(1)	☐ 212(j)
☐ Attached	☐ 212(a)(3)(D)(iv)	☐ 212(g)(2)	

41. I claim to be:
☐ A Family-Sponsored Immigrant
☐ An employment based Immigrant
☐ A diversity Immigrant
☐ A special category (Specify) _____
(Return resident, Hong Kong, Tibetan, Private Legislation, etc.)

☐ I derive foreign state chargeability under Sec. 202(b) through my _____

I am subject to the following:
☐ Preference: _____
☐ Numerical limitation: _____
(foreign state)

I understand that I am required to surrender my visa to the United States Immigration Officer at the place where I apply to enter the United States, and that the possession of a visa does not entitle me to enter the United States if at that time I am found to be inadmissible under the Immigration laws.
I understand that any willfully false or misleading statement or willful concealment of a material fact made by me herein may subject me to permanent exclusion from the United States and, if I am admitted to the United States, may subject me to criminal prosecution and/or deportation.
I, the undersigned applicant for a United States Immigrant visa, do solemnly swear (or affirm) that all statements which appear in this application, consisting of Optional Forms 230 PART I and 230 PART II combined, have been made by me, including the answers to items 1 through 41 inclusive, and that they are true and complete to the best of my knowledge and belief. I do further swear (or affirm) that, if admitted to the United States, I will not engage in activities which would be prejudicial to the public interest, or endanger the welfare, safety, or security of the United States; in activities which would be prohibited by the laws of the United States relating to espionage, sabotage, public disorder, or in other activities subversive to the national security; in any activity a purpose of which is the opposition to or the control, or overthrow of, the Government of the United States, by force, violence, or other unconstitutional means.
I understand all the foregoing statements, having asked for and obtained an explanation on every point which was not clear to me.

The relationship claimed in Items 14 and 15 verified by
documentation submitted to consular officer except as noted:

_____
(Signature of applicant)

Subscribed and sworn to before me this _____ day of _____, 19_____ at:_____

_____
(Consular Officer)

TARIFF ITEM NO. 20

Affidavit of Adoptive Parent

AFFIDAVIT BY ADOPTIVE PARENT OR PROSPECTIVE ADOPTIVE PARENT

I, _____, certify that I am the
　　　　　(Name)
adoptive parent or prospective adoptive parent of a child,

_____, on whose behalf I have
　　　　　(Name if known)
filed or will file an I-600 Petition (Petition to Classify
Orphan as Immediate Relative) according said child status as an
orphan as defined by Section 101(b)(1)(F).

I have read the statement on the reverse of this form and I am
aware of the vaccination requirement set forth in Section
212(a)(1)(A)(ii) of the Immigration and Nationality Act. In
accordance with Section 212(a)(1)(A)(ii), I will ensure that my
foreign adopted child receives the required and medically
appropriate vaccinations within 30 days after his or her
admission into the United States, or at the earliest time that
is medically appropriate.

Signed this _____day of _____, ____, at _____.
　　　　　　　　　(date)　　　　(month)　(year)　　　(location)

_____
(Signature of parent)

Subscribed and sworn to (or affirmed) before me this _____ day
　　　　　　　　　　　　　　　　　　　　　　　　　　　　　(date)
of _____,____, at _____.
　(month)　(year)　　　(location)
My Commission expires on _____.
　　　　　　　　　　　　　　(date)

_____
(Signature of Notary Public or Officer Administering Oath)

Form M-370

Color Photo Specifications

U. S. IMMIGRATION & NATURALIZATION SERVICE

COLOR PHOTOGRAPH SPECIFICATIONS

IDEAL PHOTOGRAPH
◄

IMAGE MUST FIT INSIDE THIS
BOX ►

THE PICTURE AT LEFT IS IDEAL SIZE, COLOR, BACKGROUND, AND POSE. THE IMAGE SHOULD BE 30MM (1 3/16IN) FROM THE HAIR TO JUST BELOW THE CHIN, AND 26MM (1 IN) FROM LEFT CHEEK TO RIGHT EAR. THE IMAGE MUST FIT IN THE BOX AT RIGHT.

THE PHOTOGRAPH
* THE OVERALL SIZE OF THE PICTURE, INCLUDING THE BACKGROUND, MUST BE AT LEAST 40MM (1 9/16 INCHES) IN HEIGHT BY 35MM (1 3/8IN) IN WIDTH.

* PHOTOS MUST BE FREE OF SHADOWS AND CONTAIN NO MARKS, SPLOTCHES, OR DISCOLORATIONS.

* PHOTOS SHOULD BE HIGH QUALITY, WITH GOOD BACK LIGHTING OR WRAP AROUND LIGHTING, AND MUST HAVE A WHITE OR OFF-WHITE BACKGROUND.

* PHOTOS MUST BE A GLOSSY OR MATTE FINISH AND UN-RETOUCHED.

* POLAROID FILM HYBRID #5 IS ACCEPTABLE; HOWEVER SX-70 TYPE FILM OR ANY OTHER INSTANT PROCESSING TYPE FILM IS UNACCEPTABLE. NON-PEEL APART FILMS ARE EASILY RECOGNIZED BECAUSE THE BACK OF THE FILM IS BLACK. ACCEPTABLE INSTANT COLOR FILM HAS A GRAY-TONED BACKING.

THE IMAGE OF THE PERSON
* THE DIMENSIONS OF THE IMAGE SHOULD BE 30MM (1 3/16 INCHES) FROM THE HAIR TO THE NECK JUST BELOW THE CHIN, AND 26MM (1 INCH) FROM THE RIGHT EAR TO THE LEFT CHEEK. IMAGE CANNOT EXCEED 32MM BY 28MM (1 1/4IN X 1 1/16IN).

* IF THE IMAGE AREA ON THE PHOTOGRAPH IS TOO LARGE OR TOO SMALL, THE PHOTO CANNOT BE USED.

* PHOTOGRAPHS MUST SHOW THE ENTIRE FACE OF THE PERSON IN A 3/4 VIEW SHOWING THE RIGHT EAR AND LEFT EYE.

* FACIAL FEATURES **MUST BE IDENTIFIABLE.**

* CONTRAST BETWEEN THE IMAGE AND BACKGROUND IS ESSENTIAL. PHOTOS FOR VERY LIGHT SKINNED PEOPLE SHOULD BE SLIGHTLY UNDER-EXPOSED. PHOTOS FOR VERY DARK SKINNED PEOPLE SHOULD BE SLIGHTLY OVER-EXPOSED.

SAMPLES OF UNACCEPTABLE PHOTOGRAPHS

INCORRECT POSE

IMAGE TOO LARGE

IMAGE TOO SMALL

IMAGE TOO DARK
UNDER-EXPOSED

IMAGE TOO LIGHT

DARK BACKGROUND

OVER-EXPOSED

SHADOWS ON PIC

Immigration & Naturalization Service
Form M-378 (6-92)

Medical Examination for U.S. Visa

MEDICAL EXAMINATION OF APPLICANTS FOR UNITED STATES VISAS

	PLACE
	DATE OF EXAMINATION *(Mo., Day, Yr.)*
At the request of the Amercian Consul at	CITY / COUNTRY

At the request of the Amercian Consul at

I certify that on the above date I examined	NAME *(Last in CAPS)* *(First)* *(Middle)*	DATE OF BIRTH *(Mo., Day, Yr.)*	SEX ☐F ☐M	
	WHO BEARS PASSPORT NO.	ISSUED BY	ON	

GENERAL PHYSICAL EXAMINATION

I examined specifically for evidence of the conditions listed below. My examination revealed:

☐ No apparant defect, disease, or disability
☐ The conditions listed below were found *(Check boxes that apply)*

CLASS A CONDITIONS *(Give pertinent details under remarks)*　　　　　　**CLASS B CONDITIONS**

☐ Chanorold
☐ Gonorrhea
☐ Granuloma Inguinale

☐ Hansen's Disease, Infectious
☐ Lymphogranuloma Venereum
☐ Syphilis, Infectious

☐ Tuberculosis, Active
☐ Human Immunodeficiency Virus (HIV) Infection

☐ Tuberculosis, Not Active
☐ Hansen's Disease, Not Infectious
☐ Other Physical Defect, Disease or Disability:
_____
_____

☐ Mental Retardation
☐ Insanity
☐ Sexual Deviation

☐ Previous Occurance of One or More attacks of Insanity
☐ Psychopathic Personality

☐ Mental Defect
☐ Narcotic Drug Addiction
☐ Chronic Alcoholism

EXAMINATION FOR TUBERCULOSIS

CHEST X-RAY REPORT

☐ Normal　　☐ Abnormal　　☐ Not Done

Describe findings:

TUBERCULIN SKIN TEST *(See USPHS Instructions)*

☐ No Reaction

☐ Reaction _____ mm

☐ Not Done

DOCTOR'S NAME *(Please print)*

DOCTOR'S NAME *(Please print)*	DATE READ
	DATE READ

SEROLOGIC TEST FOR SYPHILIS

☐ Reactive Titer (Confirmatory test performed - Indicate treatment under Remarks)
☐ Nonreactive
☐ Not Done

TEST TYPE:

SEROLOGIC TEST FOR HIV ANTIBODY

☐ Positive (Confirmed by Western Biot or equally reliable test)
☐ Negative
☐ Not Done

TEST TYPE:

DOCTOR'S NAME *(Please print)*	DATE READ	DOCTOR'S NAME *(Please print)*	DATE READ

OTHER SPECIAL REPORT(S) *(When needed)*

DOCTOR'S NAME *(Please print)*

REMARKS

APPLICANT CERTIFICATION

I certify that I understand the purpose of the medical examination and I authorize the required tests to be completed. The information on this form refers to me.

_____ Signature _____ Date

DOCTOR'S NAME *(Please type or print clearly)*	DOCTOR'S SIGNATURE	DATE

OPTIONAL FORM 157
Revised 2-88
DEPT. OF STATE

CHAPTER 13

Health Problems of Orphans from Developing Countries

T he general health of children adopted internationally depends a great deal upon the condition of the child at the time of relinquishment, the quality of the orphanage or foster care, and the amount of time the child spends in these situations. The international pediatric specialists we've consulted agree that the usual problems they see in newly adopted children are colds, ear infections, malnutrition, and parasites. These are quickly remedied with a loving home and medical attention. Babies and children come from impoverished environments and often arrive at orphanages and foster homes with malnutrition, lice, scabies, skin problems, worms or parasites, diarrhea, and infectious diseases. Sometimes the orphanage or hospital where the child lives may expose him to all these health conditions and even more.

This chapter covers acute medical conditions that adoptive parents might need to cope with during their first weeks or months with their child. You probably won't have to deal with the exotic ones mentioned in this chapter, but at least you'll know the signs and symptoms to watch out for. Descriptions of long-term medical and developmental problems and their treatment are beyond the scope of this book. The Bibliography cites organizations that provide information on chronic medical conditions, such as maternal lifestyles and their effect on the fetus, as well as fetal alcohol syndrome, fetal alcohol effect, premature births, and low birth weight. Other issues prospective adoptive parents need to educate themselves about are the effects of parental abuse and neglect, institutionalization, and developmental disabilities and delays, especially speech delays.

In addition, a few web sites provide excellent resources regarding the health, development, and treatment of children adopted internationally. Visit **www.orphandoctor.com** or **www.comeunity.com/adoption/health** for more information on the health of orphans from developing countries.

U.S. health insurance coverage is now regulated by a federal health insurance act, Public Law 104-91, which, among other things, limits the ability of some group insurance providers to exclude coverage of pre-existing conditions in adopted children. Most group insurance plans will cover adopted children — sometimes even while the children are still abroad. Contact your insurance provider for complete details of your plan's coverage. Adoptive parents must notify their insurance carriers within 30 days of the child's placement or adoption.

Children of developing nations get all the diseases U.S. children do with an important difference. Many foreign children have never had the series of vaccinations commonly administered to U.S. children. Consequently, complications and disabilities are sometimes caused by entirely preventable childhood diseases, such as measles or poliomyelitis. Their effects, as well as birth defects, injuries, and common illnesses often go untreated since the poor cannot afford medical care. In addition, simple conditions are often complicated by the effects of poor nutrition. Most disabled orphans face a bleak future in these countries. As adopted children, they have made some spectacular recoveries.

In the United States, all children are eligible for free orthopedic correction or surgery for burns from the Shriners Hospital network. Middle-income families whose quality of life will change if they must pay for a child's expenses themselves may apply to the nearest Shriners Hospital for Crippled Children. Donations from the Shriners make it possible for these hospitals to serve newborns and children up to sixteen years of age. The Shriners maintain 21 hospitals on the U.S. mainland, one in Hawaii, one in Mexico City, and one in Manitoba. Families apply to the Shriners Medical Board and Board of Governors, who review and accept applications within two to three weeks.

Many states also have federally funded programs for children with disabilities (usually called Children's Special Health Care Services). Some states have free eligibility for adopted children while others have a sliding scale for fees.

The immigration evaluation for visa approval is not a stamp of approval of the child's health. Most of the health conditions affecting internationally adopted children are not "excludable conditions" and may not be noted at the visa physical.

The American Academy of Pediatrics recommends the following for all newly arrived, adopted, immigrant children, regardless of age, country of origin, or apparent health.

> *Blood tests for*
> > *HIV 1 and 2*
> > *Syphilis*
> > *Hepatitis B*
> > *Hepatitis C*
> > *Complete blood count*
> *Stool samples for ova and parasites*
> *Skin test (Mantoux) for tuberculosis*
> *Update of all immunizations*

In addition, see the nearby box for a more thorough list of recommended screening tests.

Recommended Screening Tests

About two weeks after children arrive home, the following tests should be administered, even if the child appears healthy and normal. In addition, a dental exam should be scheduled for any child over 18 months of age.

Complete Physical Examination
Documentation of bruises, old scars, scars from surgeries, deformities, rickets, or abuse.

Recommended Screening Tests For All International Adoptees
- Assessment for vision, hearing (parents need to be aware that recurrent ear infections may interfere with hearing) and dental health for children over 18 months old
- Blood count, complete with erythrocyte indices
- Evaluation for anemia, iron deficiency, iodine deficient hypothyroidism, lead poisoning, malnutrition, rickets, thalassemia
- Examination of child with suspected prenatal exposure to alcohol for fetal alcohol syndrome or alcohol-related disorders
- Examination/testing of child with signs or symptoms of sexual abuse.
- Growth assessment
- Hepatitis B profile
- Hepatitis C serology for children from Eastern Europe, countries of the former Soviet Union, and China
- HIV 1 and 2 screen in all children; PCR or viral culture in a child under two years
- Immunizations review and update
- Fecal examination for ova and parasites, three times at least one week apart
- PPD (Mantoux) skin test for tuberculosis for all children, regardless of whether they had the BCG (Bacille Calmette-Guerin) vaccine
- Urinalysis
- VDRL screen for syphilis

Recommended Assessments for Development and Mental Health
- Development to be followed at one to three-month intervals for the first year after arrival.

   The majority of internationally adopted children from institutional care are mildly to severely delayed. Formal developmental testing should be performed on any and all children with suspected developmental delays through Early Childhood Intervention (ECI) or other programs. (See information on ECI that appears earlier in this chapter.) Federal law mandates that any child over age 3 must be offered testing in his or her native language.
- Assessment of mental health for older children, those with known prior abuse or loss, and any child with behavior that is developmentally inappropriate

Testing and Referrals
Planning for testing for new or previously diagnosed conditions and referrals to specialists

International Adoption Medicine

A short time ago, only a handful of doctors in the United States had experience dealing with the medical problems of children born abroad and adopted by U.S. families. Today, however, a growing number of doctors and clinics are building their practices serving the needs of families adopting internationally. These clinics can be invaluable resources for information, especially if your child has a medical condition that is not easily diagnosed or not commonly found in the United States. These physicians, for example, may be able to provide your local pediatrician with recommendations for tests, screenings, age determinations, etc. In addition to offering treatment, many international adoption clinics and pediatric specialists also offer preadoption consultations, medical reviews of referral information (see box in Chapter 8), advice on immunizations and travel preparation, and post adoption medical evaluations. Contact information for a few of these can be found in the nearby box in this chapter.

If you are interested in having a clinic or doctor review the medical information and videos of the child you have been assigned, please call first for specific instructions and information on service fees or donations before mailing any items. Be sure to send a self-addressed, prepaid envelope if you want the information returned. You can also contact the Joint Council for International Children's Services for additional medical contacts at 202-429-0400 (**www.jcics.org**) or visit **http://www.comeunity.com/adoption/health/index.html** for a more detailed list of doctors and clinics. There are more than two dozen clinics in the United States and Canada and the number of experienced practitioners in this field grows every year.

The following sections include introductory information about common and more severe illnesses that parents adopting internationally could have to deal with. For more information on health and developmental problems of orphans in developing countries visit **www.orphandoctor.com** or **http://www.comeunity.com/adoption/health/index.html**.

Immunizations

Most countries begin immunizations at birth with the BCG or tuberculosis vaccine. Other immunizations are typically given by the World Health Organization (WHO) schedule, which is different than the U.S. schedule (fewer diseases covered, doses at younger ages, and closer intervals). If your child has not been immunized, wait until you are home to begin the series of inoculations. Regardless of whether your child has an existing record of immunizations, you should consult your pediatrician about reimmunizing upon your return home. Many pediatricians do not accept vaccination records from developing countries because the vaccines may not have been kept refrigerated or they may have expired before being used. Both circumstances diminish their effectiveness. Infants and toddlers may be revaccinated without harm. Blood serum tests may be conducted on older children to determine their immunity to diphtheria, tetanus, measles, mumps, rubella, and chicken pox. The tests may indicate a need for booster vaccines.

Determining the Age of Children

In the case of abandoned children, or those without records, a doctor must make an educated guess as to the child's age. Neglected and malnourished children are usually quite short for their age and, generally, look and act much younger than they actually are.

This is to the child's benefit since he or she has a lot of catching up to do, both physically and socially. U.S. doctors and dentists can make educated guesses about a child's age by looking at teeth and bone x-rays, although the variation in these tests is great — typically plus or minus six to twelve months. However, because of catch-up growth, it is usually best to delay deciding on an age for as long as possible, preferably a year.

Malnutrition

Most children arriving in the United States from institutional care have mild caloric deprivation or mild to serious psychosocial dwarfism. Given love, nourishment, and medical care, they rapidly develop into normal little kids. Although the relationship of severe malnutrition in infancy and childhood to brain damage is a well established fact, seriously affected children are not typically selected for adoptions. Studies of severe malnutrition in infancy and childhood do show that children may experience persistent and permanent cognitive, behavioral, and social defects — the severity of the effects are impacted by the age of onset of malnutrition, the length of time of caloric deprivation, and other existing health conditions, such as premature birth and fetal alcohol syndrome (FAS). However, the damage of even severe malnutrition may be ameliorated by the age of rehabilitation (the younger the better), better social environments, and adequate educational support. Long-term studies of malnourished children show generally good outcomes, especially if the child is adopted before the age of three years. Prospective adoptive parents with concerns about the effects of malnutrition should visit with parents who have adopted foreign children who were once in this condition.

Many adopted children have phenomenal appetites and will eat whatever is presented to them. Some children will not know when to stop eating. They may gain weight initially, although their weight will level off as catch-up growth ensues and they begin growing taller. Serve them well balanced meals and snacks. A daily multi-vitamin tablet is also helpful. If the child shows no acceleration in growth, an underlying illness such as tuberculosis or parasites may be suspected.

U.S. pediatricians use the National Center for Health Statistics growth chart, which is also used by the World Health Organization. This chart indicates population standards divided into the fifth, tenth, twenty-fifth, fiftieth, seventy-fifth, ninetieth, and ninety-fifth percentiles. Ninety percent of the population should be covered by these charts. By plotting the child's growth, the doctor knows what percentile is normal for this child and can also see if the child's growth has slowed. In normal growth, the child's measurements follow along one of the percentile lines on the chart. If growth slows, the measurements cross percentile lines. The doctor can see if the child has recovered by plotting his or her return to normal. This system depends on taking repeated measurements in order to establish the normal patterns of growth.

Malnourished or neglected children, of course, do not have a normal growth pattern. Adoptive parents are usually very disappointed at their first appointment with a pediatrician because their child does not measure up to ideal U.S. standards. Upon placement in a nurturing adoptive home, however, the children's sizes change dramatically, due to the advent of "catch-up" growth. Catch-up growth may continue for years after placement. Your child's recovery from malnutrition is complete when height and weight are in proportion to each other, and the child is growing at a steady pace in a typical growth diagram.

Developmental Delays

The majority of internationally adopted children are mildly to severely delayed due to malnutrition, neglect, or illness. Upon your return, make contacts with Early Childhood Intervention (ECI) specialists through your county or public school system. Ask them to send their literature for review and consider having them evaluate your child's developmental status.

ECI programs were established by public law to help children from birth to age 3 who have either been diagnosed with a delay or who have a diagnosis or condition (such as premature birth or malnutrition) that might lead to a delay in gross or fine motor development, language development, cognitive development or other related areas. Every state has some form of an ECI program, although the details of how they are operated vary from state to state. Most programs will conduct an initial screening free of charge and recommend whether or not further intervention is recommended. Most visits and therapy occur in your home. If your child is too old to qualify for the ECI program in your state, similar services may be offered through your public school system, even for children as young as 4 and 5 years of age.

To find out about the ECI program in your state, ask your social worker or adoption agency or visit **htpp://www.pierrerobin.org/ECIStateresources.html** to get the phone number for the early childhood office in your state.

General information about developmental delays and ECI programs can be found at **www.nectas.unc.edu**. Also, see the section on screening tests at the end of this chapter.

Common Worms and Parasites

Adopted orphans have had as many as five varieties of parasites at once, some active, some in a cyst-like stage, and some in an ova (egg) stage. Most chronic parasitic infections produce no symptoms at all. The child's stool should be tested two or three times, two to three weeks apart after arrival. For diaper changes, be certain to lay the baby on a washable or disposable surface and wash your hands thoroughly afterwards. If needed, antiparastic drugs can be special ordered by your pharmacy or from the Parastic Drug Division of the Centers for Disease Control and Prevention in Atlanta at (404) 639-3311. Adoptive parents and siblings also should be tested if they exhibit any symptoms after the arrival of the adopted child. Within the first month, if an infant or child has profuse diarrhea (more than one stool every two hours) or there is obvious blood or pus in the stool, seek help immediately. Begin an oral rehydration solution (ORS) such as Pedialyte, while taking the child to the nearest medical care.

The most common worms and parasites found among adopted children are amoebas, roundworm, tapeworm, pinworm, giardia, hookworm, lice, and scabies.

Amoebas (one-celled organisms): The symptoms of amoebas are dysentery, dizziness, nausea, weight loss, or failure to gain weight. Left untreated, amoebas can cause colitis, bleeding ulcers, and in rare cases a liver abscess. The treatment is Metronidazole. Amoebas are transmitted through contaminated food or water.

Roundworm (ascaris): There are usually no symptoms. Infection is often discovered when the child passes a large, white, pencil-sized worm. The worms may be passed months or years after immigration, much to the consternation of parents. Treatment is Mebendazole. Roundworms are not typically contagious with normal hygiene.

Pinworm (enterobiasis): Pinworms are tiny thread-like worms in the stool. They may cause the child to scratch around the anus. Treatment is Mebendazole. Pinworms are highly contagious, especially to other children.

Giardia lamblia (one-celled protozoa): Symptoms include stomach cramps, nausea, vomiting, weight loss, bloating, fatigue, and foul-smelling gas. Children often have no symptoms at all. Nonsymptomatic giardia can multiply and cause the above problems. The treatment is Metronidazole Furazolidone. Giardia is contagious (typically to the mother!) and is often transmitted by poor attention to hand washing.

Hookworm (ancyclostomatidae): Symptoms are iron deficiency anemia, abdominal, and pulmonary symptoms. Treatment is Mebendazole. Hookworm is not contagious.

Tropical tapeworm (hymenolepsis nana): This worm is usually asymptomatic and is not contagious with normal hygiene. Treatment is Niclosamide or Praziquantel.

Lice: Detected by looking for white eggs or nits at the base of the hair in a good light. It is a good idea to take along Nix cream rinse and a fine-tooth comb just in case. Some toddlers and older children have had them and have infested their new families and schools.

Scabies: Adoptive parents who did not read this section have infected their friends and family with scabies by not treating the baby and by passing him or her around for everyone to hold. Scabies is caused by tiny mites that lay eggs under the skin. Symptoms include blistering of the skin and intense itching. Partially treated scabies and scabies complicated by impetigo may be very difficult to diagnose. Any persistent, itchy rash should be suspect. The treatment is a bath and applications of Elimite (permethrin lotion). A steroid cream will help with the itching as it may take up to two or three weeks to eliminate all of the eggs and mites from the skin.

Schistosomiasis (Bilharziasis): Schistosomiasis is caused by microscopic blood flukes (worms) present in fresh water lakes and streams of Asia, Africa, the Antilles, and the northeastern and eastern parts of South America. Snails are the intermediate hosts for these worms, which penetrate human skin and later develop into larger worms in the abdominal blood vessels. Schistosomiasis is usually only seen in older children who have worked in the fields — not in institutionalized children. Symptoms are not usually present. Treatment is Praziquantel.

Whipworm (trichuris): These are contagious. Symptoms include nausea, stomach pain, diarrhea, anemia, and, infrequently, rectal prolapse. Whipworm is treated with Mebendazole.

Infectious Diseases

Shigellosis (bacillary dysentery): This acute bacterial disease occurs worldwide. It is highly contagious under poor sanitary conditions. Most infections and deaths are in children under ten years of age. Symptoms include diarrhea, fever, vomiting, cramps, and tenesmus (straining). In severe cases, stools contain blood, mucus, and pus. The treatment includes fluid and electrolyte replacement. Antibiotics are not usually necessary.

Helicobacter pylori: The symptoms are abdominal pain, gastritis, or gastrointestinal bleeding; children show no symptoms when infected with this bacterium. The treatment is a course of triple antibiotics. Left untreated, the disease is mildly contagious and is the cause of most gastric ulcers.

Salmonella: The symptoms are severe abdominal pain, nausea, vomiting, and diarrhea, often with blood in the stool. Treatment is supportive. Antibiotics may actually prolong the disease.

Acquired Immune Deficiency Syndrome (AIDS): All children should be evaluated for the presence of HIV infection after arrival in the adoptive home. Tests in other countries are not reliable and should always be repeated. A positive ELISA or screening test in a baby under eighteen months of age may indicate the mother's infection, rather than the baby's. The incidence of true infection is very low. Fewer than 2 dozen cases have been documented over the past decade.

Hepatitis: Hepatitis is an inflammation of the liver. Some types of hepatitis can cause permanent liver damage. Tests for hepatitis conducted in another country should be considered unreliable.

Hepatitis A — Prevalent in all countries, including American day care centers, hepatitis A is transmitted by contaminated food and water. The majority of infected children are asymptomatic. Hepatitis A does not cause chronic liver disease and is only contagious for a few days or weeks at the time of infection. Routine testing is not recommended.

Hepatitis B — Hepatitis B is prevalent in many developing countries and is transmitted through contact with blood or body fluids. Hepatitis B may also be transmitted by mother to fetus. Five to ten percent of Asian and Eastern European children have chronic infection. Many more children have been exposed to the disease. Children who test positive for hepatitis B should be tested for hepatitis D, a disease found only in the presence of chronic hepatitis B. Medical problems are highly unusual for most children with hepatitis B. Most of the intervention in the first twenty years of life is merely monitoring for possible clearing of infection or the rare early complication. Because hepatitis B is also found in the American population, newborns here are inoculated.

Hepatitis C — Hepatitis C is spread by direct blood contact. It's possible for an infected mother to transmit the disease to her child during birth, although the incidence is low (about 5%). Hepatitis C causes chronic infection in up to 80 percent of people, but it takes 30-40 years for complications to develop. Interferon and other drugs are used to treat and manage hepatitis C.

Malaria: Malaria is carried by certain kinds of mosquitoes in coastal and jungle areas in most tropical and subtropical regions. Malaria may not be apparent for weeks to months after infection. Symptoms are often nonspecific (fever, malaise, diarrhea, etc.). Malaria should always be considered in any febrile illness that is not responding to treatment as expected. Malaria is not common among internationally adopted children.

Infantile paralysis (poliomyelitis): This disease no longer exists in North or South America, but is still prevalent in the former Soviet Union, Eastern Europe, and all parts of Asia except Japan. Paralysis in a Latin American child is more likely to be cerebral palsy or other neurological conditions. Sudden paralysis in Asia is most likely due to polio. However, the diagnosis should always be confirmed after arrival in the United States.

Syphilis: If your child's medical history states that the child had syphilis — which is usually acquired from the birth mother — make sure that the child is tested again in the United States. Treatment abroad may have been inadequate.

Tuberculosis (TB): Tuberculosis cases turn up often, especially in Chinese and Eastern European orphanages. The staff is the main source of infection. Unlike adults, children with tuberculosis do not spread the disease. Active tuberculosis must be treated for at least two weeks before an orphan immigrant visa will be issued. Because of the high rate of drug resistant tuberculosis worldwide, a doctor or clinic specializing in infectious disease should manage cases of active tuberculosis.

In all countries except in North America, a BCG (tuberculosis vaccine) is given at birth or soon after. The BCG scar looks like an old smallpox scar on the shoulder, back, or upper thigh. All children, regardless of BCG scar history, need an evaluation for tuberculosis after arrival, usually a PPD or Mantoux test. Occasionally, a chest x-ray is also needed. The 4-prong "tine" test is not appropriate for immigrant children.

U.S. bacteria and viruses: Newly arrived orphanage babies should be protected from well meaning U.S. visitors who have colds and flu. These illnesses can become critical in babies already weakened from malnutrition and/or parasites.

Other Health Concerns

Anemia (low hemoglobin): Anemia in most children is due to iron deficiency; it should be treated and followed. Some children, especially African or Asian children, will have other blood disorders, such as thalassemia, hemoglobin disorders, and G-G-PD deficiency.

Circumcision: Most of the world does not routinely circumcise. Ask your doctor if this operation is really necessary for your particular boy. The risks include possible mutilation of the penis, hemorrhage, and local infection.

Lactose intolerance: Lactose intolerance is the inability to digest the milk sugars found in most formula and cow's milk. It is fairly common in all dark-skinned populations and in Asia. Mother's milk, soybean formulas, or yogurt are substituted. Tolerance to cow's milk may eventually be attained, especially if the lactose intolerance was due to infection or malnutrition rather than inherited.

Mongolian spots: Adoptive parents who do not read this section are aghast when they change their baby's first diaper and see what looks like bruises. Babies of Asian, Indian, or African ancestry may have blue/black spots on their bottoms and along their spines called Mongolian spots. The spots may also occur on their shoulders, as well as the backs of their hands and the tops of their feet. These spots gradually disappear as the baby grows older.

Rickets: Rickets is a disease of infancy and childhood, which prevents the proper development of bone. The disease, which is prevalent in Chinese, Romanian, and Russian orphanages, is caused by inadequate exposure to sunlight and insufficient intake of Vitamin D. Signs of rickets include bow legs, raised bony bumps on the ribs, exaggerated roundness of the forehead, and a poorly shaped, sweaty head. Rickets can be diagnosed by blood tests, physical exam, or x-ray. The disease is treated with milk and food fortified with calcium and Vitamin D and exposure to natural light.

Sickle-cell disease: Sickle-cell disease is a serious anemia due to a recessive gene and is found in African, Latin American, Mediterranean, as well as other non-Caucasoid groups. Other hemoglobin or red blood cell diseases, such as alpha or beta thalassemia syndromes, are common in Asians. Anemia not responding to iron is often the first clue to the condition.

Skin pigmentation: Cuts and scrapes on dark skin heal at the same rate as on light skin, but may require many more weeks for the pigmentation to return or may become hyperpigmented as they scar. Even brown, black, or olive children may have delicate complexions that sunburn and windburn easily. Severe malnutrition can cause a genetically olive-skinned, black-haired child to be pale and blond or red-haired. With a balanced diet, the pigment gradually becomes normal.

Teeth: Some orphans need a lot of expensive dental work. Others have perfect teeth. Most dentists believe the birth mother's diet has a great influence over her child's first set of teeth. The practice in lower classes of weaning babies with bottles of sugar water contributes to tooth decay. Orphans with yellowed teeth may have been treated with tetracycline, a drug that can cause this kind of side effect. Upon returning home, a dental exam should be scheduled for any child over 18 months of age.

International Adoption Medical Professionals

International adoption specialties are relatively new in pediatrics but are certainly increasing. Most of the physicians listed below have traveled extensively in the countries that place children for adoption; many are adoptive parents themselves. Most have excellent written materials regarding common medical issues involved in international adoption. They are generally available for pre-adoption and post-adoption consultations. Many clinics and doctors will review videos and medical records of children.

Parents can consult with these doctors via phone, fax, and e-mail, sometimes at no charge. Parents are strongly urged to have their internationally adopted children evaluated by medical professionals as soon as possible after arrival in the United States. Professionals with experience evaluating these children can suggest specific interventions and referrals (occupational therapists, speech/language pathologists, etc.), can recommend general and country specific tests (for parasites, infectious diseases, etc.), and can provide family counseling on medical issues. We strongly recommend that the medical professional who works with you and your child have a solid degree of familiarity with the special needs and concerns of internationally adopted children. Ask other parents in your area who have adopted internationally for recommendations of medical professionals. The physicians listed here may be able to provide your physician with recommendations for tests, screenings, age determinations, etc. The list below represents some of the best and best known. This is not meant to be an all-inclusive list, and we will inevitably have overlooked some fine resources. You can also contact the Joint Council for International Children's Services for additional medical contacts or visit **www.comeunity.com/adoption/health/index.html**.

Illinois

Todd Ochs, M.D.
841 Bradley Place
Chicago, IL 60613-3902
Phone: 773-975-8560
Fax: 773-975-5989
Email: t-ochs@nwu.edu

Kentucky

Deborah Borchers, M.D., F.A.A.P.
Eastgate Pediatric Center
139 Louise Drive
Fort Mitchell, KY 41017
Phone: 513-753-2820
Fax: 513-753-2829

Massachusetts

Laurie Miller, M.D.
International Adoption Clinic
The Floating Hospital for Children
750 Washington Street, Box 286
Boston, MA 02111
Tel: 617-636-8121
Fax: 617-636-8388
URL: **www.nemc.org/adoption**

Michigan

Jerri Ann Jenista, M.D.
551 Second Street
Ann Arbor, MI 48103
Tel: 734-668-0419
Fax: 734-668-9492

Minneapolis

Margaret Hostetter, M.D., Co-Director
University of Minneapolis Adoption Clinic
MMC 296
420 Delaware Street, SE
Minneapolis, MN 55455-0378
Tel: 612-624-1112
Fax: 612-624-8927

Dana Johnson, M.D., Ph.D., Co-Director
University of Minnesota
International Adoption Clinic
MMC 211
420 Delaware Street, SE
Minneapolis, MN 55455-0378
Tel: 612-626-2928
Fax: 612-624-8176
Email: johns008@maroon.tc.umm.edu

New Jersey

Lisa Nalven, M.D.
Valley Health Center for Child
  Development and Wellness
505 Goffle Road
Ridgewood, NJ 07450
Tel: 201-447-8151
Fax: 201-612-1092

Ohio

Karen Olness, M.D.
Rainbow Center for International Child Health
11100 Euclid Ave. MS 6038
Cleveland, OH 44106-6038
Tel: 216-844-3224
Fax: 216-844-7601
Email: RCIC@po.cwru.edu
URL: www.uhhs.com/toheal/rcic.html

New York

Winthrop Pediatric Associates, PC
International Adoption Program
222 Station Plaza North, Ste. 611
Mineola, NY 11501
Tel: 516-663-9570
Fax: 516-663-3793
Email: ggrella@winthrop.org

Andrew Adesman, M.D., Director
Evaluation Center for Adoption
Schneider Children's Hospital
269-01 76th Ave.
New Hyde Park, NY 11040
Tel: 718-470-4000
Fax: 718-343-3578

Dr. Jane Aronson, F.A.A.P., Director
International Pediatric Health Services, PLLC
151 East 62nd Street, Ste. 1A
New York, NY 10021
Tel: 212-207-6666
Fax: 212-207-6665
Email: orphandoctor@aol.com
URL: www.orphandoctor.com

Pennsylvania

Sarah Springer, M.D.
Department of Pediatrics
Mercy Hospital of Pittsburgh
1515 Locust Street
Pittsburgh, PA 15219
Tel: 412-575-5805
Fax: 412-232-7389

Washington, D.C.

Nina Scribanu, M.D.
International Adoption Health Resource Center
3307 M Street, N.W.
Washington, D.C. 20007
Tel: 202-687-8635
Fax: 202-687-8899

Texas

Bruce A. Eckel, M.D., DABP, Medical Director
North Texas International Adoption Clinic
1160 N. Bonnie Brae
Denton, TX 76201
Tel: 940-898-1477
Fax: 940-382-4091

Heidi Schwarzwald, M.D.
Texas Children's Hospital
6621 Fannin Street
Houston, TX 77030
Tel: 832-824-1000
Fax: 832-825-1281

CHAPTER 14

After Your Return Home: Postplacement, Readoption, and Citizenship

Under the Family Medical Leave Act, new parents are entitled to twelve weeks of unpaid leave from their jobs, providing that the company they work for has more than 50 employees. Medical insurance and other benefits are maintained during your leave. You'll need this time to relax and bond with your child, to schedule appointments with the pediatrician, and to fill out and file the appropriate forms with the Social Security Administration, IRS, and INS.

First Steps on Returning Home

One of the first things you'll want to do on arriving home is to be sure that your child has been properly added to your health insurance plan. If your health insurance company needs a letter to confirm the date of your child's placement, ask your agency to send it on your behalf. Insurance carriers must be notified within 30 days of the child's placement or adoption. Be aware that group health insurance coverage is regulated by Public Law 104-191, which mandates that group insurance carriers cannot exclude pre-existing conditions or undiagnosed conditions in adopted children.

In some foreign countries, the child's name is not changed on the adoption decree or on the new birth certificate. Since it can take six months or more to readopt or reaffirm in order to legally change the name, it's best to file for a social security number and U.S. citizenship (if necessary) for your child as soon as possible. Amend them after you readopt or reaffirm. Table 14-1 includes a list of government forms that may be useful during the postplacement stage of international adoption. More information on readoption and filing for citizenship can be found later in this chapter.

The procedures for getting a social security card for your child may vary slightly from office to office and from bureaucrat to bureaucrat. Call your local office to verify the procedures and required documents ahead of time. To find the Social Security office nearest you, consult the government offices section of your phone book or visit **www.ssa.gov/locator.**

To apply for a social security number for your child, order Form SS-5, Application for a Social Security Card, from the Social Security Administration (1-800-772-1213), pick up the form at your local social security office, or download the form from the administration's web site at **www.ssa.gov**. A sample of this form is found at the end of this chapter. In order to complete the filing, you will need photocopies of the translations of the adoption or guardianship decree, the birth certificate, the child's passport including the page showing the INS stamp, and your own identification, such as a passport, driver's license, or military I.D (but not a birth certificate). If they want to see originals, take them in person. If the Social Security office tells you they need proof of U.S. Citizenship, apply for a U.S. passport for your child. Details for applying for a passport are at the end of this chapter. Don't leave the originals at the Social Security Administration or mail them in with the form. You'll need them again later. Later, if you need to change the child's name, you will need to notify the Social Security Administration. Your child will retain the same social security number.

It typically takes 10-14 days after the office receives your documents, for your child's card to be issued.

If you don't have your child's social security number by the time you file your tax return, you will need IRS Form W-7, Individual Taxpayer Identification Number, to claim your child as a dependent on your tax return. You'll also need IRS Form 8839 "Qualified Adoption Expenses," along with your agency receipt for the legal expenses incurred in order to qualify for a tax credit, which can be as much as $10,000. To request updated forms from the IRS, call 1-800-TAXFORM, or you can download IRS forms from its web site at **www.irs.ustreas.gov/**. You may also want to consider starting a savings plan for your child's college education.

This is also the time to make out a will or revise your current one. Most lawyers advise you to choose separate individuals to act as guardian of your child and as executor of your estate. Read your life insurance policy. Take a look at the beneficiaries of your life insurance, 401(k) and other investment or retirement funds. This is the time to make changes.

Registration of Your Child at the Embassy

Kazakhstan, Russia, Ukraine and possibly other countries of the former Union of Soviet Socialist Republics require adoptive parents to register their children with their country's embassy in Washington D.C. While the United States does not keep records of adopted children who leave, these countries do. The embassy, or your agency, will provide the registration form in which you identify yourself and state the child's original name and birth place and the new names you have given the child. Depending on the country, the registration form requires notarization and other legalization prior to filing at the embassy. To ignore or procrastinate registration is to jeopardize the future placements of orphans from that country.

Postplacement Supervision

Your adoption agency will also send you forms to fill out and return. These will likely include a postplacement supervision contract, five or more monthly progress reports to fill out on your child after the first month, a publicity release form, a form confirming your child's date of U.S. citizenship and possibly other forms as well.

Step 21
Participate in
postplacement
supervision.

Table 14-1: Government Forms - Postplacement

Form Number	Name of Form	Purpose
IRS Form W-7	Individual Taxpayer Identification Number	Tax filing
IRS Form 8839	Qualified Adoption Expenses	Tax filing
INS Form N-643	Application for Certificate of Citizenship on Behalf of an Adopted Child	Naturalization and proof of citizenship
INS Form N-600	Application for Certificate of Citizenship when only one parent is a citizen	Naturalization and proof of citizenship
INS Form N-656	Application for Replacement of Naturalization or Citizenship Document	Name change after Citizenship Certificate is issued or to replace lost Citizenship Certificate
INS Form G-844	Request for the Return of Original Documents	Return of documents given to the INS on entry into the United States
SSA Form SS-5	Application for a Social Security Card	Social security number
INS Form G-731	Inquiry about status of I-551 Alien Registration Card	Green card status
INS Form G-639	Freedom of Information/ Privacy Act Request	Access to your INS records
INS Form I-90	Application to Replace Alien Registration Card	Replace lost card or one that was never received

Helpful Contacts

Toll-free number for INS forms: 800-870-3676
To download INS forms: **www.ins.usdoj.gov**

Toll-free number for Social Security Administration: 800-772-1213
To download INS forms: **www.ssa.gov**

Toll-free number for IRS tax forms: 800-TAXFORM
Toll-free number for IRS assistance: 800-829-1040
To download IRS forms: **www.irs.ustreas.gov**

Each state has its own requirements regarding the frequency and length of post-placement supervision. Some states require supervisory contacts over a period of six months to one year. Three to six contacts may be required during this time period. A sample of a typical postplacement supervision report guide is included at the end of this chapter.

In addition, the national child-placing authorities in each foreign country have specific requirements as to the kind of information they wish to see, as well as how often and for how long. Your social worker will coordinate your state requirements with those of the foreign country. The nearby table shows a sample of postplacement requirements for some of the child-sending countries (see Table 14-2). Timely and informative supervisory reports benefit the orphans who wait. Child-placing authorities view these reports as examples of how children are loved and cared for in the United States. They also use these reports to judge the quality of an adoption agency. Depending upon your state requirements and those of the foreign country, your social worker will make one to six postplacement contacts or more, if required by the country of origin of your child. After the first six months, they may accept reports that you write on your child's development, with the inclusion of pediatric visits. Check with your agency.

If you are having any problems with your child, tell the social worker. One of the tasks that this person has been schooled for is helping families make satisfactory adjustments. The social worker will summarize the information she gathers at the interviews as well as referral information in postplacement reports. These are needed for the adoption or readoption in the U.S. courts and may also be translated and sent to your child's foreign agency.

Adoption agencies are licensed in their states under the child-placement standards in that state. The agencies must follow regulations governing the standards for the placement of a child in an adoptive home. The intent of state licensing departments is to cover the pre- and postplacement studies written by a social worker. The legal adoption in court is governed by the legal code on adoption procedures in the child's country of origin.

Readoption or Reaffirmation in Your County of Residence

Step 22
Readopt your child in
your state of residence.

Not only is there no national adoption law in the United States, adoption procedures are not even consistent among the counties in each state. The Clerk of Court in your county of residence and a civil lawyer with experience in foreign adoption can advise you on the best way to proceed. Readoption or reaffirmation of the foreign adoption may be necessary. Readoption in the child's state of residence can be important for a number of reasons, including future custody disputes, distribution of property, survivor's benefits, and child support. And, a state court decree would also be entitled to full faith and credit in other states, an advantage not available to decrees of foreign nations. However, the ratification by the United States of the Hague Convention and its implementation legislation will provide a U.S. norm for international adoptions in the future. Member countries will recognize each other's adoption decrees.

If you have a final foreign adoption decree and the child has an IR-3 visa, it may be possible for the court to recognize, reconfirm, or validate it. This could save you time and money. Discuss your options with an attorney experienced in international adoption.

If your child immigrated with an IR-4 visa, you may engage a lawyer to handle the adoption or readoption, or, if local laws allow it, you may handle your own case. The latter is called a *pro se* adoption.

If you do hire a lawyer, try to find a family practice attorney with international adoption experience. Your attorney will request appropriate forms and documentation from your adoption agency. The requirements for pre- and postplacement studies by the state licensing department and the requirements set down in the state legal code for local adoptions do not necessarily match. This causes a lot of confusion for the adoptive parents. Judges and lawyers inexperienced in international adoption usually request

ICCC Postplacement Requirements

The International Concerns Committee for Children (ICCC), *Report on Foreign Adoption, 1999*, has more to say on postplacement supervision.

"Many countries require that follow-up documentation be returned to the foreign courts to monitor the child's progress for a designated length of time. This is not pure whimsy or curiosity. If these children were left in their birth-countries it is likely that they would be "sold" as servants, or "encouraged" to augment their family's income, or simply to survive by themselves, becoming shoeshine boys or criminals. The documents and reports required allow the placing organizations to prove to the courts that this is not the case in the child's adoptive country, and that the child is, in truth, being loved and cherished for the unique person he is, and not being exploited."

"Failure to comply with these various postplacement requirements means it is entirely possible for foreign governments to shut down further foreign adoptions because no assurance is forthcoming that the children are in any better circumstances or their future is any more favorable than if they were left in their birth countries."

"In short, it is essential these requirements be followed to the letter if future adoptions are going to be allowed at all! Even when postplacement documentation is not required it is strongly encouraged. Not only would pictures, letters, etc., be greatly appreciated by the placing organization who — let's face it — are themselves not only the cause of your dear child being yours, but are very possibly the reason he is alive at all. Former caretakers exult in seeing the rosy face and sturdy limbs of a child who may have arrived to them on literally the edge of death. All of these caretakers live with children's deaths every day and it is never easy and never without anguish."

"If you have adopted a child from another country, please write to the source from which you adopted and tell them, with photographs if possible, how your child is doing. Apparently some really wild rumors surface from time to time about the reasons U.S. citizens want children. Medical experimentation is not the most far-out example. Write every six months if you can, especially if you adopted from an independent source rather than from one of the well established orphanages or government agencies. Even if you adopt from the latter, it is an extremely good idea to correspond. You will do a real favor to all hopeful adoptive parents who come after you, and to your child, who may wish to visit them some day."

a new home study and handle the adoption or readoption of a foreign-born child as they would a private adoption. The judge appoints *ad litems* (usually attorneys not connected with the case) to represent the child, the birth mother and the birth father. Birth relatives are notified of the impending adoption via publication in the county court gazette for a requisite number of months, but not contacted again abroad. Once the situation has been discussed, the judge may write a waiver for the additional home study or ask for an update. Your adoption agency will be requested to send the existing home study and postplacement reports to your lawyer or to the court for the adoption or readoption of your child.

Pro Se Adoption

Pro se adoption (adopting your child without using a lawyer) procedures vary from state to state and probably from county to county. Not all counties allow *pro se* adoptions. *pro se* adoption may be applied by parents who received a permanent guardianship or custody transfer. Children with final foreign adoption decrees may also be readopted *pro se* as may children brought into the United States under guardianships or custody arrangements held by international adoption agencies.

The best source of information on how to adopt your child without a lawyer is the Clerk of Court. Your social worker may also have this information, or he or she may know a postadoptive parent who will advise you.

Ask your social worker to send the necessary adoption papers to you after your last postplacement meeting. From an office form supply company, purchase the forms required by your court. You can contact the Clerk of Court to determine what forms are necessary. Send the completed and notarized court-required forms to the Clerk of Court. (If you are conducting a *pro se* adoption, enter *pro se* in the blank for the name of the lawyer.) With the form, enclose the filing fee (usually about $250.00). If you are conducting a *pro se* adoption, you will also need to enclose a letter to the judge of the District Court, Juvenile Division, explaining why you wish to represent yourself. (For example, you wish to exercise your constitutional right, and you need to save the lawyer's fee.) You may wish to add that you are adequately prepared because you have read your state adoption laws and you have discussed them with your social worker.

Adoption Hearings

The adoption hearing takes about ten minutes. If possible, ask the Clerk of Court for a photocopy of the questions to be asked at the hearing. Be prepared to pay about $200.00 in court costs in addition to the filing fee and $35.00 for a new birth certificate (in some states). At the hearing, you or your lawyer will attest to the legality of the foreign adoption, guardianship, or other legal arrangements made for your child abroad. Under oath, you will verify all of the facts listed on the adoption forms. You will state that your child has been examined by your family physician and that you are satisfied with the child's mental and physical health. You may also be asked if you are responsible for any other minors living in your home, as well as other questions the judge may decide to ask. In most states, a new birth certificate is issued. If you have second thoughts about the child's name, now is the time to change it.

Reaffirmation of the Adoption and Name Changes

If your child immigrated with an IR-3 visa and your state recognizes, reconfirms or validates foreign adoption decrees, you may wish to reaffirm or request a name change rather than readopt. The child's name is changed and recorded at the state Bureau of Vital Statistics. A new birth certificate will show your name and the child's new name. The only catch is that you will need to find an attorney who has paved the way in court for such cases or is willing to try.

Table 14-2: Number of Postplacement Reports Required by Selected Countries

Country	Social Worker Reports	Parent Reports	Translation
Bolivia	Yes — 5	Yes — 5 for the first year, plus one semi-annually for the next two years	Yes
Bulgaria	Yes — 5	Yes — 5, plus bi-annual reports for the next two years.	No
China, Mainland	Yes — 5	Yes — One annually on the anniversary of placement. Ends with proof of citizenship.	Yes
Colombia, Medillin	Yes — 5	Yes — 5	No
Ecuador	Yes — 5	Yes — 5, plus one per year for the next four years.	Yes
Guatemala	Yes — 5	Yes — 5	Yes
Honduras	Yes — 5	Yes — 5, plus one per year until child reaches 18.	Yes
Kazakhstan	Yes — 5	Yes — 5, and also at 6, 12 ,24, and 36 months.	Yes
Peru	Yes — 5	Yes — 5, plus a bi-annual report for four years legalized by Peruviuan Consulate.	Yes
Romania	Yes — 5	Yes — 5, plus 1 every six months for two years.	No
Russia	Yes — 5	Yes — at 11 months and then bi-annually for two years.	No
Ukraine	Yes — 5	Yes — 5, plus at least once a year.	No
Vietnam	Yes — 5	Yes — One every month for first five months, plus one per year until child reaches age 18	No

U.S. Citizenship

Step 23

Obtain proof of
citizenship for your
child, or file for U.S.
citizenship if your child's
adoption was not final
at the time he or she
entered the country.

Since Congress passed the Child Citizenship Act of 2000 (effective February 27, 2001), children entering the United States with an IR-3 visa become U.S. citizens the moment they set foot (or are carried) on U.S. soil. This act also granted citizenship retroactively to children under the age of 18 with a final adoption decree whose parents procrastinated and did not apply for U.S. citizenship. Unfortunately, proving your child's status as a U.S. citizen is not automatic. It is everyone's hope that INS will eventually streamline this process in view of the new law. However, in the meantime, parents of children in this category must still obtain proof of citizenship through an application for a certificate for U.S. citizenship or a U.S. passport. It will save time and money to apply for the passport; however, some lawyers are not as comfortable with this option, since passports expire every 5 years until the child is 16 years old. (Adult passports are valid for 10 years.)

However, a child's passport is also an I.D. that can be used in lieu of a birth certificate and to travel abroad, whereas the Certificate of Citizenship belongs in a safety deposit or strong box. If you decide to apply for a Certificate of Citizenship for your child, follow the procedure outlined below for filing Form N-643, Application for Certificate of Citizenship on Behalf of an Adopted Child. You may want to apply for both a passport and certificate.

The Child Citizenship Act does not confer automatic citizenship for children who enter the United States on an IR-4 visa. If your child arrived with an IR-4 visa, you will need to apply for citizenship for as soon as your child has a U.S. adoption decree. In this case, you will receive an Alien Registration Card in the mail. You triggered the issue of the card when you turned in the envelope with your original adoption documents from the U.S. Consulate to an INS official at the airport. You will need this card at the child's citizenship hearing. The card is mailed to the same address you listed on Form I-600, Petition to Classify an Orphan as an Immediate Relative, at the time of filing. If you didn't receive the form, order INS Form G-731, Inquiry about the Status of I-551 Alien Registration Card. If you lost the card, order INS Form I-90, Application to Replace Alien Registration Card.

If both parents are U.S. citizens, order Form N-643, Application for Certificate of Citizenship on Behalf of an Adopted Child, by using the INS's toll-free ordering number (800) 870-3676 or download the form from the INS web site at **www.ins.usdoj.gov/**. (See sample at the end of this chapter.) The filing fee is $145.00. If only one parent is a citizen, order Form N-600 ($185.00). Send in photocopies of the required documents listed on the form and include the following statement: "Copies of the documents being submitted are exact photocopies of original documents. I understand that I may be required to submit original documents to an immigration official at a later date." Sign and date this statement.

Once your documents have been received and processed by INS, you will be notified of the citizenship hearing. Take the originals requested on Form N-643 or N-600 to present to the official. The child's alien card is surrendered in lieu of the Certificate of Citizenship. Keep the Certificate of Citizenship in a safe place. Although it states that this document cannot be photocopied, it is now permissible to do so for legal purposes. The entire process of applying for and receiving citizenship can take anywhere from three to twelve months, depending on the INS office workload. U.S. citizenship bestows rights and privileges and protection. As a U.S. citizen, your child now qualifies for federal programs, grants, college loans, and can travel internationally and return to the United States without restrictions.

Forward information regarding your child's date of citizenship to your U.S.-based international adoption agency. Both the U.S. agency and the foreign child-placing entity need this information to close their files.

Documents Required for U.S. Citizenship Application

Certified copies or originals of the following documents will be required:

1. Adoptive parents' birth certificate(s)

2. Adoptive parents' marriage license, if applicable

3. Child's birth certificate

4. Child's adoption decree

5. Child's foreign passport

6. Child's alien registration card. (Children who enter the United States with an IR-3 visa are not always sent an alien card, since the child is an automatic U.S. citizen and does not need to be naturalized.)

Take your identification and passports along, as well as all documents (both foreign and U.S.) pertaining to the child's adoption or guardianship, in case the court wishes to examine them.

Once citizenship is awarded, be certain to store the child's documents in a safe place. A safe-deposit box would probably be best. Type the citizenship number and the name and location of the bank where the safe-deposit box is located on a sheet of paper and file it elsewhere for easy reference.

If you would like a flag flown over the U.S. Capital in your child's honor, contact your local U.S. representative regarding the proposed date. They will send you an order form with a selection of sizes and fabrics. After your child's special day, the flag will be sent to her or him as a memento.

Documents for Child's U.S. Passport

If you have a final adoption decree for your child, you may apply for a U.S. passport for your child immediately after arriving in the United States. Use a zero in the space for social security numbers if necessary. Since this will be your child's first passport, you will need to apply in person at the nearest passport office. Visit the state department web site at **http://travel.state.gov** and click on the heading Passport Services to find the passport office nearest you.

Five items are required for the passport application.

1. Certified final adoption decree

2. Child's foreign passport with INS I-155 stamp or child's alien card

3. Child's birth certificate(s)

4. Valid identification of adoptive parent, such as a U.S. passport. (If a couple is adopting, identification will be needed for both parents.)

5. Passport photo of child

Passports for children younger than age 16 cost $70 and are valid for 5 years. After age 16, passports are valid for 10 years.

Celebration

Once you have obtained citizenship for your child, you have completed the adoption requirements from A to Z. Now is the time to unfurl the Stars and Stripes! Decorate cakes in red, white, and blue for this day and on every anniversary of this memorable occasion. Take pictures of these activities for your child's Life Book.

Changes to or Replacement of the Naturalization/Citizenship Document

If, at any time after receiving the child's citizenship documents, you need to either replace the Certificate of Citizenship because it has been lost or damaged or you need to change the child's name on the document, you'll need to file Form N-565, Application for Replacement of Naturalization/ Citizenship Document, from the INS. The instructions on the form will explain the number, size, and poses of the photographs required. You will also need to send them a copy of the damaged document if one exists. If you need to make a name change, you will also need to submit copies of the original service document and a copy of the court order, or your marriage or divorce certificate, showing the name change. After you submit the completed form, required photocopies, and the $155.00 filing fee, you may be called in for a hearing prior to being issued a new Certificate of Citizenship.

OMB No. 1115-0152

U.S. Department of Justice
Immigration and Naturalization Service

Certificate of Citizenship on Behalf of Adopted Child

START HERE - Please Type or Print	FOR INS USE ONLY

Part   Information about adopted child.

Last Name	First	Middle

Address:

Street Number		Apt. #

City	State or Province

Country	ZIP/Postal Code

Date of Birth (Mo/Day/Yr)	Place of Birth (City, Country)

Social Security #	A#

Personal Description:

Sex   ☐ Male   ☐ Female   Height   Ft. _____   In. _____

Marital Status	Visible Marks or Scars

Information about Entry:

Name at Entry (If different from Item A)

Date of Entry	Place of Entry

Date of Adoption (Mo/Day/Yr)	Place of Adoption (City, Country)

Part B. Information about the Adoptive Parents (if there is only one parent write "None" in place of the name of the parent which does not apply.)

Last Name of Adoptive Father	First	Middle

U.S. Citizen by: ☐ Birth in the U.S.

☐ Birth abroad to USC parents (List certificate of citizenship number or passport number)

☐ Naturalized or derived after birth (List naturalization certificate number)

Last Name of Adoptive Mother	First	Middle and Maiden

U.S. Citizen by: ☐ Birth in the U.S.

☐ Birth abroad to USC parents (List certificate of citizenship number or passport number)

☐ Naturalized or derived after birth (List naturalization certificate number)

FOR INS USE ONLY

Returned	Receipt
Resubmitted	
Reloc Sent	
Reloc Rec'd	
☐ Applicant Interviewed	

Action Block

Recommendation of Officer:

☐ Approval   ☐ Denial

Concurrence of District Director or Officer in Charge:

☐ I do   ☐ do not   ☐ concur

Signature

Certificate # _____

To Be Completed by **Attorney or Representative**, if any
☐ Fill in box if G-28 is attached to represent the applicant
VOLAG#
ATTY State License #

Form N-643

U.S. Citizenship, Page 2 of 2

Part B. *Continued.*

Date and Place of Marriage of the Adoptive Parents

Number of Prior Marriages of Adoptive Father	Number of Prior Marriages of Adoptive Mother

Is residence of parents' the same as the child's? ☐ YES ☐ NO (If no, explain on a separate sheet of paper.)

If the residence address is different from Item A, list actual residence address.   Daytime Telephone #

Part C.   Signature. (Read the information on penalties in the instructions before completing this section.)

I certify that this application, and the evidence submitted with it, is true and correct. I authorize the release of any information from my records, or that of my child which the Immigration and Naturalization Service needs to determine eligibility for the benefit I am seeking.

Signature	*Print Name*	*Date*

Part D.   Signature of person preparing form, if other than above. *(Sign below)*

I declare that I prepared this application at the request of the above person and it is based on all information of which I have knowledge.

Signature	*Print Name*	*Date*

Firm Name
and Address

DO NOT COMPLETE THE FOLLOWING UNTIL INSTRUCTED TO DO SO AT THE INTERVIEW

AFFIDAVIT.   I, the (parent, guardian) _____ do swear or affirm, under penalty of the perjury laws of the United States, that I know and understand the contents of this application signed by me, and the attached supplementary pages numbered ( ) to ( ) inclusive; that the same are true and correct to the best of my knowledge, and that corrections numbered ( ) to ( ) were made by me or at my request.

Signature of parent or guardian _____   Date _____

Person Examined	Address	Relationship to Applicant

Sworn or affirmed before me on _____ at _____

Signature of interviewing officer _____ Title _____

Form SS-5

Application for a Social Security Card

SOCIAL SECURITY ADMINISTRATION
Application for a Social Security Card

Form Approved
OMB No. 0960-0066

1

		First	Full Middle Name	Last
NAME ⟶ TO BE SHOWN ON CARD				
FULL NAME AT BIRTH IF OTHER THAN ABOVE		First	Full Middle Name	Last
OTHER NAMES USED				

2

MAILING ADDRESS ⟶
Do Not Abbreviate

Street Address, Apt. No., PO Box, Rural Route No.

City	State	Zip Code

3 **CITIZENSHIP** ⟶ (Check One)

☐ U.S. Citizen   ☐ Legal Alien Allowed To Work   ☐ Legal Alien **Not** Allowed To Work (See Instructions On Page 1)   ☐ Other (See Instructions On Page 1)

4 **SEX** ⟶   ☐ Male   ☐ Female

5 **RACE/ETHNIC DESCRIPTION** ⟶ (Check One Only - Voluntary)

☐ Asian, Asian-American or Pacific Islander   ☐ Hispanic   ☐ Black (Not Hispanic)   ☐ North American Indian or Alaskan Native   ☐ White (Not Hispanic)

6 **DATE OF BIRTH** — Month, Day, Year

7 **PLACE OF BIRTH** (Do Not Abbreviate)   City   State or Foreign Country   FCI   Office Use Only

8

A. MOTHER'S MAIDEN NAME ⟶   First   Full Middle Name   Last Name At Her Birth

B. MOTHER'S SOCIAL SECURITY NUMBER ⟶   ☐☐☐ — ☐☐ — ☐☐☐☐

9

A. FATHER'S NAME ⟶   First   Full Middle Name   Last

B. FATHER'S SOCIAL SECURITY NUMBER ⟶   ☐☐☐ — ☐☐ — ☐☐☐☐

10 Has the applicant or anyone acting on his/her behalf ever filed for or received a Social Security number card before?

☐ Yes (If "yes", answer questions 11-13.)   ☐ No (If "no", go on to question 14.)   ☐ Don't Know (If "don't know", go on to question 14.)

11 Enter the Social Security number previously assigned to the person listed in item 1. ⟶   ☐☐☐ — ☐☐ — ☐☐☐☐

12 Enter the name shown on the most recent Social Security card issued for the person listed in item 1. ⟶   First   Middle Name   Last

13 Enter any different date of birth if used on an earlier application for a card. ⟶   Month, Day, Year

14 **TODAY'S DATE** — Month, Day, Year

15 **DAYTIME PHONE NUMBER** — ( ) Area Code   Number

16 I declare under penalty of perjury that I have examined all the information on this form, and on any accompanying statements or forms, and it is true and correct to the best of my knowledge.

YOUR SIGNATURE ▶

17 **YOUR RELATIONSHIP TO THE PERSON IN ITEM 1 IS:**
☐ Self   ☐ Natural Or Adoptive Parent   ☐ Legal Guardian   ☐ Other (Specify)

DO NOT WRITE BELOW THIS LINE (FOR SSA USE ONLY)

NPN			DOC	NTI	CAN		ITV
PBC	EVI	EVA	EVC	PRA	NWR	DNR	UNIT

EVIDENCE SUBMITTED

SIGNATURE AND TITLE OF EMPLOYEE(S) REVIEWING EVIDENCE AND/OR CONDUCTING INTERVIEW

_____ DATE

DCL _____ DATE

Form **SS-5** (3-2001)   EF (07-2002)   Destroy Prior Editions

Postplacement Supervision Guidelines

GUIDELINES FOR POSTPLACEMENT SUPERVISION

One report per month, written by a social worker, will be required for five months. These reports should be based on two face-to-face interviews with the entire family, one of which must take place in the family's home, and three telephone interviews. If the child is over the age of one year, all of the interviews must be face to face.

After the initial visit, subsequent contacts will cover the same topics — a progress report on the child's development, the family's adjustment, and language acquisition and age appropriate education. Include the integration of the child into the community, as well as the utilization of ECI (Early Childhood Intervention) programs, resources of the public or private school system, and other community resources.

Attach copies of the results of the recommended physical for internationally adopted children, including information on height, weight, and immunizations, as well as periodic check-ups, treatments, or therapies.

*Contact No.:*_____   (State whether the contact is made in the home
                                with all members present, face-to-face, or by telephone.)

Date: _____   (Date contact was made.)

*Family Name:*_____

Address: _____

_____

Phone Number: _____

Child's Original Name: _____

Child's Present Name: _____

Date of Birth: _____

Date of Placement: _____

*Name of Child-Placing Entity Abroad:*_____

Postplacement Supervision Guidelines

INFANTS UNDER ONE YEAR

- *General appearance.*
- *Habits, behavior, and personality characteristics.*
- *Favorite games and toys.*
- *New developmental milestones or skills.*
- *Sleeping and eating patterns.*
- *Unusual or problematic behavior and your suggestions to modify the behavior.*

Parental Adjustment

- *Adjustments for the parent(s) and any siblings in sharing time and new responsibilities.*
- *Quality of time that parent(s), child, and any siblings enjoy together. Is the family bonding? What is the attachment of the parents to the child like and vice versa?*

See final paragraphs in "Older Children" category for advising parents on the legal and citizenship processes as well as your evaluation and recommendations.

OLDER CHILDREN & FUTURE ISSUES

- *General appearance.*
- *Personality, behavior, favorite activities, sports, and toys.*
- *Attainment of developmental milestones and skills.*
- *Positive and/or negative habits and behaviors.*

Child's Adjustment

- *Language, racial, and cultural differences in the family and neighborhood.*
- *Emotional, social, and physical changes since placement.*
- *Child's personality and integration of past experience with the present living situation.*
- *Evidence of the child's attachment to the family.*

Parental Adjustment

- *Emotional and social adjustments.*
- *Methods of coping with increased responsibility and changing roles.*
- *Feelings of attachment toward the child.*
- *Discussion with parents regarding the differences in the development of institutionalized children.*
- *Discussion with parents of how children learn.*
- *Ability to individualize the special needs of birth child or children and adoptive child.*
- *Interpretation of any community prejudices against the child.*
- *Child-rearing practices regarding discipline, setting limits, and household rules.*

Postplacement Supervision Guidelines

- *Parents' response to the manifestations of the loss and separation trauma in the child. For example, parents' reaction to the child's sleep disturbances, withdrawal, aggression, not eating, inconsolable crying, screaming, bed-wetting, and regression in toilet training.*
- *Child's readiness for and enrollment and adjustment to a nursery, day care, or school.*

EVALUATION OF THE PLACEMENT

- *Family's feelings about their preparation for this experience. Is the child as they visualized? How have their ideas changed?*
- *Child's preparation for placement in the United States. Does the family believe it was adequate?*
- *Changes in residence, number of adult household members, health, or income since the placement.*
- *General appraisal of the placement.*

Recommendations

- *Prognosis for the future. How has placement changed and benefited the child, the new parent(s), and the rest of the family?*
- *Discussion with parents to help the child understand the meaning of adoption at age and language appropriate levels.*
- *Your recommendation for adoption, readoption, or reaffirmation. (Request a Waiver and Citation of Consent to Adoption if required in your county.)*
- *Explanation of the steps required to obtain the child's U.S. citizenship.*

Final Observations: Comment upon the manner in which the child or children are being raised. If this is a sibling group, a child over two years of age, or a handicapped child, state whether you recommend that postplacement supervision continue until the adoption is consummated.

Final Report: Indicate that this is the final report and that "The family understands and agrees with termination of postplacement services." Mention any specific recommendations or referrals that you have made to the family. Are these in place, or do they have a plan to follow through?

Social Worker's Name and Credentials

CHAPTER 15

Parenting the Adopted Child

This chapter includes a brief overview of what you might expect as you and your child begin to adjust to one another. There are many other excellent resources that can provide a more in-depth discussion of child development, attachment, and adoptive adjustments. Many social workers and child psychologists have much experience and expertise to offer on the issues of bonding and attachment in families. Let your social worker or adoption agency know if you experience any problems. These professionals are able to help adoptive parents through the critical first months of an adoptive adjustment and can be called upon later if further help is needed. Prospective parents can help prepare themselves for the first few months of the adoptive adjustment by reading and talking to postadoptive parents of children of the age group and culture in which they are interested. In addition, recommended books on adoption and adoptive parent magazines are listed in the Bibliography. Concise guidelines and tools are available as well. A postplacement progress questionnaire, a checklist for medical tests, a Life Book outline, and a Forever Family Certificate are available to adoptive families through the Joint Council on International Services for Families and Children.

Abandoned children, who have usually been malnourished over an extended period, are usually small for their ages and physically weak. Unfortunately, their early (birth to three months) emotional and developmental needs were probably never met. Typical orphanage infants and children are normal in their mental development, yet lag behind in fine and gross motor skills. Children like these overcome their physical problems quite rapidly in adoptive homes. At the same time, however, the adoptive parents must temporarily forget their child's chronological age and tend to their child's emotional needs, just as they would to a baby's physical and emotional needs. Thus, parents nurture their children and establish mutual trust, love, and cooperation.

Bonding, the process of attachment to a family, gives children the chance to grow and to change within a family over an extended period of time. In bonding, adoptive children decide to trust their parents to not disappear. Bonding is a process that can take up to five years. Working adoptive couples and singles must plan on one parent spending at least six months at home to carry on this bonding process with the child before returning to a career. Yet, keep in mind, it is quality of attention given to the child rather than the quantity of time that leads to a strong bond.

Parenting institutionalized children who are culturally and ethnically different from yourself is a unique challenge, especially when the child is past the baby stage and already has a personality, memories, habits, and a different language. Quite often they have developed survival behaviors that are far beyond what is expected of a child of that age in a family. Five-month-olds may hold their own bottles; two-year-olds may never indulge in a temper tantrum; three-year-olds may share without a fuss; and four-year-olds may never ask for help, even when they get hurt. You may have to teach your child how to be a child — more specifically how to be your child.

Household Rules for Older Children

Before you emigrate your child, think about age-appropriate household rules. List what the child will and will not be allowed to do. This is particularly important for school-age children who are accustomed to institutional rules and schedules and feel insecure without them. All children feel more relaxed when they know what their new parents expect of them.

Explain these rules the first day your child moves in. A weekly family meeting to highlight each member's progress, to plan family activities, and to maintain or revise the rules is beneficial to everyone, even if it has to be conducted in hand and body signals because of language barriers.

Help from someone who speaks the child's native language is usually seen as threatening to a child under five or six. They have found security and loving attention with you. They don't know what the native speaker's motives are and may interpret it to mean that they are about to be moved again. A native speaker usually makes the child feel insecure.

Siblings

Prospective brothers and sisters are either happy or neutral when they hear about a new sibling. Many adoptive parents take their children along on the adoption trip. This helps some children feel important, especially if they take responsibility for entertaining the new sibling, in order to give their parents a break. Other children have immediately become jealous and difficult, which has added to the stress of the adoption experience. A family meeting should be held before the new child comes home to establish everyone's responsibilities with the new sibling. Household rules should be developed with everyone's ideas making a contribution. Most orphans are used to a structured environment in an institution. The new child will feel more comfortable with a household routine. Siblings will be able to feel important by cooperating with the care of their new brother or sister.

Toys should be sorted out by siblings and decisions made regarding what the newcomer can play with. Perhaps some favorites should be put out of sight for a while, as well as other items precious to the siblings. Most problems with new children have to do with the destruction of possessions that are important to the established children. Their inability to share toys may be a symptom of the inability to share parental attention. The happiest children are those who are taken out individually for an ice-cream cone or a walk. They feel that they are valued members of the family. And you can enjoy each other's company away from the demands of the house and the rest of the family.

A family picnic is another great way to share time together. I've never met a child who didn't like picnics. Let everyone help pack the basket and have as many picnics as you can.

The oldest child of a large, adoptive sibling group needs special attention in this respect, since this child has carried the responsibility of the family on his or her small shoulders. The child needs to let go of this responsibility as soon as he or she can trust you. Then the child can relax and be a child.

Stages in an Adoptive Adjustment

Once your child is in your custody, you may notice some puzzling behavior. Various stages occur in the adoptive adjustment of a child, in varying degrees, depending upon the age, sex, culture, and history of the child.

Compliant: Children's initial presence in an adoptive setting is one of quiet submission. The parent has little to complain about, as the child is good.

Rejecting: Crying and searching for lost caregivers. Children may tell their new mother or father by words or actions, "You're not my parent. You can't tell me what to do."

Disoriented: The child's new environment is in conflict with their old environment concerning what is expected of them. The child is frightened and defensive and may act aggressively.

Nondiscriminatory: These children are always happy and friendly to everyone. They imitate the fads and behaviors of peers and charm their new family, neighbors, and teachers.

All-American boy or girl: Eventually, children reject their old culture more vehemently. They don't want to talk about their past. They say that they are a regular American kid. Adoptive parents must create a climate of acceptance of all kinds of people since the children need a connection with their past.

Adjustment: Children achieve balance by knowing who they were and who they are in order to function in the United States, in their new family structure, and with their new language.

Adoptive Adjustments: Things that Parents Go Through

Like children, parents also go through an adjustment process. The parents' initial behavior is one of anticipating the child's needs and providing consistent care and nurturing. Although "rejecting" children are the most difficult to deal with, they are also the ones most in touch with their feelings. In all cases, your kindness, unconditional love and one-on-one personal attention will bring the child out of numbness and into a close relationship with you. Consistently maintain eye contact and verbal and physical expressions of love and caring to win their confidence.

The number one factor in the adoptive adjustment of parents is their expectation of what the child will be like and the degree to which the child is like or different from that dream. Often the adoptive parent feels somewhat disillusioned. The ability of the parent to resolve feelings of disappointment is the key in bonding with the child.

Adoptive parents must realize that their child will always be different from his or her North American friends and classmates because their child:

has already lost several mother figures.

was raised under a different set of child-raising beliefs.

was born in a foreign country.

spoke another language.

does not match the adoptive parents racially or culturally.

has had more than one set of parents.

experienced a disrupted family.

has learned a different way to act with adults.

has experienced serious emotional and/or physical trauma.

has national loyalties to another country.

All of these problems are potential concerns to the adoptive parents and to a child, depending somewhat on his or her age and history. To achieve a good adjustment within the adoptive family, the children must handle these concerns and ultimately resolve them. Your attitude toward the child's history is key. Nothing is more important to a child's self-esteem than their adoptive parent's high esteem of their birth mother. The adoptive parents' first job is to explain that their child was placed for adoption with the authorities because the birth mother trusted them to provide the care that she could not. There was nothing wrong with the child, and he or she was not rejected.

According to Ronald S. Federici, a child psychologist specializing in international adoption, 20-25 percent of orphans make routine adjustments within six to eighteen months and have no need for ongoing medical or psychological intervention. Forty-50 percent have mild attachment disorders, mild to moderate learning disabilities, speech and language disorders, and need a longer recovery period. Most social workers agree that the possibility that the family can never adjust is higher when the child is handicapped, more than three years old at the time of adoption, or part of a sibling group. Parents should not blame themselves too harshly if they have to ask to have the child removed from their home when they believe another family can do a better job. (Further information on disrupted adoptions can be found at the end of this chapter.) Fortunately, most international families can get all the help and information they need. A growing number of pediatricians, psychologists and other specialists have seen enough institutionalized children to create a body of knowledge for other practitioners. Adoptions can be on the brink of disrupting and be salvaged by skilled intervention.

Helpful Activities for Adopted Children

1. Help the child save money to send to an orphanage, church or other organization that does humanitarian work in the child's native land.

2. Find a pen pal for your child in the native land.

3. Read some relevant books together, such as *Why Am I Different* by Norma Simon or *Filling in the Blanks: A Guided Look at Growing Up* Adopted by Susan Gabel. (See Bibliography listings for children's books for other suggestions.)

4. Discuss minority or foreign-born Americans you admire. You can talk about the qualities of color and nations and all of the good things associated with them. You can discuss children you know, along with their good and bad traits and point out that the traits have nothing to do with color or national origin.

5. Go to the children's department of your public library and check out some books on the child's country with pictures. Plan an imaginary trip to that country and talk about what you would see and do there together.

6. Help your children design a Life Book (described below).

7. Attend a heritage and culture camp or participate in a homeland tour (see nearby box).

The Life Book

One of the best ways to help a child maintain a sense of identity is to create and maintain a Life Book for your child. Design the book to reflect both families and cultures. A large scrapbook is a good background for placing a copy of your child's birth documents, pictures of the people and places where the child stayed, and pictures and memorabilia connected with the child's first moments with you.

While you are abroad, buy picture postcards for the book, small maps, a small flag, and save some coins to tape into the Life Book. Tickets, menus, and any other paper tourist-type items will fascinate the child later on as you look through the book together.

Add pictures of the child's journey home, the first meeting with other new family members, the readoption, and the ceremony of citizenship. This Life Book is the most meaningful baby book an adopted child can possess since the book gives a child a sense of continuity regardless of the changes in his or her life.

Above all, start a journal once you have made the decision to adopt. Keep this as an open letter for the child to read later on. This record will help the child understand that your waiting time was a very important and meaningful period in your lives.

Your cover letter and the response from your foreign child-placing source should also be saved for the child, as well as the foreign stamps.

You and Your Child

The challenge ahead is one of adjustment for both parent and child. Foreign-born orphans, regardless of which country they are from, have similar adjustment patterns. There is information available on building close parent-child relationships. You may also find studies on adopted foreign orphans at your public library or perhaps at some adoption agencies.

One important, but often overlooked, part of the adoption adjustment involves vocabulary. "The Language of Adoption," a research paper by Marietta E. Spencer, ACSW, Children's Home Society of Minnesota, begins by saying one important aspect in developing close parent-child relationships is the use of correct terminology.

"A vital part of education for adoption must include an inspection of the words we use. Vocabulary helps give meaning to the sensitive human process. One should choose words with care. Alternatives to 'put up for adoption' might be the following:"

"To arrange for an adoption.
To make a placement plan for the child.
To find a family who will adopt the child, and so on."

"Adoption holds out the promise of the fullest realization of the child's (and family's) potential. Such full potential can only be reached if society provides a benign and supportive climate for both the adopted person and for his family."

Unfortunately, our society is not yet benign or supportive. From kindergarten through adulthood, adopted foreign children, as well as adoptive parents, need a lot of answers to a lot of questions that the children ask, those that strangers ask, and those that we ourselves ask.

Consider joining a support group of adoptive families or starting one. Together, you can discuss the problems institutionalized children have and support each other in order to support them. You can also help your children learn about their cultures with other adopted children and adults of their ethnic origin. As a group, you can also discover resources to aid you in planning transracial, cross-cultural workshops for adoption agency staff and prospective adoptive parents.

Racial Prejudice

Like many adoptive parents, we realized that our personal experience with minorities in this country had been very limited before we adopted our foreign children. We entered into a transracial, cross-cultural adoption believing that by the time our children grew up there would be less racism. Now we know that they will not see the end of prejudice and discrimination in their lifetime. Nevertheless, our lives were enriched by transracial adoption. Our family befriended people we would not have otherwise met. As our children grew, they chose friends because of their personalities and good character. Race was never their criteria for friendship. When they were old enough to date, they followed the same process of selection. Two are married now to people of different ethnicities and religion. Our family is living out our vision of social change. Our twin daughters rose to important positions in our adoption agency. They are also as thoughtful and considerate as any parent could wish.

Interestingly, girls are still more sought after than boys in international adoption; about 80 percent of prospective parents prefer to adopt girls. Is it because mothers want to re-experience the joys of their childhood with a little girl? Would the presence of an Asian or Latin female in their social group be more benign than a male? Or, should we believe the reason advanced by cynics — that boys carry on the family name, sire future generations, and, therefore, should look like a member of the family?

Prospective adoptive parents who inquired about adoption almost always mentioned their relatives as either being supportive or dead set against a transracial, cross-cultural adoption. After months of hearing some of these callers complain that they could not consider adopting a foreign child because of their relatives, I began asking them how they personally felt about Asian, Hispanic, African-American, or other minority groups in the United States. Now that we are placing Asian children and white children from Eastern Europe, we must look at political and religious hatreds, as well.

Not until several years after we adopted our foreign children did we realize that we had been thinking of adoption as a single event, done once and for all. We began talking about the additional responsibility of adoptive parents of foreign children as we helped organize their paperwork. We needed to help parents help their children to develop feelings of self-esteem and a sense of identity with both their old family and their new family.

One way to accomplish this is to find friends within the minority groups in our communities to provide adult role models for our middle-school-age children. The prospective adoptive parents who are unwilling to mingle with minorities or foreigners are not likely to feel comfortable in future social situations with their adopted children. Postadoptive parents tend to neglect this aspect of their children's lives.

Most of our inquirers usually mentioned whether they already had, or planned to have, biological children. Had the couple already decided how to handle the problem if a grandparent showed a preference for their genetic grandchildren? Or, had they given some thought to the opposite problem: the foreign adopted child might be given too much attention by everyone and the biological child would feel left out?

Some of the parents considering adoption wondered if the schoolteachers in their communities might believe that children from certain minority groups were intellectually gifted, while children from other groups were intellectually inferior. Other prospective parents confided that minority children were such a rarity in their communities that teachers might overindulge a foreign adopted child.

Most of the time, adoptive parents gave a great deal of thought to their transracial, cross-cultural adoptions. And, usually, once they understood the prospective adoptive parent's feelings, the relatives were emotionally supportive. If their relatives were truly against the idea, the prospective adopters had to ask themselves if they were strong enough to function well without the emotional support and the child care that their extended family would have provided. Fortunately, very few parents considering adoption had to make such a difficult decision. The children were welcomed into loving, extended families. And, some of the grandparents even flew overseas with their children to help with the care and the adoption of their new grandchild.

Whether your extended family supports your adoption plan or not, you do need to make some arrangements concerning your will as well as who shall care for the child should you and your spouse die before the child reaches adulthood. If you have a relative or friend who agrees to accept this responsibility, a letter to this effect can be attached to your will. If you do not have anyone to assume your parental duties, consider writing a letter to your adoption agency, which may agree to re-place your child in a permanent home. Without these provisions, your child could, upon your death, become a ward of the state and be placed in long-term foster care.

Cross-Cultural and Interracial Workshops

To help widen their own awareness and to continue to help other parents and children learn more about the child's country of origin, some parents have volunteered to organize cross-cultural and interracial workshops on an annual basis. Some ideas for similar workshops are listed below.

Purpose: To grow in awareness and understanding of cultural differences. Adoptive parents need to discover some links to the people and culture of their child's native country.

Organization: Gather educational materials for a display. Include a map, posters of children, and other book and non-book materials. Those from UNICEF are colorful, informative, and inexpensive.

Preworkshop reading: Have the workshop participants read some of the anthropological studies of families in Asia, Europe, or Latin America and discuss the book they chose with the group. Or have the group read a novel written by a native of the country you are adopting from that describes family and other social interactions.

Music: Play folk music indigenous to these countries. You can probably find tapes and records at the public library.

Featured guest: Present a pro-adoption foreigner from a developing country who is willing to answer questions concerning the conditions that lead to child abandonment and adoption. Prepare a list of questions about the conditions in the guest's country to discuss before his or her presentation concerning child raising.

Films: Present a slide show or rent a video. Slide presentations complete with scripts showing children struggling for survival in extreme poverty are available through UNICEF at very low cost.

Group leaders: Ask the foreign featured guest, a social worker, and a postadoptive couple who have at least three years experience as adoptive parents to answer questions during the group discussion sessions.

Group discussion: Discuss the following questions:
How can we be one another's teachers:
  in researching foreign cultures?
  in finding immigrants who are willing to teach us culture and customs?
  in seeking awareness and understanding of racial and cultural differences?
  in learning child-raising methods of other cultures as a comparison?
  in discovering how children are taught in other cultures?

Adopted children's interest in these groups may drop off when children are in elementary school. At this point, the family is involved in church and athletic activities and the child just wants to fit in and be an American kid.

In the meantime, parents should continue to collect information on the subject. As children approach adolescence and relate to changing social groups, they will need this for thought and discussion in order to eventually define themselves.

Culture Camps and Homeland Tours

Many adoption agencies and adoptive parent support groups sponsor culture camps, which can be anything from a week-long stay to a weekend day camp. Some are for children only, while others are for children and parents together. Some camps are geared specifically for children from one particular country, while other camps are for children adopted from any country outside of the United States.

Your adoption agency may be able to provide information about nearby culture camps, or for a more complete list, visit **www.adoptioncamps.com** or send a query to one of the on-line, country-specific adoption support groups.

Homeland tours are also becoming popular, especially to those countries that have sent thousands of orphans here. Some of these trips lead to meetings with the children's birth mothers. Many adopted children feel anxious about these trips, regardless of whether or not their original family is found, because they don't know what to expect. A better alternative might be to educate the children about their country of origin as best as you can and put off the journey until they're young adults. At that point, they'll have a better understanding of the socio-economic problems that caused their mothers to make an adoption plan.

If you decide that your child or young adult is ready for a homeland tour, your agency can make recommendations for a reputable organization. Their representative abroad may make the arrangements. Further resources for organizations that sponsor homeland tours can be found on the Internet. Be sure to check the organization thoroughly. Trained counselors should be on hand to guide the children through the emotional joys and pitfalls of these trips, especially if there is a potential meeting with birth relatives.

Disruptions of Adoptive Families

Not every adoptive placement succeeds. In our agency's history of more than 2,500 placements, only nine have disrupted. Other agencies cite similar statistics. The reasons have been varied. One child had a serious hearing loss, which was not noticed by the U.S. Embassy-approved doctor. The adoptive parents did not wish to deal with the handicap. Another was an eight-year-old beggar girl who was not easy to transform into a Girl Scout. Another neglected and abused eight-year-old Panamanian boy was uncivilized at home and unruly at school. Another child turned up with hepatitis B and was rejected. A sibling set of three pubescent boys proved impossible for their mother to control. And we were forced to remove an infant when the adoptive parents split up and neither was capable of raising the child alone. On three separate occasions, Romanian and Russian boys of three years old were returned by their first set of adoptive parents for hyperactive, destructive behavior. In all of these cases, our agency was able to help locate new adoptive families for the children. The children adjusted well in their new families, probably because the new families were more tolerant and their expectations were not as high.

The main reason adoptive parents reject children after adoption is not health, but behavior. Sometimes the reactive behavior of the existing children rather than that of the newcomer is more than the parents can tolerate and they decide that the new child has to leave.

Keep your social worker informed of any concerns. Get counseling. Most problems can eventually be resolved. However, if your family agrees that the placement can never succeed, you will need to make plans. If you do not have a final foreign decree, your agency must be contacted. If they hold managing conservatorship, they will take the child into foster care until they can arrange a new placement. The agency must be given all the child's original documents, passport, and alien registration card in order to re-place the child and notify the authorities of the child's change of address.

If you have a foreign decree or U.S. adoption decree, you will need to enlist the assistance of your agency, or another private or public agency, depending upon the needs of the child. If you are able to secure the help of an adoption agency in order to re-place the child in a new home, you must give them the child's previously listed documents. In addition, you will need to sign relinquishments of parental rights in order to terminate your parental rights in court. Only then can the child be placed in an adoptive home.

In our experience, second placements have been successful. The new adoptive parents are already aware of the child's problems and are ready, willing, and able to help the child overcome them. A family meeting held before the child moves in is mandatory in order to establish household rules. The children, unfortunately, blame themselves for having been rejected. They are generally eager to comply with a new living arrangement in the hope of permanence. If at all possible, the first adoptive family should make a preplacement visit with the new adoptive family prior to the placement. They should be there when the transfer is made. If the first family has other children, they should be part of the process so that they don't worry after the transfer is made. If possible, the children should also be allowed to make a postplacement visit to be certain that the child is OK. If a family cannot be found for the child, you or your agency will need to call your state agency to obtain a list of public and private church-run residential homes.

However, the majority of adoptive parents know their limitations and have the right motives: love for children. To them, children are worth all the paperwork, the expense, and the waiting. They're worth the worry and the endless tending. They feel enriched by their racial and/or national diversity and pleased that succeeding generations will probably be of mixed ethnicity.

Figures from the U.S. State Department show that U.S. citizens adopt more than 19,000 foreign children each year. According to sociologists researching this type of adoption, the odds are in favor of happy, cross-cultural, transracial families.

Internationally adopted children will always be "extraordinary Americans." They're resilient survivors of relinquishment, abandonment, and institutionalization. They're brave children raised by some of the most exemplary women and men in the United States. These "extraordinary Americans" grow up with respect for their homelands as well as loyalty toward the United States. As they grow to voting age and rise to responsible positions in the private sector and government, they offer hope for a broader and gentler perspective toward global problems.

Contacting Birth Parents

Secure, well-functioning international adoptive parents do everything possible to enhance their child's emotional well-being. They choose just the right words to tell the child about his or her adoption, create Life Books, sign up for annual culture camps to familiarize the child with his or her homeland, and try to answer the child's questions with honesty, love and patience in a way that's appropriate for his or her age. Now that the practice of open domestic adoptions in the United States is commonplace, some parents even try to contact their child's foreign birth mother.

Wait a minute! International adoption is a far cry from domestic adoption. American birth parents and adoptive parents meet before the child is born and develop a relationship with one another. Although children born in developing countries need to know at an early age that they were adopted, they're unable to grasp the entire concept until they reach adulthood. We walk a tight rope when it comes to balancing the child's need to know with telling too much. Some adoptive parents continually dialog about the foreign birth mother and name her. She's an invisible presence. Too much information can overwhelm children and fill them with worry. "Did she love me? Is she still poor? Doesn't she have enough to eat or a place to sleep?"

When a foreign judge grants a foreign adoption decree, the matter is closed and the records are sealed. The parties involved are not pledged to meet at a future date. Well meaning international adoptive parents tend to do too much too soon. I've heard from parents who helped their child write letters to their birth mother in hope of a response. They've tracked the mother down through a foreign embassy and taken the child abroad to find her. Unfortunately, the trips raise even more questions in the mind of a child unequipped to deal with the socio-economic reasons behind international adoption.

Let your children know they were adopted, but don't dwell on the details. Enjoy your children and help them thrive, secure in your family environment. You are the parent who planned, prepared, and paid to adopt your child. You're entitled.

Only an emotionally mature adult of 25 or beyond can fully grasp all of the ramifications of an international adoption. Most states permit children who don't know their birth parents to contact them when they reach 18 or 21. Although no laws exist to cover such searches internationally, let these ages be your guide and opt for the oldest.

COMPENDIUM

Adoption Information for Participating Countries

nformation in this Compendium is based on research from international sources and information from the U.S. Department of State. Much of this information is available on the State Department web site (**www.travel.state.gov**). This web site offers direct links to detailed international adoption information for many different countries as well as direct links to the web sites of U.S. Embassies around the world. To access this information, click on the link for Other Services under the menu for State Department. Then click on the link for International Adoption. You can also receive additional information by calling the Office of Children's Issues in the U.S. Department of State at 202-736-7000.

Foreign sources selected for inclusion in the Compendium were based on the political and legal situations for individual countries relating to international adoption at the time of writing. Keep in mind, however, that political and legal situations for individual countries are subject to rapid change. In addition, contact information such as addresses and phone numbers may change. Be sure to consult the State Department web site or the U.S. Embassy located in the country in which you are interested for the latest information on adoption policies and procedures.

Countries not listed in the Compendium typically do not place children outside of their countries, either because few children are available for adoption, or because legal requirements make it difficult for non-nationals to adopt unless they reside in the country or because of other restrictions. For example, Islamic religious law restricts adoption in many African and Middle Eastern countries.

For each country listed in the Compendium, we have tried to list available information on the adoption process and the adoption authority, if one exists, and accredited organizations. Contact information for the U.S. Embassy and visa issuing post for each country is also listed. In addition, we've provided available information on the number of orphan visas recently issued for each country and summary information on each country's geography, capital, demography, language, currency, and major religions.

If information is not available or is not relevant to that particular country, the section may be omitted. For example, not every country has an adoption agency or a government authority in charge of adoption. In such cases, write to the U.S. Consulate in that country for a list of attorneys who practice family law and speak English.

When evaluating the following information, keep in mind that the personal philosophy and policies of foreign judges, attorneys and child-placing entities are as important as the national adoption laws concerning international adoption. Whether an adoption proceeds quickly or slowly depends upon the judge, the lawyer, and the child-placing entity, in that order.

Instructions for the dossier of documents generally required by foreign child-placing entities and courts can be found in Chapter 7. Additional requirements for some countries might include a psychological evaluation; a letter from your adoption agency stating the agency's commitment to supervise the child for a specific period of time; a copy of the agency's license; a letter of authorization from your state; and possibly a copy of your state's adoption laws.

When contacting countries overseas, keep in mind that the time zones may be 12-24 hours ahead of U.S. time zones. When phoning or faxing from the United States, it will usually be necessary to dial 011, followed by the country code, which appears in brackets [ ], the city code, which appears in parentheses ( ), and then the phone or fax number. Some countries may have only a city code or a country code, rather than both. When dialing some countries, especially many Caribbean countries, it is only necessary to dial a 1, followed by the country or city code, rather than 011.

Divisions of the Compendium

The organization of the Compendium is based on the geographic designations used in the Report of the Visa Office.

Africa — We list only those countries that place significant numbers of adopted children.

Asia — The geographic designation of Asia includes the countries of Asia as well as the Middle East. Those countries not listed have no history of orphan visas because of Islamic religious laws or other restrictions. Israel does not permit adoption of children by anyone living outside of Israel.

Europe — Most of the sources listed are in Eastern Europe. Western European countries are not listed due to a shortage of babies available for adoption. For the most part, the countries of Europe are presented in alphabetical order. However, Russia and other members of the Commonwealth of Independent Sates (CIS) are grouped together, as are republics of the former Yugoslavia. We did not list countries of the CIS that have never allowed international adoption

Latin America — This section of the Compendium includes Mexico and the countries of Central America, South America, and the Caribbean. Those countries not listed have never allowed international adoption or have laws or residence requirements that greatly restrict the possibility of international adoption.

Oceania — This section of the Compendium includes only the Marshall Islands, a country shown considerable interest by prospective adopters.

Index to Countries in the Compendium

Africa
Ethiopia
Kenya
Liberia
Sierra Leone

Asia
Cambodia
China
Hong Kong
India
Japan
Korea
Laos
Lebanon
Nepal
Philippines
Sri Lanka
Taiwan
Thailand
Vietnam

Europe
Albania
Bulgaria
Estonia
Greece
Hungary
Latvia
Lithuania
Poland
Romania
Russian Federation (CIS)
* Armenia
* Belarus
* Georgia
* Kazakhstan
* Moldova
* Ukraine
* Uzbekistan
Yugoslavia
(Former Republic)
* Bosnia and Herzegovina
* Croatia
* Macedonia
* Serbia-Montenegro
* Slovenia
Turkey

Latin America
Belize
Bolivia
Brazil
Chile
Colombia
Costa Rica
Dominican Republic
Ecuador
El Salvador
Grenada
Guatemala
Haiti
Honduras
Jamaica
Mexico
Nicaragua
Panama
Paraguay
Peru
Trinidad and Tobago
Venezuela

Oceania
Marshall Islands

AFRICA

According to Cheryl Shotts, Director of Americans for African Adoptions (**www.africanadoptions.org**), Islamic laws have an impact on the adoption laws and procedures in each country. In countries such as Sudan, where the religious law and the law of the nation are the same, adoption by persons who are non-Muslims and non-residents is impossible. In countries where adoption is possible, such as Ethiopia, adoptive parents can be of any religion.

In 2001, 234 orphans from the entire African continent were adopted by U.S. citizens. While civil wars, famine, refugee problems and AIDS ravage many parts of Africa and leave thousands of orphans in their wake, adoption of these children can be difficult. Refugee camps under the auspices of the United Nations shelter many of such children, They cannot be adopted unless there is documented evidence to prove that their parents have relinquished or abandoned them or died.

Important Note: As discussed in the introduction to the Compendium, the political and legal situations regarding international adoption for individual countries are subject to rapid change. In addition, contact information such as addresses and phone numbers may change. Be sure to consult the State Department web site (**www.travel.state.gov**) or the U.S. Embassy located in the country in which you are interested for the latest information on adoption policies and procedures.

ETHIOPIA

Geography: East African country of 1,221,918 square kilometers bordered by Sudan, Somalia, and Kenya

Capital: Addis Ababa

Demography: 4,200,000

Language: Amharic

Currency: Birr

Major Religions: Christianity, Islam, Judaism

Orphans Admitted into the United States

Fiscal year 1998: 96	Fiscal year 2000: 95
Fiscal year 1999:103	Fiscal year 2001: 158

Adoption Information: Most adoptions are handled by proxy through two U.S. agencies approved by the Ethiopian government. Ethiopian authorities require the usual documents, as well as two passport-size photos of each spouse and a statement explaining why you prefer to adopt an Ethiopian child. Another form, called "Obligation of Adoption or Social Welfare Agency," must be signed by your local adoption agency. With this form, the adoptive parents promise to submit progress reports to the Ethiopian Children and Youth Affairs Organization (CYAO).

These documents are authenticated at the Ministry of Foreign Affairs in Ethiopia. Then they are submitted to the Children, Youth and Family Affairs Department (CYFAD) for approval. Upon approval, a child may be located for the adoptive parents. A Contract of Adoption is signed between the CYFAD and the adopting parents or their legal representative, after which they file for a court date. The adoption may be initiated by power of attorney and consummated by the prospective parents or their representative. CYFAD issues a final decree. Then the international adoption agency arranges for the child to be immigrated to the adoptive parents, usually by airline personnel.

Adoption Authority

Children's Youth and Family Affairs Department (CYFAD), which is under the Ministry of Labor and Social Affairs. It is located in the capital city of Addis Ababa. Tel: [251] (1) 505-358.

U.S. Embassy/Visa Issuing Post

U.S. Embassy, Ethiopia
Entoto Street
P.O. Box 1014
Addis Ababa, Ethiopia

Tel: [251] (1) 550-666
Email: consaddis@state.gov

Consular Section:
Tel: [251] (1) 553-100
Fax: [251] (1) 551-094

KENYA

Geography: An East African country of 224,961 square miles bordered by Somalia, Sudan, Uganda and Tanzania.

Capital: Nairobi

Demography: Population of more than 28 million people from more than of 40 different ethnic groups.

Languages: English, Swahili and tribal languages

Currency: Shilling

Major Religions: Roman Catholic (28 percent), Protestant (26 percent), Animists (18 percent), Muslim (6 percent)

Orphans Admitted into the United States:

Fiscal year 1998: 5
Fiscal year 1999: 9
Fiscal year 2000: 17
Fiscal year 2001: 15

Adoption Information: Kenyan law specifically states that that an adoption order shall not be made in favor of a sole applicant who is male or an applicant who is of a different race than the child unless there are extenuating circumstances. Although it still remains an issue, the courts are beginning to take a more liberal view of racial differences between potential adopters and the child. Overall, when considering an adoption case, Kenyan courts view the welfare of the child as paramount. Those interested in adopting a child in Kenya may wish to hire an attorney familiar with Kenya's legal system, as the court's interpretation of adoption laws can vary widely depending on the case. The U.S. Embassy in Nairobi maintains a list of attorneys, but is not aware of any specializing in adoptions.

Those applying for the adoption of a child must be 25 years of age or older and must be at least 21 years older than the child. Both the adoptive parent and the child must be resident in Kenya at the time of the proposed adoption. The required length of residency for the adoptive parent is generally six months. The child must be in the continuous care and possession of the applicant for at least three consecutive months immediately proceeding the date of the submission to the court of the application for the adoption order. The court system is responsible for adoptions.

U.S. Embassy/Visa Issuing Post
U.S. Embassy, Kenya
P.O Box 30137
Nairobi, Kenya

Tel: [254] (2) 537-800
Fax: [254] (2) 537-810

LIBERIA

Geography: West African country bordering Sierra Leone, Guinea, and the Ivory Coast.

Capital: Monrovia (population 500,000)

Demography: 3,000,000. Freed slaves from the United States originally settled the country.

Languages: English and tribal languages

Currency: Dollar

Major Religions: Animist (70 percent), Muslim (20 percent), Christian (10 percent)

Orphans Admitted into the United States:
Fiscal year 1998: 7   Fiscal year 2000: 25
Fiscal year 1999: 14   Fiscal year 2001: 20

Adoption Information: There are no marriage requirements or specific age requirements; any adult may file a petition to adopt a child who is legally cleared for adoption. Following the filing of the petition, the court serves notice on all interested parties and orders an investigation. Upon receipt of the investigation, the court schedules the hearing and serves notice on all interested parties. The petitioners and children are required to attend the hearing. The court must be satisfied that the "moral and temporal interests" of the child will be satisfied by the adoption.

Note: Civil wars have ravaged Liberia since 1980. Check with the State Department travel advisory (**www.travel.state.gov**) for updated information on adoptions and travel to this region.

Adoption Authority

The government office responsible for adoptions in Liberia is the Ministry of Justice. All petitions for adoptions are filed in the Probate Court, which issues a decree of adoption if all legal requirements are met.

U.S. Embassy/Visa Issuing Post

U.S. Embassy, Liberia
111 United Nations Drive
Mamba Point
Monrovia, Liberia

SIERRA LEONE

Geography: A small African country of 27,925 square miles on the Atlantic Coast. Sierra Leone is bordered by Guinea, Liberia and the Ivory Coast.

Capital: Freetown

Demography: 3,100,000

Languages: Mende, Temne, Vai, English, Krio (pidgin)

Currency: Leone

Major Religions: Tribal religions, Islam, Christianity

Orphans Admitted into the United States

Fiscal year 1998: 17	Fiscal year 2000: 23
Fiscal year 1999: 28	Fiscal year 2001: 51

Adoption Information: Most adoptions are handled by proxy through an adoption agency. When the final decree is issued, the child is escorted to the adoptive parents by approved airline personnel. Current adoption information may be obtained from the U.S. Consulate.

Note: At the time this book was published, Sierra Leone continued to suffer from a civil war involving armed forces from Nigeria as well as UN troops and was not a safe place to travel. Check travel advisories from the State Department (**www.travel.state.gov**) for updated information.

U.S. Embassy/Visa Issuing Post

U.S. Consulate
Corner of Walpole and Siaka Stevens Streets
Freetown, Sierra Leone

Tel: [232] (22) 226-481
Fax: [232] (22) 225-471

ASIA

The geographic designation of Asia is used by the U.S. Visa Office to describe the countries of Asia and the Middle East. Countries not listed, particularly in the Middle East, either do not permit or do not encourage intercountry adoptions. Islamic countries usually do not allow adoptions by foreigners except in the case of adoption by relatives.

Important Note: As discussed in the introduction to the Compendium, the political and legal situations regarding international adoption for individual countries are subject to rapid change. In addition, contact information such as addresses and phone numbers may change. Be sure to consult the State Department web site (**www.travel.state.gov**) or the U.S. Embassy located in the country in which you are interested for the latest information on adoption policies and procedures.

CAMBODIA

Geography: A Southeast Asian country of 181,035 square kilometers, bordered by Thailand, Vietnam, and Laos.

Capital: Phnom Penh

Demography: Population of 8,500,000 is made up of people of Cambodian and Thai descent.

Languages: Cambodian (Khmer), French

Currency: Riel

Major Religion: Buddhism

Orphans Admitted into the United States

Fiscal year 1998: 249	Fiscal year 2000: 402
Fiscal year 1999: 249	Fiscal year 2001: 407

Adoption Information: Applicants must be 25 years old and 21 years older than the child. If the adopting parent is married, a doctor's letter stating that the wife is no longer able to have children is also required. The adopting parent(s) must also provide information about the adopted child until it reaches majority age, as requested by the Ministry of Foreign Affairs.

Important Note: In 2001, the United States INS suspended the approval of adoption petitions in Cambodia. A year later, Cambodia suspended adoptions for American families. The future of Cambodian adoptions remains unclear at this time, although a task force from the United States was dispatched to determine to what extent, through mutual cooperation, cases could be considered for adjudication, consistent with U.S. law. Although a number of cases that were in progress before the suspension have been released and the children have joined their adoptive families, there are many unresolved cases that are still under investigation. Check the State Department web site (**www.travel.state.gov**) for more up-to-date information regarding adoptions from this country.

U.S. Embassy
U.S. Embassy, Cambodia
16, Street 228 (between Streets 51 and 63)
Phnom Penh, Cambodia

Tel: [855] (23) 216-436 ext. 38
Fax: [855] (23) 218-931 or 217- 085

U.S. Visa Issuing Post
U.S. visas are issued at the U.S. Embassy in Bangkok, Thailand.

U.S. Embassy, Consulate Section
120-122 Wireless Road
Bangkok, Thailand

Tel: [66] (2) 205-4287 and [2] 205-4753
E-mail: adoptionsCambodia@state.gov

CHINA

Geography: Land mass of 9,561,000 square kilometers bordering Mongolia, Russia, Korea, India, Nepal, Burma, Laos, and Vietnam.

Capital: Beijing

Demography: Population of 1,300,000,000, of which 93 percent are Han (ethnic Chinese). The remaining 68 million are distributed among 55 minority groups ranging in size from the 12 million Zhuang to some groups numbering fewer than 1,000.

Languages: Mandarin Chinese, Cantonese, Chuang, Uigar, Yi, Tibetan, Miao, Mongol, Kazakh

Currency: Yuan (Renmin)

Major Religions: Confucianism, Buddhism, Taoism, Islam

Orphans Admitted into the United States
Fiscal year 1998: 4,206   Fiscal year 2000: 5,053
Fiscal year 1999: 4,101   Fiscal year 2001: 4,681

Adoption Information: Most children available for adoption are abandoned females. Prospective adoptive parents must apply through an international adoption agency approved by the China Center of Adoption Affairs (CCAA). This is the central authority in charge of adoption throughout all of the provinces. This authority reviews and approves a group of dossiers of prospective adoptive parents from an adoption agency and matches them to a group of orphans. Presently, the requirements for parents are as follows. To qualify for a baby around one year, adoptive parents must be between the ages of 30 and 45. Couples between the ages of 45 to 50 may adopt children between one and three years old. Applicants between 50 and 55 may adopt children between three and six years old. Further guidelines of the CCAA involve the number of children already in the family, income requirements and the percentage of single applicants they will accept. At the present time, there are more applicants than there are orphans waiting for placement. The CCAA imposed a quota for the number of children allowed per agency for the year 2002. It was not clear whether or not the quota system would be continued for 2003 and beyond

Adoption Authority
China Centre for Adoption Affairs (CCAA)
103 Beiheyan Street
Dongcheng District
Beijing, China 100006

Tel: [86] (10) 6522-3102 or [86] (10) 6513-0607

U.S. Embassy/Visa Issuing Post
U.S. Embassy, China
American Citizen Services
2 Xiu Shui Dong Jie
Beijing, China 100600

Tel: [86] (10) 6532-3831 X 229
Fax: [86] (10) 6532-4153

* U.S. visas are issued by the U.S. Consulate in Guanzhou

HONG KONG

Geography: Located at the southern tip of China, Hong Kong is made up of three geographic areas: the New Territories, Kowloon Peninsula, and Hong Kong Island. Hong Kong became a part of China again on July1, 1997. According to the Sino-British joint declaration of 1984, the transfer of control should allow for the current social and economic policies of Hong Kong to continue for 50 years.

Capital: Victoria (694,500), an island of only five square miles.

Demography: Population of 4,400,000, the majority of which are of Chinese descent, with East Indian and European minorities.

Languages: Chinese and English

Currency: Hong Kong Dollar

Major Religions: Confucianism, Buddhism, Christianity

Orphans Admitted into the United States
Fiscal year 1998: 27
Fiscal year 1999: 14
Fiscal year 2000:14
Fiscal year 2001: 27

Adoption Information: The Adoption Unit of the Social Welfare Department is the government authority in Hong Kong responsible for arranging the adoption of children by local residents and coordinating with non-governmental organizations for the adoption of children by foreigners. Children to be adopted by foreigners must first be relinquished by the parents to the Director of Social Welfare.

Married couples or single individuals who are at least 25 years of age, in good health, and financially capable of raising a child to independence are eligible to adopt. However, the Social Welfare Department does mention that candidates are more likely to be successful if they are able to stay in Hong Kong for a continual period of 12 months or more to complete the adoption process.

Adoption Authority
Adoption Unit
Social Welfare Department
38, Pier Road
Harbor Building, 4F
Central, Hong Kong

Tel: [852] 2852-3107 (No city code is needed for Hong Kong)
Fax: [852] 2851-9189
E-mail: grau@swd.gov.hk
URL: **www.info.gov.hk/swd**

U.S. Consulate General/Visa Issuing Post
U.S. Consulate General
26 Garden Road
Central Hong Kong

Tel: [852] 2841-2211
Fax: [852] 2845-4845
E-mail: acshnk@netvigator.com

INDIA

Geography: A republic of southern Asia that was once a British colony. With 1,261,482 square miles, India covers most of the Indian subcontinent.

Capital: New Delhi (324,283)

Demography: The population of 853,100,000 includes six major ethnic groups and millions of tribal people.

Languages: Hindi is the official language and English is widely spoken by educated people; however, a total of 141 different languages and dialects are spoken in India.

Currency: Rupee

Major Religions: Hinduism, Islam, Sikhism, Buddhism, Jainism, Zoroastrianism, Animism, Christianity

Orphans Admitted into the United States
Fiscal year 1998: 478   Fiscal year 2000: 503
Fiscal year 1999: 499   Fiscal year 2001: 543

Adoption Information: International agencies have to be accredited by the Central Adoption Resource Agency (CARA). After that they have to link up with an Indian licensed adoption agency that places children domestically. An Indian agency can only place as many children internationally as they have already placed domestically. Children leave India with a guardianship unless the adopters are Hindu, since Indian law allows only Hindus to adopt. Children placed under guardianship with non-Hindus can then be adopted in their new country of residence.

Adoption Authority

Central Adoption Resource Agency (CARA)
Ministry of Social Justice and Empowerment
West Block 8, Wing II, 2nd floor
R.K. Puram
New Delhi, India 110066

Tel: [91] (11) 610-5346 or 618-0194
Fax: [91] (11) 618-0198
E-mail cara@bol.net.in

U.S. Embassy/Visa Issuing Posts

U.S. Embassy, India
Shantipath
Chanakyapuri 110021
New Delhi, India

Tel: [91] (11) 419-8000
Fax [91] (11) 419-0017

American Consulate General

American Consulate, Bombay
Lincoln House
78 Bhulabhai Desai Road
Mumbai (Bombay)
India 400026

Tel: [91] (22) 363-3611
Fax: [91] (22) 363- 3618

American Consulate General

American Consulate, Calcutta
5/1 Ho Chi Minh Sarani
Kolkata (Calcutta), India 700071

Tel: [91] (33) 288-1200
Fax: [91] (33) 288-1600

American Consulate General

American Consulate, Madras
Mount Road
Chennai (Madras), India 600006

Tel: [91] (44) 827- 7835
Fax: [91] (44) 825-0240

JAPAN

Geography: An island empire consisting of four large islands, eight small islands, and two island groups, covering 142,798 square miles.

Capital: Tokyo (11,350,000)

Demography: 123,500,000

Language: Japanese

Currency: Yen

Major Religions: Shintoism, Buddhism, Christianity

Orphans Admitted into the United States

Fiscal year 1998: 39	Fiscal year 2000: 36
Fiscal year 1999: 37	Fiscal year 2001: 39

Adoption Information: The law does not prohibit foreigners from adopting, and no specific government requirements exist. Either a final decree or guardianship may be obtained. One or both parents may travel to Japan to immigrate the child, or the child may be escorted.

Adoption Authority

The Family Court and the Child Guidance Center (often located in the City or Ward Office) are the governmental offices responsible for adoption in Japan. They have jurisdiction over the placement of children, home studies and adoption.

U.S. Embassy/Visa Issuing Post

U.S. Embassy, Japan
10-5-1 Akasaka Minato-ku
Tokyo, Japan 107-8420

Tel: [81] (3) 3224-5000
Fax: [81] (3) 3505-1862

KOREA

Geography: The Republic of Korea, commonly referred to as South Korea, occupies the southern half of the Korean Peninsula, covering 38,452 square miles.

Capital: Seoul (4,100,000)

Demography: 31,683,000

Language: Korean

Currency: Won

Major Religions: Confucianism, Buddhism, Chondogyo, Christianity

Orphans Admitted into the United States

Fiscal year 1998: 1,829	Fiscal year 2000: 1,797
Fiscal year 1999: 2,007	Fiscal year 2001: 1,770

Adoption Information: All international adoptions in Korea must be arranged through one of the four Korean adoption agencies listed below, which are authorized by the Korean government. These Korean agencies have child-placing agreements with many adoption agencies in North America and Western European countries.

Adoptive couples must be between the ages of 25 and 44 and married for at least three years. In addition, the adoptive couple should have no more than five children, including the child or children to be adopted and the couple should not have an age difference of more than 15 years. Korean authorities may make exceptions in some cases. The following factors may be considered when making exceptions to the age limit: (1) at least one parent is under 45, (2) the adoptive parents have previously adopted a Korean orphan, and (3) the parents are willing to adopt an orphan with serious medical problems.

Adoption Authority

Family Welfare Bureau
Ministry of Health and Social Affairs
77 Sejong-Ro, Chongro-Ku
Seoul, Korea

Adoption Agencies

Eastern Child Welfare Society, Inc.
Holt Children's Services
Korea Social Services
Social Welfare Society, Inc.

A list of local U.S. contacts affiliated with these organizations can be found on the State Department web site (**www.travel.state.gov**). Click the link for Other Services under the main menu and then click the link for International Adoption.

U.S. Embassy/Visa Issuing Post

U.S. Embassy, Korea, Consular Section
82, Sejong-Ro, Chongro-ku
Seoul, Korea 110-050

Tel: [82] (2) 397-4114
Fax: [82] (2) 738-8845
URL: **http://usembassy.state.gov/seoul**

LAOS

Geography: A country in Southeast Asia, formerly a part of French Indochina, with 236,789 square kilometers

Capital: Vientiane

Demography: Population of about 4,000,000

Languages: Lao, French, English

Currency: New Kip (LAK)

Major Religions: Buddhism, tribal religions

Orphans Admitted into the United States
Fiscal year 1998: 0   Fiscal year 2000: 0
Fiscal year 1999: 1   Fiscal year 2001: 0

Adoption Information: The Ministry of Justice of the Lao People's Democratic Republic notified the U.S. Embassy of the Lao government's suspension of adoption of Lao children by foreigners, pending review of the Lao adoption law. The suspension will not be lifted until the Laos National Assembly completes its review. At the time this book was published, the U.S. Embassy had received no indication that such a review had begun or was scheduled to begin. Consult the State Department web site (**www.travel.state.gov**) or the U.S. Embassy in Laos for more up-to-date information.

U.S. Embassy
U.S. Embassy, Laos
Box 114, Rue Bartholonie
Vientiane, Laos PDR

Tel: [856] (21) 212-581
Fax: [856] (21) 212-584

LEBANON

Geography: A republic on the Arabian Peninsula that borders Turkey and covers 4,015 square miles

Capital: Beirut

Demography: 2,800,000, the majority of whom are of Arab descent. Most of the rest are Turk and Armenian minorities.

Languages: Arabic and French

Currency: Lebanese Pound

Major Religions: Christianity and Islam

Orphans Admitted into the United States
Fiscal year 1998: 17   Fiscal year 2000: 13
Fiscal year 1999: 14   Fiscal year 2001: 15

Adoption Information: Laws concerning adoptions are handled by religious authorities. Islamic law does not provide for adoption; however, adoption is allowed by the various Christian denominations. Christian orphanages may have children available for adoption. The Lebanese Surete General requires that all adoptive parents must travel to Lebanon to complete the adoption procedure and to accompany the child out of Lebanon.

U.S. Embassy/Visa Issuing Post
U.S. Embassy, Lebanon
Antelias, P.S. Box 70-840
Beirut, Lebanon

Tel: [961] (4) 542-600 or 543-600
Fax: [961] (4) 544-209 (Consular Section)

*U.S. Visas for Lebanon are issued at the U.S. Embassies in Damascus, Syria; Tel Aviv, Israel; Abu Dhabi, United Arab Emirates; or Nicosia, Cyprus.

NEPAL

Geography: Mountain kingdom in the Himalayas between China and India

Capital: Kathmandu

Demography: More than 13 million of Nepalese and Tamang descent

Languages: Nepali, Maithali, Tamang, Newari, Than

Currency: Nepalese Rupee (NPR)

Major Religions: Hinduism, Buddhism

Orphans Admitted into United States

Fiscal year 1998: 19   Fiscal year 2000: 3
Fiscal year 1999: 9   Fiscal year 2001: 6

Adoption Information: In 1999, the government of Nepal imposed new adoption requirements that effectively precluded U.S. citizens from adopting in Nepal. At the time of writing, the U.S. Department of State was continuing work with the government of Nepal to try to find a solution that would allow adoptions by U.S. citizens to resume. Consult the State Department web site (**www.travel.state.gov**) for more up-to-date information.

Adoption Authority

Nepal Children's Organization (NCO)
P.O. Box 6967
Bal Mandir, Naxal
Kathmandu, Nepal

Tel: [977] (1) 411-202
Fax: [977] (1) 414-485

U.S. Embassy/Visa Issuing Post

U.S. Embassy, Nepal
Pani Pokhari
Kathmandu, Nepal

Tel: [977] (1) 413-836
Fax: [977] (1) 319-963

PHILIPPINES

Geography: An island republic covering 115,707 square miles in the Malay Archipelago island group. The Philippines became independent from the United States in 1946.

Capital: Manila, on the island of Luzon (2,000,000)

Demography: 62,400,000 people of Indonesian and Malayan ethnic backgrounds

Languages: Filipino (Tagalog), English, Spanish, Bisayan, Ilocano, Bikol, and many other dialects

Currency: Piso

Major Religions: Roman Catholic, Islam, Protestant, and tribal religions

Orphans Admitted into the United States

Fiscal year 1998: 200	Fiscal year 2000: 173
Fiscal year 1999: 195	Fiscal year 2001: 219

Adoption Information: Foreigners may not adopt children in the Philippines except in the following circumstances: Former Filipinos who seek to adopt a relative by consanguinity, or who seek to adopt the legitimate child of their Filipino spouse, or who are married to Filipino citizens and seek to adopt a relative jointly with their spouse.

Aliens not included in the foregoing exceptions may adopt Filipino children in accordance with the rules on intercountry adoptions as may be provided by law. In general, to process an intercountry adoption, a U.S. citizen must be physically outside the Philippines and process the adoption through a licensed agency in conjunction with the Philippine Department of Social Welfare and Development. It will no longer be possible for American citizens living in the Philippines to identify a child and adopt through the Philippine courts, except as noted above. Either a guardianship or final adoption decree is issued. Adoptions are initiated through accredited agencies.

Adoption Authority
Bureau of Child and Youth Welfare
Department of Social Welfare and Development
Batasang Pambansa Complex
Constitution Hills
Quezon City, Philippines

Competent Authority
Office of the Solicitor General of the Philippines
134 Amoorsolo Street
Legaspi Village
Makati City, Philippines

U.S. Embassy/Visa Issuing Post
U.S. Embassy, Philippines
1201 Roxas Road
Ermita, Manila
Philippines

Tel: [632] 523-1001
Fax: [632] 522-4361

SRI LANKA

Geography: An island republic at the tip of the Indian subcontinent covering 25,332 square miles

Capital: Colombo (551,200)

Demography: 12,300,000

Languages: Sinhalese, Tamil, English

Currency: Sri Lankan Rupee (LKR)

Major Religions: Buddhism, Hinduism, Christianity

Orphans Admitted into the United States

Fiscal year 1998: 2	Fiscal year 2000: 5
Fiscal year 1999: 5	Fiscal year 2001: 4

Adoption Information: The District Court of Colombo and the District Court of Colombo South are empowered to make orders of adoption of Sri Lankan children by persons not resident and domiciled in Sri Lanka. Foreign applicants cannot find children for adoption privately. Allocation of children can only be made from the Sri Lankan State Receiving Homes and Voluntary Children's Homes that are registered by the Department of Probation and Child Care Services for over five years and only by specific authorization of the Commissioner of Probation.

Adoption Authority

Department of Probation and Child Care Services
P.O. Box 546
Chatham Street
Colombo 1, Sri Lanka

U.S. Embassy/Visa Issuing Post

U.S. Embassy, Sri Lanka
210, Galle Road
Colombo, 03 Sri Lanka

Tel: [94] (1) 448-007
Fax: [94] (1) 437-345 or 436-943

TAIWAN

Geography: An island off the coast of China, which is claimed by China as a "renegade province."

Capital: Taipei (1,604,543)

Demography: 14,577,000

Languages: Mandarin Chinese, Taiwanese, Formosan, and Hakka dialects

Currency: New Taiwan Dollar

Major Religions: Confucianism, Buddhism, Taoism, Christianity

Orphans Admitted into the United States

Fiscal year 1998: 30   Fiscal year 2000: 28

Fiscal year 1999: 32   Fiscal year 2001: 42

Adoption Information: Since the United States recognized the People's Republic of China as the official government of all China, we no longer have consular representation. The American Institute in Taiwan (AIT) acts as a U.S. liaison office. Childless couples or those with one child who have been married three years and are under 42 years of age may apply for adoption. Either a guardianship or final adoption decree is issued.

The American Institute in Taiwan

Travel Service Section
7 Lane 134
Hsin Yi Road, Section 3
Taipei, 106 Taiwan

Tel: [886] (02) 2709-2000
Fax: [886] (02) 2784-2306

Private Adoption Agencies in Taiwan

Catholic Welfare Services
Room 907, Central Building (9th Floor)
2 Chung Shan North Road, Section 1
Taipei, Taiwan

Tel: [886] (02) 2311-0223
Fax: [886] (02) 2371-0338
E-Mail: Rosa0125@ms.22.hinet.net

Christian Salvation Service
14F-3, #415 Hsin Yi Road, Section 4
Taipei, Taiwan

Tel: [886] (02) 2729-0265
E-Mail: csstte@ms14.hinet.net

The Pearl Buck Foundation
Room 950, Central Building (9th floor)
2 Chung Shan North Road, Section 1
Taipei, Taiwan

Fax: [886] (02) 2331-8690

The Home of God's Love
P.O. Box 9
Lo-Tung 265, Taiwan

Tel: 039-514-652
Email: teskales@ms6.hinet.net; Bevanna@ms15.hinet.net

U.S. Embassy/Visa Issuing Post
American Consulate General
26 Garden Road, Box 30
Hong Kong

Tel: [852] 2841-2412 (No city code is needed for Hong Kong)
Fax: [852] 2845-1598

*Check with the Office of Children's Issues (202-736-7000) or the Visa Office of the U.S. Department of State for visa issuing information.

THAILAND

Geography: A kingdom in Southeast Asia on the gulf of Siam. This country, which was formerly named Siam, covers 198,445 square miles.

Capital: Bangkok (2,000,000)

Demography: 55,700,000 persons of Thai and Chinese descent

Languages: Thai, Lao, Chinese, Khmer, Malay

Currency: Thai Baht

Major Religions: Buddhism, Islam, tribal religions

Orphans Admitted into the United States
Fiscal year 1998: 84   Fiscal year 2000: 88
Fiscal year 1999: 77   Fiscal year 2001: 74

Adoption Information: The adoptive couple must be over 30 years of age, married at least five years, and be 15 years older than the child. Both prospective parents must travel to Thailand for a stay of about two weeks until a final decree is issued and the child's visa is obtained. Documents must be submitted via an approved agency. All adoptions in Thailand are managed by the Department of Public Welfare. The first step in the process is direct communication with that office. For complete information and appropriate forms, write to the address below.

Adoption Authority
Child Adoption Center
Department of Public Welfare
Rajvithee Road
(Rajvithee Home for Girls)
Bangkok 10400, Thailand

U.S. Embassy/Visa Issuing Post
120-122 Wireless Road
Bangkok 10330 Thailand

Tel: [66] (2) 205-4287 or 205-4753
Fax: [66] (2) 254-1171

VIETNAM

Geography: A country in Southeast Asia of 128,066 square miles that shares borders with China, Laos, and Cambodia.

Capital: Hanoi

Demography: Population of approximately 80,000,000

Languages: Vietnamese, Thai, Muong, Chinese, Khmer, French, and local dialects

Currency: Dong. The U.S. dollar is also widely accepted and used in large cash transactions.

Major Religions: Buddhism, Taoism, Confucianism, Roman Catholicism

Orphans Admitted into the United States

Fiscal year 1998: 603	Fiscal year 2000: 724
Fiscal year 1999: 709	Fiscal year 2001: 737

Adoption Information: Vietnam is in the process of changing its adoption laws and as part of that process has warned of a temporary suspension in international adoptions while the new laws are put in effect. However, many provinces in Vietnam have continued to place children, and the date for the implementation of the suspension and new laws has changed numerous times. Check with the State Department (**www.travel.state.gov**) or the U.S. Embassy in Vietnam for the latest information before beginning the process.

When Vietnam's new laws take effect, a newly created central adoption authority will replace provincial offices currently administrating the adoption process. Children will be referred and placed from the central authority instead of through provincial authorities, as has been the case in the recent past. In addition, foreign international adoption agencies will need to apply for a license through the Ministry of Justice in Hanoi. Licensed agencies will be investigated for their past work in Vietnam as well as their humanitarian efforts in that country. Licenses will have to be renewed yearly and the adoptions will then be carried out in the province in which the agency is working.

U.S. Embassy
U.S. Embassy, Vietnam
7 Lang Ha Road
Ba dinh District
Hanoi, Vietnam

Tel: [84] (4) 772-1500
Fax: [84] (4) 772-1510

U.S. Consulate, Hanoi
2nd floor, Rose Garden Tower
6 Ngoc Khan Street
Hanoi, Vietnam

Tel: [84] (4) 831-4590
Fax: [84] (4) 831-4578

Visa Issuing Post

U.S. Consulate General
#4 Le Duan Street
District 1
Ho Chi Minh City, Vietnam

Tel: [84] (8) 822-9433
Fax: [84] (8) 825-0938

U.S. Immigration Office for Orphan Visas

Saigon Centre, 9th floor
65 Le Loi Street
Ho Chi Minh City, Vietnam

Tel: [84] (8) 821-6237
Fax: [84] (8) 821-6241

EUROPE

As sources have opened in Eastern European countries and as new U.S. Embassies are being established, new possibilities for international adoption have appeared. We are listing countries where information has become available. Please note that although some of the countries formerly a part of the Soviet Union and now part of the Commonwealth of Independent States (CIS) are located in Asia, they are listed here because orphan visas for these countries will still be issued by the U.S. Embassy in Moscow. However, visas for Latvia, Lithuania, Belarus, and Ukraine will be issued by the U.S. Embassy in Warsaw, Poland. Visas for Estonia will be issued by the U.S. Embassy in Helsinki, Finland, and visas for Moldova are issued in Bucharest, Romania.

Important Note: As discussed in the introduction to the Compendium, the political and legal situations regarding international adoption for individual countries are subject to rapid change. In addition, contact information such as addresses and phone numbers may change. Be sure to consult the State Department web site (**www.travel.state.gov**) or the U.S. Embassy located in the country in which you are interested for the latest information on adoption policies and procedures.

ALBANIA

Geography: A small Balkan country bordering the former Yugoslavia and Greece

Capital: Tirana

Demography: The population of 3,200,000 are mainly descendants of the Illyrians of Central Europe. The rest are Greek.

Language: Albanian (Tosk and Gheg)

Currency: Lek

Major Religions: Islam, Eastern Orthodox, Roman Catholic

Orphans Admitted into the United States
Fiscal year 1998: 10   Fiscal year 2000: 22
Fiscal year 1999: 18   Fiscal year 2001: 16

Adoption Information: A law passed in January 1993 regulates all foreign adoptions, which are overseen by the Albanian Adoption Committee (AAC). The authority of this committee began in July of 1995. A register of children eligible for adoption exists. For the first six months, children on the register are available for adoption by Albanian citizens residing in Albania. After six months, they become eligible for international adoption. Adoptions can only be handled through a foreign agency licensed by the Albanian Adoption Committee. Prospective adoptive families are not allowed to go to an orphanage to select a child without authorization by the committee. In general, the Adoption Committee will work through a licensed foreign agency. Bethany Christian Service and International Children's Alliance are two agencies recognized by the Adoption Committee. Contact the U.S. Consulate for names of other U.S.-based international agencies working in Albania.

Adoption Authority
> Albanian Adoption Committee (AAC)
> Ms. Ilmije Mara
> Komiteti Shqiptar I Biresimeve
> Kryeministria
> Tirana, Albania

U.S. Agencies Accredited by the AAC
> Bethany Christian Service
> 901 Eastern Ave., N.E.
> Grand Rapids, MI 49503-1295
>
> Tel: (616) 459-6273
> Fax: (616) 224-7585
>
> International Children's Alliance
> 1101 17th Street, N.W., Suite 1002
> Washington, D.C. 20036
>
> Tel: (202) 463-6874
> Fax: (202) 463-6880
> Email: Adoptionop@aol.com

U.S. Embassy/Visa Issuing Post
> U.S. Embassy, Tirana
> Rruga e Elnasanit 103
> Tirana, Albania
>
> Tel: [355] (4) 247-285
> Fax: [355] (4) 232-222

BULGARIA

Geography: A Balkan country of 110,911 square kilometers.

Capital: Sofia

Demography: 9,000,000. The majority of the population consists of ethnic Bulgarians. Ten percent are Turk, with lesser minorities of Macedonians and Gypsies.

Languages: Bulgarian and Turkish

Currency: Lev

Major Religion: Eastern Orthodox

Orphans Admitted into the United States

Fiscal year 1998: 151   Fiscal year 2000: 214
Fiscal year 1999: 221   Fiscal year 2001: 297

Adoption Information: Adoptive parents must be at least 15 years older than the child. Parent-initiated and agency-initiated adoptions are permitted. In addition to the documentary requirements, there are other conditions of foreign adoptions in Bulgaria to keep in mind. Bulgarian regulations prohibit foreign adoptions of orphans under one year of age or by parents who have previous natural or adopted children. The Ministry of Justice can waive these prohibitions, but prospective adoptive parents should not count on waivers. In practice, most children adopted by Americans are three or four years old. For children under three, the orphanage must certify that three Bulgarian families have declined to adopt the child before it can be placed with a foreign parent.

There are many orphanages in Bulgaria, and there is no central organization for identifying available children through photographs or videotapes. Bulgarian representatives of international adoption agencies cooperate with orphanage directors to assemble this information and send it to international adoption agencies. Adoptive parents must meet an orphan in person. Adoptive parents should plan on making two trips to Bulgaria or delegating power of attorney to a lawyer or agent in Bulgaria to complete the case, as the process always takes at least six months.

After the child has been identified and the U.S. preadoption requirements have been met, a packet containing all of the documents is submitted simultaneously to the Bulgarian Ministry of Justice and the Ministry of Health (for children 0-3 years old) or the Ministry of Education (for children 3-6 years old). The Ministry of Justice must give permission for the adoption to take place, with only advisory opinions from the other ministries. When the Ministry of Justice has given approval, the case is turned over to the court for the final adoption decree and the amendment of the birth record. Foreign adoptive parents must retain a Bulgarian lawyer for the court case.

Adoption Authority

The Ministry of Public Health (children ages 0-3)
The Ministry of Education (children over 3)
The Ministry of Justice (approves all adoptions)

All three ministries are located at the district center of each town and at the district center for Sofia.

U.S. Embassy/Visa Issuing Post

U.S. Embassy, Consular Section
No.1 Kapitan Andreev Street
Sofia, Bulgaria

Tel: [359] (2) 963-1250
Fax: [359] (2) 963-2859

ESTONIA

Geography: A Baltic republic of 45,100 square kilometers, which was part of the former Soviet Union. Estonia is now independent.

Capital: Tallinn

Demography: 1,600,000 of Finno-Ugric ancestry. Two-thirds of the population is Estonian, one-fourth is Russian, and the remaining population is made up of Ukrainian, Finnish, and Belarussian minorities.

Languages: Estonian, Russian

Currency: Ruble, Kroon

Major Religions: Eastern Orthodox, Protestant

Orphans Admitted into the United States

Fiscal year 1998: 6   Fiscal year 2000: 7
Fiscal year 1999: 3   Fiscal year 2001: 10

Adoption Information: A U.S. citizen wishing to adopt a child in Estonia must first contact an approved U.S agency or organization. A list of approved agencies and organizations can be obtained from the Estonian Ministry of Social Affairs (MSA). The agency will prepare the application, assist the applicants with their legal prerequisites, obtain all the necessary civil documents, and forward them to the MSA. The MSA has a list of children in Estonia who are currently available for international adoption. A commission from the MSA will identify a child on that list and offer the prospective parent(s) the choice of adopting that particular child. If a prospective parent declines three successive offers, his or her application will be terminated. MSA will not accept applications directly from nonresident prospective parents. These are only accepted through an agency that has been approved and signed an agreement with the MSA.

Adoption Authority
Consultant of the Office of Child Protection
Ministry of Social Welfare, Republic of Estonia
Gonsiori, 29, Room 217
15027 Tallinn, Estonia

U.S. Embassy
U.S. Embassy/Consular Service
Kentmanni 20
Tallinn, Estonia

Tel: [372] 668-8100
Fax: [372] 668-8267
E-mail: consul@usemb.ee

U.S. Visa Issuing Post
U.S. visas are issued at the U.S. Embassy in Helsinki, Finland.

U.S. Embassy/Consular Section
Itainen Puistotie 14 A
Helsinki, Finland 00140

Tel: [358] (9) 171-931
Fax: [358] (9) 652-057

GREECE

Geography: A republic of 131,955 square miles in the southern part of the Balkans, including the islands of Crete, the Aegean, and Dodecanese Islands. Greece is bordered by Turkey, Bulgaria, Macedonia (former Yugoslavia), and Albania.

Capital: Athens (population 627,564)

Demography: 10,000,000 persons of European descent

Languages: Greek, Turkish

Currency: Drachma

Major Religion: Greek Orthodox

Orphans Admitted into the United States

Fiscal year 1998: 3   Fiscal year 2000: 0
Fiscal year 1999: 0   Fiscal year 2001: 0

Adoption Information: Greek children can only be adopted by persons who are either Greek citizens or of Greek origin and residents in Greece. Exceptions are made for children with health problems at the discretion of the institution sheltering the child. A list of government institutions and private orphanages can be found on the U.S. State Department web site (**www.travel.state.gov**). The only condition in such a case is that the adoptive parents be the same religion as the child. A Greek lawyer is needed to obtain a final adoption decree. (See State Department web site for list.) There is no central adoption authority.

U.S. Embassy

U.S. Embassy, Consular Section
91 Vasilissis Sophias Ave.
101 60 Athens, Greece

Tel: [30] (1) 721-2951
Fax: [30] (1) 645-6282
E-mail: consul@attglobal.net
URL: **www.usembassy.gr**

HUNGARY

Geography: A landlocked country covering 25,000 square miles, bordered by Romania, Moldova, the Czech Republic, Austria, and the former Yugoslavia.

Capital: Budapest

Demography: 10,600,000 people of Hungarian and Gypsy heritage

Language: Hungarian

Currency: Forint

Major Religion: Christian

Orphans Admitted into the United States

Fiscal year 1998: 34   Fiscal year 2000: 25
Fiscal year 1999: 18   Fiscal year 2001: 13

Adoption Information: Parent-initiated and agency-initiated adoptions are permitted. Children are available for adoption from 19 institutions located in Hungary. The U.S. Embassy can provide a list. Adoption from private sources (from parent to parent) is no longer possible. People who are interested in adopting a child from Hungary should write to one of the Children Care and Welfare Institutes (GYIVI) for information. The GYIVI provides information in writing regarding the procedure and the documentary requirements.

Once a request for adoption with the supporting documents is received, the GYIVI enters the request on a waiting list. The waiting period might be five to six years because the demand for children (especially under age 3) is much higher than the number of children available for adoption in Hungary. However, the waiting period for older children or those of non-ethnic Hungarian background is much shorter, perhaps six months to two years. When the desired child or children are located, the GYIVI notifies the prospective parents, and the parents must come to Hungary to see the child. If they accept the offered child, the GYIVI makes an official record of intention to adopt. At the same time, up-to-date documents must be presented if the original documents, which are generally required, were submitted more than a year earlier. Original documents and/or certified copies with Hungarian translations are required. If translations are done in the United States, the Hungarian Embassy in Washington, D.C. must authenticate the official translations.

Although there are no fees for the adoption itself, expenses for obtaining documents and translations and paying lawyers, if any, can be high. The embassy usually advises adoptive parents to seek the assistance of a lawyer if no friends or relatives are available to help in Hungary since the adoption procedure is time consuming and complex.

Adoption Authority
Children's Care and Welfare Institute (GYIVI)
There are 19 such institutions in Hungary. Contact the U.S. Embassy in Budapest for a list.

U.S. Embassy/Visa Issuing Post
U.S. Embassy, Consular Section
Szabadsag Ter 12
Budapest V. Hungary 1054

Tel: [36] (1) 475-4400
Fax: [36] (1) 475-4764
E-mail: usconsular,budapest@state.gov

LATVIA

Geography: A small Baltic republic of 63,700 square miles, which was part of the former Soviet Union. Latvia is now independent.

Capital: Riga

Demography: Approximately 2,700,000. More than half are ethnic Latvians; the rest are Lithuanians and ethnic Russians.

Languages: Latvian, Russian

Currency: Ruble, Lat

Major Religions: Catholic, Protestant, some Eastern Orthodox

Orphans Admitted into the United States

Fiscal year 1998: 76	Fiscal year 2000: 25
Fiscal year 1999: 58	Fiscal year 2001: 27

Adoption Information: Pursuant to the Latvian intercountry adoption law in effect since 1992, the Ministry of Justice and the Ministry of Welfare are jointly responsible for administering adoptions. Adoption of Latvian children is allowed by singles and couples if: The persons adopting are relatives of the child; or the child is ill and will receive medical treatment that is unavailable in Latvia; or no Latvian citizens have expressed a willingness to adopt the child during the first three months of its life (applies only to children available for adoption from birth); or the child has been rejected by at least two persons who had applied for adoption (applies to children available for adoption for one year). The fact that the child was rejected twice must be verified by records in the child's adoption file. Foreigners interested in adopting a Latvian child should express their interest in writing to the Ministry of Justice (see address below). Adoption procedures in Latvia can be very complex and time consuming, sometimes taking up to two years. Adoptive parents are required to make two trips.

Adoption Authority

The Ministry of Welfare
Orphans Department
28 Skolas Street
Riga, LV 1050, Latvia

Tel: [371] (2) 277-468
Contact: Ms. Norina Meksa

Civil Registration Department

Latvian Ministry of Justice
24 Kalku Iela
Riga, LV 1050, Latvia

U.S. Embassy

U.S. Embassy/Consular Section
7 Raina Boulevard
Riga, LV 1510, Latvia

Tel: [371] 703-6200
Fax: [371] 781-4088
E-mail: AskConsular@USRiga.lv

*Visas are issued by the U.S. Embassy in Warsaw, Poland. Consult the section on Poland for contact information.

LITHUANIA

Geography: A Baltic republic of 65,200 square kilometers, which was part of the former Soviet Union. Lithuania is now independent.

Capital: Vilnius

Demography: The population of 3,700,000 is made up of Eastern Baltic people of Lithuanian and Russian descent.

Languages: Lithuanian, Russian

Currency: Ruble, Litas

Major Religions: Roman Catholic, Eastern Orthodox

Orphans Admitted into the United States

Fiscal year 1998: 72   Fiscal year 2000: 29
Fiscal year 1999: 63   Fiscal year 2001: 30

Adoption Information: Agency-initiated and parent-initiated adoptions are allowed. The Lithuanian Adoption Authority is the adoption agency under the Ministry of Social Security and Labor. It maintains a registry for foreign families, wishing to adopt. Prospective adoptive parents may register in person or by writing to the agency (address below). There is a 20-day waiting period after the adoption hearing. During that time, the child remains in the institution.

Adoption Authority
Adoption Agency
Ministry of Social Security and Labor
Vivulskio 11
115 kab, Vilnius, Lithuania

Fax: [370] (2) 60-38-13

U.S. Embassy
U.S. Embassy, Consular Section
Akmenu 6 232600
Vilnius, Lithuania

Tel: [370] (2) 22-27-37
Fax: [370] (2) 22-2739

*Visas are issued by the U.S. Embassy in Warsaw, Poland. Consult the section on Poland for contact information.

POLAND

Geography: Eastern European Republic occupying 120,725 square miles, bordering Germany, the Czech and Slovak Republics, the Ukraine, Belarus, Lithuania, and the Russian region of Kaliningrad.

Capital: Warsaw

Demography: 38,400,000. Most of the population is ethnic Poles; two percent are European minorities from bordering countries, as well as Jews and Gypsies.

Language: Polish

Currency: Zloty

Major Religion: Roman Catholic

Orphans Admitted into the United States

Fiscal year 1998: 77	Fiscal year 2000: 83
Fiscal year 1999: 97	Fiscal year 2001: 86

Adoption Information: U.S. families interested in adoption must contact the Central Adoption Commission ((Publiczny Osrodek Adopcyjno-Opiekunczy). In addition to overseeing the processing of adoptions, the commission maintains a list of children residing in orphanages and available for adoption. Polish adoption procedures are complicated, time consuming and often require professional legal guidance. A competent lawyer may handle many of the legal formalities in Poland and help the adoptive parents communicate with the proper Polish authorities before they travel to Poland for the adoption hearing. The entire process may take a year or more.

Adoption Authority

Mrs. Elzbieta Podczaska, Director
Publiczny Osrodek Adopcyjno-Opiekunczy (Central Adoption Commission)
ul. Nowogrodzka # 75
02-018 Warszawa, Polska

Tel: [48] (22) 621-1075
Fax: [48] (22) 621-1075

U.S. Embassy/Visa Issuing Post

U.S. Embassy, Consular Section
ulica Piekna 12
00-054 Warsaw, Poland

Tel: [48] (22) 628-3041 (X 2038)
Fax: [48] (22) 627-4734
E-mail: adoptwrw@state.gov

*Visas for Belarus, Ukraine, Latvia, and Lithuania are also issued here.

ROMANIA

Geography: A country bordered by the Black Sea, Moldova, Hungary, the former Yugoslavia, Ukraine, and Bulgaria

Capital: Bucharest

Demography: 23,300,000, the majority of whom trace their origins to the early Romans. About 10 percent are minorities of Magyars, Szeklers, and Gypsy descent.

Languages: Romanian, Hungarian

Currency: Leu

Major Religion: Eastern Orthodox

Orphans Admitted into the United States

Fiscal year 1998: 406   Fiscal year 2000: 1,122
Fiscal year 1999: 895   Fiscal year 2001: 782

Adoption Information: A moratorium eliminated international adoptions during most of 2001 and 2002. The country is projected to open adoptions in 2003 through a newly created central authority, the Romanium Office of Adoption. Check the State Department web site (**www.travel.state.gov**) or the U.S. Embassy for more up-to-date information. You may also contact the Romanian Embassy (**www.roembus.org**) in Washington D.C. for information. Since the moratorium took effect, cases that were already in process were allowed to proceed. The Romanian Committee for Adoption (RCA) continues to redefine its role. Romanian foundations were created to shelter and place children under the auspices of the RAC and international adoption agencies; however, the future of these organizations remains unclear.

Adoption Authority

Romanian Committee for Adoption (RCA)
Piata Victoriei Nr. 1 Bucharest
Sector 1
Bucharest

U.S. Embassy/Visa Issuing Post

U.S. Embassy, Consular Section
Strada Batistei Filipescu
Sector 1
Bucharest, Romania

Tel: [40] (1) 210-4042
Fax: [40] (1) 211-3360

RUSSIA, Commonwealth of Independent States (CIS)

Other members of the Commonwealth of Independent States are marked with an asterisk and include Armenia, Belarus, Georgia, Kazakhstan, Moldova, Ukraine, and Uzbekistan. CIS countries not listed in the Compendium either do not allow international adoption or did not respond to requests for information on international adoption.

Geography: With 17,025,000 square kilometers, Russia is the largest of the former republics of the Soviet Union and is now part of the Commonwealth of Independent States. Russia reaches from the Baltic republics, Belarus, and the Ukraine in the west, to the Pacific Ocean in the east, and borders Finland in the north, and Georgia and Kazakhstan to the south.

Capital: Moscow

Demography: 147,386,000. The majority call themselves "Great Russians" (Caucasians). The rest are Mongols, Jews, Kazakhs and other ethnicities from the former Soviet Union.

Languages: Russian, plus many of the languages of the other republic

Currency: Ruble

Major Religions: Russia has been officially atheist for more than 70 years; however, the Eastern Orthodox church, some Protestant religions, and Judaism are experiencing a revival. There are some Muslim temples, as well.

Orphans Admitted into the United States

Fiscal year 1998: 4,491   Fiscal year 2000: 4,269
Fiscal year 1999: 4,348   Fiscal year 2001: 4,279

Adoption Information: Russia's laws and procedures have changed considerably since it granted the first adoption by non-citizens. By 2000, Russia required foreign adoption agencies to apply for accreditation. The U.S. State Department (**www.travel.state.gov**) maintains a list of agencies and attorneys accredited by the Ministry of Education. A new law passed in 2001 mandates that only the gender, age and health status of the child can be provided to the international adoption agency to match with their approved prospective parents. Adoptive parents make two trips. On the first trip, they meet the child and are given a summary of the health and social information. Would-be parents can bring an interpreter to consult with the orphanage director and pediatrician. They are given a translated summary of the child's records and they can take photos/videos to send to an international pediatric specialist in the United States for evaluation. Once they decide to adopt, they ask the agency's representative to ask for a court date and return home to wait for the adoption hearing. Approximately three weeks later, they present themselves at the hearing, take custody, and immigrate the child to the United States. The process described above is not cast in stone. The Russian regions do not uniformly comply with commands from Moscow. They appear to have a lot of liberty as to how they interpret the regulations.

  Regardless of the distance of the Russian region, the adoptive family must acquire a U.S. orphan visa at the U.S. Consulate in Moscow. Visas for children adopted from most other CIS countries will also be issued in Moscow; however, visas for children adopted from Ukraine, Belarus, Latvia, and Lithuania are issued in Warsaw, Poland. Visas for children adopted from Estonia will be issued by the U.S. Embassy in Finland.

Adoption Authority

  There is no central adoption authority at this time. The only central aspect of the process is the data bank of waiting children. The Ministry of Education in Moscow and the Regional Departments of Education are in charge of the orphanages. District Courts conduct the adoption procedures.

U.S. Embassy/Visa Issuing Post

  U.S. Embassy, Consular Section
  19/23 Novinsky Blvd.
  123242 Moscow, Russia

  Tel: [7] (095) 728-5567 or 728-5058
  Fax: [7] (095) 728-5247

*Armenia (CIS)

Geography: Small republic of 29,800 square kilometers, bordered by Georgia, Azerbaijan, Turkey, and Iran

Capital: Yerevan

Demography: 3,283,000 Armenians and Russians

Languages: Russian, Armenian

Currency: Ruble

Major Religion: Eastern Orthodox

Orphans Admitted into the United States
Fiscal year 1998: not available

Adoption Information: Orphans fall under the jurisdiction of the Ministry of Education. There is no child-placing authority. The Ministry of Education and the President of the Republic must approve adoptions by foreigners. There currently are no foreign adoptions from this republic. Some agencies claim to have a program in this country; however, the web site of the U.S. Department of State does not even mention Armenia in terms of international adoption.

U.S. Embassy
U.S. Embassy, Consular Section
18 General Bagramian Avenue
Yerevan, Armenia

Tel: [374] (2) 151-551
Fax: [374] (2) 151-550

*Visas are issued by the U.S. Embassy in Moscow, Russia. Consult the section on Russia for contact information.

*Belarus (CIS)

Geography: Republic of 207,600 square kilometers bordered by Lithuania, Poland, Latvia, Ukraine, and Russia

Capital: Minsk

Demography: Population of 10,200,000

Languages: Russian and White Russian (a dialect)

Currency: Ruble

Major Religion: Eastern Orthodox

Orphans Admitted into the United States

Fiscal year 1998: 2	Fiscal year 2000: 46
Fiscal year 1999: 32	Fiscal year 2001: 129

Adoption Information: Adoptions must be supervised by the Belarusian National Adoption Center (see below). Interested American citizens should find and work with a licensed adoption agency or provider that employs representatives or facilitators in Belarus. Because prospective parents are advised that they should not travel to Belarus until a suitable child has been selected for them, a representative in Belarus is absolutely essential in order to work through the adoption process.

Adoption Authority

Belarusian National Adoption Center
Mrs. Olga Karaban, Director
Platonova Str. 22, 11th floor
Minsk, Belarus

Tel: [375] (17) 232-6701
Fax: [375] (17) 231-0617

U.S. Embassy

U.S. Embassy, Consular Section
46 Starovilenskaya St.
220002 Minsk, Belarus

Tel: [375] (17) 210-1283
Fax: [375] (17) 217-7160

*U.S. Visas are issued by the U.S. Embassy in Warsaw, Poland. Consult the section on Poland for contact information.

*Georgia (CIS)

Geography: A small republic on the Black Sea bordered by Russia, Armenia, and Azerbaijan

Capital: Tbilisi

Demography: 5,449,000 people of Georgian and Russian descent

Languages: Georgian and Russian

Currency: Ruble

Major Religion: Eastern Orthodox

Orphans Admitted into the United States

Fiscal year 1998: 6   Fiscal year 2000: 4
Fiscal year 1999: 2   Fiscal year 2001: 16

Adoption Information: The Ministry of Justice, through its court system, adjudicates international adoptions, while the Ministry of Education registers children for adoption and creates a central registration databank of all orphaned and abandoned Georgian children. Healthy children are placed on the Ministry of Education's databank for six months during which time they are eligible to be adopted by Georgian citizens only. In cases in which the child's health is in danger, the Ministry of Education may request the court waive the six month waiting period and allow a foreign adoption immediately.

Contact the U.S. Embassy in Tbilisi for more information regarding adoption in this region or visit the State Department web site (**www.travel.state.gov**) for a list of U.S. adoption agencies working in Georgia.

Adoption Authority

The Ministry of Justice

The Ministry of Education

U.S. Embassy

U.S. Embassy, Tbilisi

25 Atoneli Street

Tbilisi, Georgia 380005

Tel: [995] (32) 98-99-67 X 4137

Fax: [995] (32) 92-29-53

URL: **http://web.sanet.ge/usembassy/consular.htm**

*Visas are issued at the U.S. Embassy in Moscow, Russia. Consult the section on Russia for contact information.

*Kazakhstan (CIS)

Geography: A large republic of 2,717,300 square miles bordered by Russia, China, Kyrgyzstan, Uzbekistan, and Turkmenistan

Capital: The republic's capital has moved from Almaty to the new capital city of Akmola.

Demography: Population of 16,538,000 Kazakhs and Russians

Languages: Russian and Kazakh

Currency: Ruble

Major Religions: Islam and Eastern Orthodox

Orphans Admitted into the United States

Fiscal year 1998: 54   Fiscal year 2000: 398

Fiscal year 1999: 113   Fiscal year 2001: 672

Adoption Information: U.S. agencies must be approved and be registered by the Ministry of Education in the new capital of Astana (Akmola). The ministry reviews the adoptive parent's dossier. Upon approval, they are notified and sent an invitation to travel to Kazakhstan. Both parents must be present to visit the orphanage and to select a child. They are given custody for a fourteen day bonding period. The adoption process begins on the fifteenth day and ends fifteen days later. At that point, the family travels to Moscow to obtain a U.S. Orphan Visa. Parents stay with the child for four to five weeks. Or, after the bonding period, they may place the child in foster care and go home until the child has been adopted and brought to Moscow. There they join the child in order to obtain a U.S. orphan visa. Delays in the court process may lengthen the estimates for bonding and finalization by several weeks.

Adoption Authority

Ministry of Education Committee on Guardianship and Care

Astana (Akmola), Kazakhstan

U.S. Embassy

U.S. Embassy, Consular Section
99/97A Furmanova Street
Almaty, Kazakhstan 480001

Tel: [7] (3272) 63-39-21 or 63-24-26
Fax: [7] (3272) 50-62-69
E-mail consularalmaty@state.gov

*Visas are issued by U.S. Embassy in Moscow, Russia. Consult the section on Russia for contact information.

*Moldova (CIS)

Geography: A small republic of 33,700 square kilometers bordered by the Ukraine and Romania

Capital: Chisinau (Kishinev)

Demography: Approximately 4,341,000, the majority of whom are Moldovans of Russian and Romanian descent

Languages: Moldovan, Russian, Romanian

Currency: Ruble

Major Religion: Eastern Orthodox

Orphans Admitted into the United States

Fiscal year 1998: 46
Fiscal year 1999: 63
Fiscal year 2000: 79
Fiscal year 2001: 46

Adoption Information: In order to be eligible for adoption, a Moldovan child must first be registered on the official list of orphaned or abandoned children. If after six months the child has not been adopted by a Moldovan family, he or she is then eligible to be adopted by foreign parents working through a registered adoption agency. In practice, it is impossible for a foreigner to adopt a child who is less than six months old.

All adoption agencies must register with the Moldovan Adoption Committee to be allowed to petition to adopt eligible Moldovan children. A list of agencies working in Moldova can be found on the State Department web site (**www.travel.state.gov**). Only registered agencies will be given permission to visit eligible children in orphanages and/or hospitals. Once an agency has matched a prospective family with an eligible child, the agency must submit documentation to the committee showing that the family has met all legal requirements for adoption in their own country. The committee will then review all documentation and make a final decision on the adoption. Those approved to adopt a Moldovan child must pay $1,000.00 and the equivalent of a round-trip ticket to the adoptive country so that Moldovan authorities would be able to visit the child to monitor the home environment, should the need arise.

Note: In May of 2001, Moldova instituted a temporary ban on international adoption while a new entity was created to oversee foreign adoptions in that country. At the time of printing, no information was available on the creation of the new adoption authority or the reinstatement of foreign adoption. In November or 2002, the Moldovan government expressed an interest in an agreement with the United States to allow adoptions again. Consult the U.S. Embassy in Moldova or the State Department web site for more up-to-date information.

Adoption Authority
A new agency will be created to oversee foreign adoptions.

U.S. Embassy
U.S. Embassy, Moldova
Strada A. Mateevici 103
Chisinau, Moldova MD-2009

Tel: [373] (2) 23-37-72 or 40-83-00
Fax [373] (2) 22-63-61

*Visas are issued by the U.S. Embassy in Bucharest, Romania. Consult the section on Romania for contact information.

*Ukraine (CIS)

Geography: A republic of 603,700 square kilometers bordered by Poland, Belarus, Slovakia, Romania, Russia, and Moldova

Capital: Kiev (Kiyeu)

Demography: 51,704,000, ethnic Ukrainians and Russians

Languages: Ukrainian, Russian

Currency: Ruble

Major Religion: Eastern Orthodox

Orphans Admitted into United States
Fiscal year 1998: 180   Fiscal year 2000: 659
Fiscal year 1999: 323   Fiscal year 2001: 1,246

Adoption Information: Citizens of foreign countries may adopt Ukrainian children only if they have permission from the Adoption Center (a department of the Ministry of Education of Ukraine). Children eligible for adoption must be registered with the Adoption Center for eighteen months prior to the adoption. If within this time no Ukrainian family expresses a desire to adopt them or become their guardians, the children become eligible for foreign adoption. If citizens of the foreign countries are relatives of the child or if the child is suffering from a disease (the Ministry of Health protection has a list of diseases), the waiting period may be waived. Citizens of countries that have signed bilateral agreements on adoption have priority.

Citizens of foreign countries interested in adopting a child residing in Ukraine should submit their request to the Adoption Center of the Ministry of Education of Ukraine. The Adoption Center is operated as part of the Ministry of Education and is the only legal Ukrainian authority that maintains a database of children available and qualified for both domestic and international adoptions. Note: The head of the Adoption Center in Kiev was replaced late in 2002. Changes in the regulations are underway. Contact the U.S. Embassy in Ukraine for more up-to-date information regarding adoption or consult the State Department web site (**www.travel.state.gov**).

Adoption Authority
> Adoption Center
> 27 Taras Shevchenko Boulevard
> Kiev, Ukraine 252032
>
> Tel: [380] (44) 246-54-31 or 246-54-32
> Fax: [380] (44) 246-54-52

U.S. Embassy
> U.S. Embassy, Consular Section
> 10 Yuriya Kotsiubynskoho
> Kiev, 04053 Ukraine
>
> Tel: [380] (44) 490-4000
> Fax: [380] (44) 244-7350
> URL: www.usemb.kiev.ua

*Visas are issued by the U.S. Embassy in Warsaw, Poland. Consult the section on Poland for contact information.

*Uzbekistan (CIS)

Geography: A republic of 447,400 square kilometers bordered by Kazakhstan, Turkmenistan, Tajikistan, Kyrgyzstan, and Afghanistan

Capital: Tashkent

Demography: Population of 19,906,000 Uzbekis and Russians

Languages: Uzbeki and Russian

Currency: Ruble

Major Religion: Islam

Orphans Admitted into the United States

Fiscal year 1998: 1	Fiscal year 2000: 1
Fiscal year 1999: 0	Fiscal year 2001: 1

Adoption Information: The government office responsible for adoptions in Uzbekistan is the Ministry of Education. Parent-initiated adoptions are permitted; however, in reality, there are very few adoptions by foreigners. The following steps outline the Uzbeki adoption process:

An agent or the prospective parents select a child from an orphanage and present the child's documents to the adoption inspector of the regional Department of Education (Rayonniy Otdel Narodnovo Obrazovaniya, or RAYONO) for review;

The inspector passes the documents to the city's mayor's office (Hokimiste) for approval;

The city Hokimiste sends approval to a local district (Hokimiate), which grants final authority for the adoption;

The local ZAGS (registration office of civil acts) issues a certificate of adoption based on the local Hakimiate's decision (Note: the certificate can also legalize a name change based on the adopting parents' wishes.);

UVVG (the Administration for Exit, Entry, and Citizenship, formerly known as OVIR) issues a passport to the child based on the local Hokimiate's permission, the ZAGS certificate, and a notarized invitation for permanent residence abroad.

Adopted orphans retain their Uzbekistan citizenship until they reach the majority age of sixteen. In order to monitor the rights of its citizens adopted overseas, in 1992 the Cabinet of Ministers officially delegated this responsibility to the Red Crescent Society (an Islamic version of the Red Cross). The Red Crescent Society, in turn, delegated this responsibility to a sub-organization called Tayanach. Tayanach, a not-for-profit organization, has become an active participant in the process of foreign adoptions. Although it has no official authority to do so, this organization has been accepting the documents and bona fides of various adoption agencies and granting them permission to operate in Uzbekistan. Since it works to ensure that children adopted from Uzbekistan have good living conditions and receive necessary medical treatment once overseas, it also requests regular reports about the children's life and health abroad during the first five years after adoption.

Adoption Authority
Ministry of Education
Tashkent, Uzbekistan

U.S. Embassy
U.S. Embassy, Consular Section
82 Chilanzarskaya Street
Tashkent, Uzbekistan 70000

Tel: [998] (71) 120-5450
Fax: [998] (71) 120-6335

*Visas are issued by the U.S. Embassy in Moscow, Russia. Consult the section on Russia for contact information.

YUGOSLAVIA (Former Republic

Now less than half its original size, this newly reshaped Balkan country is now referred to as Serbia-Montenegro and consists of the republics of Serbia and Montenegro, as well as Kosovo. The former republics of Croatia, Slovenia, Macedonia, and Bosnia and Herzegovina are now independent countries.

*BOSNIA AND HERZEGOVINA

Geography: A newly formed republic of southeastern Europe that borders Croatia and Serbia-Montenegro. Bosnia and Herzegovina (the Bosnian abbreviation is ÒBIHÓ) is divided into two entities — the Republika Srpska (RS) and The Federation of Bosnia and Herzegovina.

Capital: Sarajevo

Demography: Population of approximately 3,594,000

Languages: Croatian, Serbian, Bosnian

Currency: BH Dinar

Major Religions: Islam, Roman Catholic, and Eastern Orthodox

Orphans Admitted into the United States
Fiscal year 1998: 0   Fiscal year 2000: 1
Fiscal year 1999: 0   Fiscal year 2001: 1

Adoption Information: Both the Republika Srpska (RS) and The Federation of Bosnia and Herzegovina have inherited the old family law of the former Yugoslavia, which, among other things, regulates adoption. While there is nothing in the Bosnian law that specifically prohibits foreigners from applying to adopt a Bosnian child, the law stresses that there has to be overwhelming justification and exceptionally compelling reasons for a foreigner to be able to adopt a Bosnian child. Just what an "overwhelming justification" might be is judged on a case-by-case basis. Foreign adoption is a particularly sensitive subject to Bosnian authorities and to the people of Bosnia. Having lost so many lives in the recent war, Bosnians have strong feelings against permitting Bosnian children to be removed from their homeland. Therefore, Bosnian law gives absolute priority to adoptions by Bosnian citizens. There are no indications that either the RS or the Federation is considering liberalizing their adoption laws to make foreign adoptions easier.

Adoptions by foreigners must be approved by the Ministry of Social Policy, which is not the case for adoptions by local Bosnian citizens. In practice, it is extremely difficult or almost impossible to obtain this approval. The main reason is the fact that neither the government of the Federation nor that of the RS considers it beneficial for native-born children to be uprooted, to lose contact with other relatives, or to lose their identity through losing their citizenship. Furthermore, in a country that is still recovering from a long and brutal conflict, it can be extremely difficult to determine if the whereabouts of a parent is simply unknown or if the child is truly an orphan. In fact, relatively few of the children in Bosnian orphanages or children's homes are true orphans in the sense of having lost both parents. Many are the children of parents who are unable to care for them at home, but continue to take an interest in their welfare

Adoption Authority
Ministry of Social Policy (for foreign adoptions)

U.S. Embassy/Visa Issuing Post
U.S. Embassy, Consular Section
Alipasina 43
71000 Sarajevo
Bosnia and Herzegovina

Tel: [387] (33) 445-700
Fax: [387] (33) 221-837

*CROATIA

Geography: Large republic split off from former Yugoslavia bordered by Slovenia, Hungary, Romania, Bosnia and Herzegovina, and Serbia

Capital: Zagreb

Demography: Approximately 1,700,000 Croatians and Serbs

Languages: Croatian, Serbian, Slovenian

Currency: Kuna

Major Religions: Eastern Orthodox, Roman Catholic

Orphans Admitted into the United States

Fiscal year 1998: 3	Fiscal year 2000: 1
Fiscal year 1999: 2	Fiscal year 2001: 1

Adoption Information: Under normal circumstances, only Croatian citizens may adopt children from Croatia. In some "extraordinary circumstances" persons of Croatian ethnic origins who have lived in Croatia for some time or persons willing to adopt children with special needs have been allowed to adopt. No more than three or four orphan visas have been issued per year.

Adoption Authority

Minisarstvo Radai Socijalne Skrbi Hrvatske
(Croatian Ministry of Labor and Social Service)
Prisavlje 14
10000 Zagreb
Attn. Ms. Helena Ujevic

U.S. Embassy/Visa Issuing Post

U.S. Embassy, Consular Section
Andrije Hebrangar 2
10000 Zagreb, Croatia

Tel: [385] (1) 661-2300
Fax: [385] (1) 455-0774

*MACEDONIA

Geography: A former republic of Yugoslavia bordering Albania, Greece, Bulgaria, and Kosovo

Capital: Skobje

Demography: Approximately 1,500,000 Macedonians of Serbian, Greek, and other minorities

Languages: Serbian, Greek, Albanian

Currency: Macedonian Dinar

Major Religions: Greek Orthodox, Roman Catholic, and Muslim

Orphans Admitted into the United States
    Fiscal year 1998: 8   Fiscal year 2000: 4
    Fiscal year 1999: 0   Fiscal year 2001: 2

Adoption Information: The waiting list of qualified Macedonian couples seeking to adopt Macedonian children far exceeds the availability. In fact, in recent times, the only foreign couples who have successfully adopted Macedonian children have been persons holding dual nationality (Macedonian and another) and who have long-standing family and ethnic ties to Macedonia. Nonetheless, responsible officials are not totally closed to the possibility of adoption by foreigners, but are considering future procedures and revision to law in order to ensure the best interests of those few children who may become available for intercountry adoption.

Adoption Authority
    Ministry of Labor and Social Affairs
    14 Dame Gruev St.
    1000 Skobje, Macedonia

    Tel: [389] (2) 106-226

U.S. Embassy/Visa Issuing Post
    U.S. Embassy, Macedonia
    Ilindenska, b.b.
    1000 Skobje, Macedonia

    Tel: [389] (2) 116-180
    Fax: [389] (2) 213-767

*SERBIA-MONTENEGRO

Geography: The largest of the former Yugoslavia republics, Serbia also still controls Kosovo, Montenegro, and Vojvodina.

Capital: Belgrade

Demography: Approximately 10,800,000 Serbs, Kosovans, Montenegrins, and Vojvodinans

Languages: Serbian, Croatian, Slovenian, and other languages and dialects of former Yugoslavia

Currency: Dinar

Major Religions: Eastern Orthodox, Roman Catholic

Orphans Admitted into the United States
    Fiscal year 1998: 4   Fiscal year 2000: 0
    Fiscal year 1999: 0   Fiscal year 2001: 3

Adoption Information: An excerpt from a U.S. Consulate report states that according to the Law of Marriage and Marital Affairs, adoption of orphans by foreign citizens is only allowed under unusual circumstances. For example, a few exceptions may be made for diplomats and foreign citizens of Yugoslav origin or dual nationals when an adoptive parent is not found within national boundaries.

U.S. Embassy/Visa Issuing Post
U.S. Embassy, Consular Section
Kneza Milosa 50
11000 Belgrade
Serbia-Montenegro

Tel: [381] (11) 645-655
Fax: [381] (11) 645-332

*SLOVENIA

Geography: Formerly a part of Yugoslavia, this republic became independent and, for the most part, escaped the civil war that followed the break up. Slovenia shares a border with Italy, Austria, Croatia, and Hungary.

Capital: Ljubljana

Demography: 1,625,000 people of Slovenian, Italian, and Croatian ethnicity

Languages: Slovenian, Serbian, Croatian

Currency: Slovenian Dinar

Major Religion: Roman Catholic

Orphans Admitted into the United States

Fiscal year 1998: 0   Fiscal year 2000: 0
Fiscal year 1999: 0   Fiscal year 2001: 0

Adoption Information: Usually only Slovenians can adopt children who have been relinquished to a "competent body." There are no central institutions for adoption, rather 52 centers of social work carry out social services. An unusually high number of Slovenian couples are waiting to adopt.

U.S. Embassy/Visa Issuing Post
U.S. Embassy, Consular Section
P.O. Box 254
Prazakova 4
61000 Ljubljana, Slovenia

Tel: [386] (61) 301-427
Fax: [386] (61) 301-401

TURKEY

Geography: A nation located between southwestern Europe and the Middle East Peninsula

Capital: Ankara

Demography: 55,900,000 persons of Mediterranean, Caucasian, and Mongoloid heritage

Language: Turkish

Currency: Turkish Lira

Major Religion: Islam

Orphans Admitted into the United States

Fiscal year 1998: 2   Fiscal year 2000: 4
Fiscal year 1999: 5   Fiscal year 2001: 3

Adoption Information: Adoptions are governed by the Turkish Civil Code, which requires the adopting parents to be at least 35 years of age, at least 18 years older than the child to be adopted, and have no biological children. Singles may also adopt. The final adoption decree is issued in court. Only private attorneys and not agencies may assist.

Note: The Parliament is working on the new Civil Code, which may include major changes to adoption laws.

Adoption Authority

T.C. Basbakanlik Sosyal Hizmetler
ve Cocuk Esirgeme Kurumu Genel Mudurlugo
Anafartala Cad. N. 70 Ulus
Ankara, Turkey

Tel: [90] (312) 231- 9665
Fax: [90] (312) 231-0650

U.S. Embassy/Visa Issuing Post

U.S. Embassy, Consular Section
110 Ataturk Blvd.
Kavaklidere
06100 Ankara, Turkey

Tel: [90] (312) 455-5555
Fax: [90] (312) 468-6131

American Consulate, Istanbul

Mesrutiyet Caddesi No. 104/10
Tepebasi
80050 Istanbul, Turkey

Tel: [90] (212) 251-3602
Fax: [90] (212) 251-3632

LATIN AMERICA

The geographic designation of Latin America includes Mexico, the countries of Central and South America, and the Caribbean Islands.

Important Note: As discussed in the introduction to the Compendium, the political and legal situations regarding international adoption for individual countries are subject to rapid change. In addition, contact information such as addresses and phone numbers may change. Be sure to consult the State Department web site (**www.travel.state.gov**) or the U.S. Embassy located in the country in which you are interested for the latest information on adoption policies and procedures.

BELIZE

Geography: Located on the east coast of Central America, Belize is about the size of Massachusetts and is bordered by Mexico and Guatemala. A former British colony known as British Honduras, Belize gained its independence in 1981.

Capital: In 1975, the capital was moved from Belize City, which is on the coast, inland to Belmopan, which offers more protection from hurricanes. The U.S. Consulate is still located in Belize City (40,000).

Demography: The population of about 187,000 is made up of Creole (African/English), Mestizo, Maya, and Carib-Indian groups, as well as East Indian, African, Asian, and Caucasian minorities.

Languages: English, Spanish, and Mayan

Currency: Belizean dollar

Major Religion: Anglican

Orphans Admitted into the United States
Fiscal year 1998: 4   Fiscal year 2000: 7
Fiscal year 1999: 5   Fiscal year 2001: 5

Adoption Information: Belizean adoption law is not fully delineated and is in the process of revision. While U.S. citizens may adopt in Belize, Belizean adoption law requires that both the adoptive parents and the child reside in Belize. However, Belizean law does not specify residence requirements, which have often been liberally interpreted to mean being physically present long enough to accomplish the adoption. Adoptive parents must be at least 25 years of age and 21 years older than the child. The process of adoption in Belize can take as long as two years. Cases are processed by the Belize Supreme Court and do not require the services of a private attorney.

U.S. Embassy/Visa Issuing Post
U.S. Embassy
29 Gabourel Lane
Belize City, Belize

Tel: [501] (2) 35321
Fax: [501] (2) 30802

BOLIVIA

Geography: Bolivia is the fifth largest country in South America. It is bordered by Brazil on the north and east; Paraguay on the southeast; Argentina on the south; and Chile and Peru on the west.

Demography: More than half of Bolivia's 7,300,000 people are Amerindians; the rest are mestizos and people of European descent.

Capital: La Paz

Languages: Although Spanish is the official language, Aymará and Quechuan are more widely used. Little English is spoken.

Currency: Bolivian Peso

Major Religion: Roman Catholic

Orphans Admitted into the United States

Fiscal year 1998: 73	Fiscal year 2000: 60
Fiscal year 1999: 44	Fiscal year 2001: 35

Adoption Information: The government of Bolivia passed a new adoption law (known as the "Codigo de Nino, la nina y Adolescente" on January 19, 2002. Similar to provisions under the old law, foreign adoption agencies must be approved by the government, and adoptions must be carried out via such agencies. An updated listing of such agencies may be obtained from the Vice Ministerio de Asuntos Genero Generacionales y Familia. There is still disagreement between Bolivia's ministries as to whether a bilateral agreement between countries is required when the countries have not yet ratified the Hague Convention.

Adoption Authority
Vice-Ministerio de Asuntos de Genero Generacionales y Famila
Casilla 5960
La Paz, Bolivia

Tel: [591] (2) 376-862
Fax: [591] (2) 366-763

U.S. Embassy/Visa Issuing Post
U.S. Embassy, Consular Section
Avenida Arce No. 2780
Esquina Cordero
La Paz, Bolivia

Tel: [591] (2) 430-251 (Embassy)
Fax: [591] (2) 433-854

BRAZIL

Geography: Colossal Brazil is the largest country in Latin America and the fifth largest country in the world. Its 21 states, four territories, and federal district are slightly larger than the continental United States.

Capital: Brasilia

Demography: 150,400,000. About 60 percent of the Brazilian people have European ancestry (Italian, Portuguese, Spanish, and German); more than 25 percent are of mixed ancestry (European, African, and Indian). About 10 percent of the people are black, and one percent are Amerindian. Most of the people who live in northern, northwestern, and central Brazil are Indians; those in the northeastern coastal area are of African ancestry; those in the southeastern area are of European ancestry; and those within the triangle formed by Bras'lia, Sao Paulo, and Rio de Janeiro are mixed. Brazil's estimated population of 150 million is about half of the entire population of Latin America. One-half of all Brazilians are less than 25 years of age.

Languages: Portuguese; some English is spoken in major cities.

Currency: Real (BRC)

Major Religion: Roman Catholic

Orphans Admitted into the United States

Fiscal year 1998: 103	Fiscal year 2000: 26
Fiscal year 1999: 64	Fiscal year 2001: 33

Adoption Information: According to the Federal Statute on the Child and the Adolescent, the government offices responsible for international adoptions in Brazil are the State Judiciary Commissions of Adoption (CEJA), which are the sole organization authorized to approve foreign adopting parents in each of Brazil's 21 states. Persons over 21 years of age may adopt as long as they are at least 16 years older than the child. A final adoption decree has to be issued in order for the child to leave Brazil. Adoptions can be arranged either directly between the court and the adopters or through approved U.S. adoption agencies. Brazilian judicial authorities maintain a register of children available for adoption and a second register for persons wishing to adopt. Judges require adoptive parents to live in Brazil with the child for at least 15 days for children under two years and at least 30 days for older children. Most Brazilian orphans are three years of age or older and of mixed-race. Preference in adoption is given to Brazilian citizens. Adoptions from Brazil dropped dramatically in 1999 and 2000 until passage of legislation in the U.S. brought U.S. laws into accordance with the Hague Convention.

Adoption Authority
State Judiciary Commissions of Adoption (CEJA) for each of the 21 states.

U.S. Embassy
Avenida das Nacoes 3
Lote 3
Brasilia, Brazil

Tel: [55] (61) 321-7272

Visa Issuing Post
U.S. Consulate General
Avenida Presidente Wilson, 147, Castelo
Rio de Janeiro RJ, Brazil, 20030-020.

Tel: [55] (21) 2292-7117
Fax: [55] (21) 2524-1972

CHILE

Geography: Chile is the southernmost country of Latin America. It occupies a long, narrow ribbon of land between the Pacific Ocean and the Andes Mountains.

Capital: Santiago

Demography: About one-third of Chile's 13.2 million people are mestizos; two percent are Araucanian Indians; and most of the rest are descended from Spanish or other European settlers.

Languages: Spanish; some English is spoken in the cities.

Currency: Peso

Major Religion: Roman Catholic

Orphans Admitted into the United States
Fiscal year 1998: 30   Fiscal year 2000: 10
Fiscal year 1999: 20   Fiscal year 2001: 3

Adoption Information: Couples interested in adopting in Chile must apply and be approved by SENAME, which keeps the national registry of children eligible for adoption. Couples using an adoption agency, should be certain that the agency is working in close relationship with SENAME. SENAME matches available children with families who wish to adopt. Blood relatives are always given priority, followed by Chilean families, then non-Chilean families. After a child is matched with a family, there is a hearing in front of judge where the adoption decree is signed. A new birth certificate, with the adoptive parents' names, is issued and can be used to obtain the child's Chilean passport. Obtaining a new passport is the longest stage of the process and U.S. families should plan to remain in Chile for a few additional weeks after the adoption is final.

Adoption Authority
> Servicio Nacional de Menores de Chile (SENAME)
> Unidad de Adopción
> Huerfanos 587
> Santiago, Chile
> Telephone: [56] (2) 398-4447

U.S. Embassy/Visa Issuing Post
> Consular Section - Immigrant Visas
> Avenida Andrés Bello 2800
> Santiago, Chile

> Tel: [56] (2) 335-6550
> Fax: [56] (2) 330-3005
> URL: www.usembassy.cl
> E-mail: SantiagoVisa@state.gov

COLOMBIA

Geography: Colombia is the fourth largest country in South America, with coastlines on both the Atlantic and Pacific oceans. Colombia shares a border with Panama.

Capital: Bogotá

Demography: Of Colombia's population of 33,000,000, about 40 percent are mestizo; 30 percent white, mostly of Spanish descent; 15 percent mulatto; seven percent Amerindian (Colombia has 398 distinct tribes); and five percent are of African descent. Bogotá has a high percentage of mestizos, while Medellín has a high percentage of people with European ancestry, and Cali has a tri-ethnic mixture of mestizos, and people of African or European descent.

Languages: Spanish; English is spoken in major cities.

Currency: Peso

Major Religion: Roman Catholic

Orphans Admitted into the United States

Fiscal year 1998: 351	Fiscal year 2000: 246
Fiscal year 1999: 231	Fiscal year 2001: 266

Adoption Information: Singles are accepted, although couples are preferred. For married couples, at least one of the adopting parents must be over 25 years of age. In practice, newborns are assigned to younger couples, and older children are assigned to older couples. The child to be adopted must not be over 16 years of age. The law establishes that only sources licensed by the ICBF (Instituto Colombiano de Bienestar Familiar (or Colombian Institute of Family Welfare) and licensed Colombian adoption agencies can offer children for adoption. A short waiting period for orphaned, abandoned, and relinquished children takes place while relatives are sought. If none appear, a certificate of abandonment is issued by the court. Then when the child is placed, a final adoption decree is soon issued, which negates the possibility of the birth parents or adoptive parents overturning the adoption. Private adoption agencies shelter abandoned children and some wards of the ICBF. Wards of the family welfare institute are usually housed in government orphanages. Since government orphanages usually provide minimal care, adopters may find it possible and desirable to arrange foster care for a child who has been assigned to them.

The ICBF, as well as most of the private agencies, works with adoption agencies rather than individuals. The exception is Casa de la Madre y el Nino, which will only place children directly with couples.

Central Adoption Authority

Instituto Colombian de Bienestar Familiar (ICBF)
Grupo Nacional de Adopciones
Avenida 68, numero 64-01
Bogota, Colombia

Tel: [57] (1) 437-7630 Ext 3158 or 3157

Competent Adoption Authorities

The following agencies are licensed by the ICBF.

Ayudame (Asociacion Amigos del Nino)
Calle 128, # 8-53
Bogata, Colombia
Apartado Aereo 102697

Tel: [57] (1) 258-3390 or 216-0538

Casa de la Madre y el Niño
Calle 48, # 28-30
Bogota, Colombia

Tel: [57] (1) 268-7400

Casa de Maria y el Niño
Calle 9 A Sur, # 24-422
Loma de los Balsos – El Poblado
Medellin, Antioquia
Colombia, Apartado Aereo 062298

Tel: [57] (94) 268-6112
Fax: [57] (94) 266-6771

Casita de Nicolas
Carrera 50, # 65-23
Medellin, Antioquia
Colombia

Tel: [57] (94) 263-8086
Fax: [57] (94) 211-4242

U.S. Embassy/Visa Issuing Post

U.S. Embassy, Consular Section — Adoptions
Calle 22 D
Bis # 47-51
Bogota, Colombia

Tel: [57] (1) 315-1566
Fax: [57] (1) 315-4155

COSTA RICA

Geography: Costa Rica is a small, mountainous country in Central America with coastlines on both the Atlantic and Pacific oceans.

Capital: San José

Demography: More than 97 percent of Costa Rica's population of 3,015,000 is either mestizo or white of European ancestry. Amerindians and blacks make up two small minority groups.

Languages: Spanish; some English is spoken in the larger cities.

Currency: Colón

Major Religion: Roman Catholic

Orphans Admitted into the United States
Fiscal year 1998: 7   Fiscal year 2000: 17
Fiscal year 1999: 41   Fiscal year 2001: 9

Adoption Information: Costa Rica's central adoption authority Patronanto Nacional de la Infancia (PANI) requires that adoptive couples must be between 25 and 60 years of age and at least 15 years older than the adopted child. Children four years old or more may be adopted. They may be younger than four if they are part of a sibling group adopted together. Both spouses must travel to Costa Rica. Adoptions can also be arranged through private attorneys or agencies; however, these must be authorized by the Patronato. Although by Costa Rican law, children do not have to be orphans to be eligible for adoption, U.S. immigration law does require this.

Once a child is assigned, the couple must stay in Costa Rica for two weeks to initiate the adoption. Then, the child can be placed in foster care and both spouses can return home, or one can stay and care for the child. One spouse must return in 45 to 60 days for the final adoption decree and to obtain the child's U.S. visa before immigrating the child.

The Patronato does not charge a fee for child care or legal work. Excellent medical and psychological evaluations on each child are provided at the time of assignment.

Central Adoption Authority
Patronato Nacional de la Infancia (PANI)
Apartado 5000
San Jose, Costa Rica

U.S. Embassy/Visa Issuing Post
U.S. Embassy, Consular Section
Calle 120 Avenida 0
Pavas, San José
Costa Rica

Tel: [506] 220-3050 X 2455 or 2456
Fax: [506] 220-2305

DOMINICAN REPUBLIC

Geography: The Dominican Republic makes up the eastern two-thirds of the island of Hispaniola in the Caribbean Sea; Haiti occupies the western third of the island.

Capital: Santo Domingo

Demography: About 65 percent of the 7,170,000 population are biracial, 20 percent are blacks, and 15 percent are whites.

Language: Spanish

Currency: Peso

Major Religion: Roman Catholic

Orphans Admitted into the United States

Fiscal year 1998: 140   Fiscal year 2000: 8
Fiscal year 1999: 16   Fiscal year 2001: 12

Adoption Information: New changes in the law require adoptive parents to reside at least 90 days in the Dominican Republic, sometimes even longer. Consent of the biological parents is required under the Dominican law to adopt a minor child. If the parents are separated or divorced, the consent of the parent having custody is essential and the noncustodial parent must be notified of the impending adoption. In the case of abandonment, the legal representative can give the consent. The representative is appointed by the Secretaria de Estado Salud or by a judicial authority. Under Dominican law, a single individual, married couple, or unmarried couple may adopt a child. A single individual must be at least 25 years old and at least 15 years older than the child. A married couple may adopt a child if one of the spouses is at least 25 years old.

Adoption Authority

Oversight Agency, System for the Protection of Children and Adolescents
Calle Moises Garcia #7 esq. Calle Galvan
Ensanche Gazcue
Santo Domingo, Dominican Republic

Tel: [809] 685-9257

U.S. Embassy/Visa Issuing Post

U.S. Embassy, Santo Domingo
Calle Cesar Nicolas Penson & Calle Leopoldo Navarro
Santo Domingo, Dominican Republic

Tel: [809] 221-2171
Fax: [809] 686-7437

ECUADOR

Geography: A small, mountainous country in South America that lies on the west coast of the continent between Colombia to the north and Peru to the south.

Capital: Quito. The largest city is Guayaquil, where the U.S. Consulate is located.

Demography: The population of 10,600,000 consists of about 40 percent mestizos, about 40 percent Amerindians, and about 10 percent whites of European ancestry.

Languages: Spanish; some English is spoken in the cities.

Currency: Sucre

Major Religion: Roman Catholic

Orphans Admitted into the United States

Fiscal year 1998: 55	Fiscal year 2000: 57
Fiscal year 1999: 61	Fiscal year 2001: 50

Adoption Information: Husbands must be between 30 and 50 years of age, and wives must be between 25 and 40. No prior divorce is permitted, and the couple must be married at least five years. Childless couples are given preference. If the couple has a biological child, they must present a statement of infertility in order to adopt a child of the opposite sex to the one they already have. If they have an adopted child, they may adopt a child of either sex. Some exceptions may be made for couples wishing to adopt a special needs child. The wait between the assignment of the child and the adoption trip is about one week. Both spouses travel to Ecuador for a stay of about two weeks in Guayaquil, or in Quito. They receive custody during their stay. The final decree is issued five to six weeks later. Children can only be placed in Ecuador through licensed Ecuadorian agencies or the National Directorate for the Protection of Minor Children (Direccion Nacional de Proteccion de Menores), which, in turn, licenses U.S. adoption agencies to place children. The Juvenile Court (Tribunal de Menores) must grant permission for the child to depart the country.

Adoption Authority
Dirreccion Nacional de Proteccion de Menores
The Tribunal de Menores (Juvenile Court)

U.S. Embassy/Visa Issuing Post
U.S. Embassy, Consular Section
Avenida 12 de Octubre y Avenida Partria
Quito, Ecuador

Tel: [593] (2) 562-890
Fax: [593] (2) 502-052

U.S. Consulate General
9 de Octubre y Garcia Moreno
Guayaquil, Ecuador

Tel: [593] (4) 323-570
Fax: [593] (4) 325-286

EL SALVADOR

Geography: Located on the Pacific coast between Guatemala and Honduras, El Salvador is the smallest and most densely populated country in Central America.

Capital: San Salvador

Demography: About 92 percent of El Salvador's 5,300,000 people are mestizos; nearly five percent are whites of European ancestry, and three percent are U.S. citizens.

Language: Spanish; some English is spoken in the major cities.

Currency: Colon

Major Religion: Roman Catholic

Orphans Admitted into the United States

Fiscal year 1998: 13   Fiscal year 2000: 9
Fiscal year 1999: 8   Fiscal year 2001: 4

Adoption Information: Adopters must be more than 25 years old, and couples must be married at least two years. Generally, an orphan's birth documents are sent to preadoptive parents shortly after the child is assigned to them. Only one spouse is required to travel to El Salvador to obtain custody of the child; adopters stay in the country about one week.

The Central Authority included in the ratification of the Hague Convention states that only residents of countries who ratified the convention and have established a central authority will be approved for an adoption.

Adoption Authority

Jefe de Seccion de Adopciones
Procuradoria General de la Republica
Centro de Gobierno
San Salvador, El Salvador

Tel: [503] 222-4444 or 222-4133

U.S. Embassy/Visa Issuing Post

U.S. Embassy, Consular Section
Final Blvd. Santa Elena
Antiguo Cuscatlan
La Libertad, El Salvador

Tel: [503] 278-4444
Fax: [503] 278-5522

GRENADA

Geography: Small island off the coast of Venezuela, consisting of 344 square kilometers

Capital: St. George's

Demography: Population of 85,000, mostly of African and mixed heritage

Languages: English, French patois

Currency: East Caribbean Dollar

Major Religions: Christian, Protestant

Orphans Admitted into the United States

Fiscal year 1998: 3	Fiscal year 2000: 2
Fiscal year 1999: 2	Fiscal year 2001: 1

Adoption Information: Although limited detailed information is available, international adoption is allowed. An initial adoption request is made through a local attorney. The U.S. Embassy in Grenada maintains a list of attorneys. Subject to the provisions of the Grenada Adoption Act, the court may authorize a foreigner who is residing in Grenada to adopt a child if the applicant is at least 25 years of age and 20 years older than the child to be adopted. An information pamphlet on adoption in Grenada is available by writing the adoption board.

Adoption Authority

The Adoption Board of Grenada
Ms. Jeannine Sylvester
Ministry of Social Services, Tanteen
St. George's, Grenada

Tel: [473] 440-7952

Orphanage

The Queen Elizabeth Home for Children
Tempe Street
St. George's, Grenada

Tel: [473] 440-2327

U.S. Embassy/Visa Issuing Post

P.O. Box 54
St. George's, Grenada

Tel; [473] 444-1173
Fax: [473] 444-4820
E-mail: usemb_gd@caribsurf.com

GUATEMALA

Geography: With 108,888 square kilometers, Guatemala is the third largest of the Central American countries. Guatemala shares a long border with Mexico and has coastlines on both the Atlantic and Pacific oceans.

Capital: Guatemala City

Demography: About 55 percent of Guatemala's 9,200,000 people are mestizos; most of the remaining 45 percent are Amerindians. The infant mortality rate is 95 per 1,000 births; 82 percent of urban children and 95 percent of rural children suffer from chronic malnutrition.

Languages: Spanish and Mayan; some English is spoken in the larger cities.

Currency: Quetzal

Major Religion: Roman Catholic

Orphans Admitted into the United States

Fiscal year 1998: 911	Fiscal year 2000: 1,518
Fiscal year 1999: 1,002	Fiscal year 2001: 1,609

Adoption Information: Couples between 25 and 50, married at least one year, as well as single women over 25, may adopt. Adoptions in Guatemala follow either the public (judicial) or the private (extrajudicial) route, depending on the status of the child to be adopted. Public adoptions, which require a court decree declaring that the child has been abandoned, are only processed when the biological parents are known to have died or deserted the child. Public adoptions are processed through the courts using a Guatemalan government recognized adoption agency or orphanage in Guatemala. This process grants considerable discretion to the judge and normally takes about a year to complete.

Under the private adoption procedure, the natural parent makes a declaration of release of the child to an attorney who represents both the natural and the adoptive parents. Guatemalan adoption law requires a document review by the Solicitor General's office (Procuraduria General) and a court-ordered social worker's report on the natural and adoptive parents. With a power of attorney, a lawyer or law firm undertakes to locate a child, or to do the legal work on a child already identified. The irrevocable consent of relinquishment of the child's remaining biological parent, usually the mother, is required.

The lawyer also submits documentation to the INS officer at the U.S. Embassy. After the approval of submitted documents, the embassy will schedule a DNA test to be conducted in order to verify the birthmother's biological relationship to the child. After receiving the test results, the INS will make a decision regarding the orphan status of the child. Upon approval of the case, the lawyer submits the case to the Solicitor General (Procuraduria General de la Nacion). After approval he draws up the final notarial decree of adoption, obtains a new birth certificate in the adopter's name, and obtains a Guatemalan passport in the child's new name.

Adoption Authority

Responsibility for adoption in Guatemala rests with a variety of government entities including Social Services, the Procuraduria General de la Nacion, and the courts.

Private Guatemalan Adoption Agencies

The following agencies are recognized by the Guatemalan government:
A.G.A.N.D (Asociacion de Ayuda para el Nino Desamparado)
(Abandonment cases only)
15 Calle # 5-20
Zona 11
Guatemala City, Guatemala

Tel: [502] 473-1880

Hogar Campestre Adventista "Los Pinos"
(Abandonment cases only)
Director Alcyon Ruth Fleck
15 Avenida # 19-62
Zona 13, Apartado Postal 35-C
Guatemala

Tel: [502] 331-0056 or 331-6197

Hogar Rafael Ayau

Tel: [502] 232- 6747
Fax: [502] 232-1789

U.S. Embassy/Visa Issuing Post

U.S. Embassy, Consular Section
7-01 Avenida de la Reforma
Zona 10
Guatemala City, Guatemala

Tel: [502] 331 1541
Fax: [502] 331-4342
URL: **www.usembassy.state.gov/guatemala**
E-mail: adopguatemala@state.gov

HAITI

Geography: Haiti occupies the western third of the Caribbean island of Hispaniola, which lies between Cuba and Puerto Rico.

Capital: Port-au-Prince

Demography: Most of Haiti's 6,513,000 people are descendants of Africans who were brought to Haiti as slaves; about five percent are biracial.

Languages: French and Creole (a French/African patois)

Currency: Gourde

Major Religions: Roman Catholic, Voodoo

Orphans Admitted into the United States

Fiscal year 1998: 121	Fiscal year 2000: 131
Fiscal year 1999: 96	Fiscal year 2001: 192

Adoption Information: Haitian law requires that a completed final adoption decree must be issued in Haiti before a child can leave the country. The adoption process normally takes from two to six months, but can stretch to longer than a year. Under Haitian law, a prospective adopting parent must be older than age 35; for married couples, one prospective parent may be under age 35, provided the couple has been married for 10 years and has no children together. The Institut du Bien Etre Social et de Recherches (IBESR) authorizes all adoptions. The IBESR is also responsible for accrediting adoption agencies and orphanages in Haiti. Documentation from both the Haitian courts and from the IBESR is essential if you are planning to adopt a child in Haiti. While it is possible to complete the adoption process without the use of a local attorney, the U.S. Embassy maintains a list of local attorneys and adoption agencies working in Haiti.

Adoption Authority
Institut du Bien Etre Social de Recherches (IBESR)

U.S. Embassy/Visa Issuing Post
U.S. Embassy, Consular Section
104 Rue Oswald Durand
Port-au-Prince, Haiti

Tel: [509] 223-6440
Fax: [509] 223-9665

HONDURAS

Geography: Second largest of the Central American countries, Honduras is bordered by Guatemala and Nicaragua. Honduras has a long coastline on the Caribbean Sea and a small strip of coastline on the Pacific Ocean.

Capital: Tegucigalpa

Demography: 5,138,000 people, of which about 95 percent are mestizos; the rest are small minorities of Amerindians and people of African descent.

Languages: Spanish; some English is spoken in the larger cities.

Currency: Lempira

Major Religion: Roman Catholic

Orphans Admitted into the United States
Fiscal year 1998: 7   Fiscal year 2000: 17
Fiscal year 1999: 16   Fiscal year 2001: 9

Adoption Information: All adoptions are processed through the Instituto Hondureño del Niño y la Familia, also known as IHNFA, which is a social welfare agency charged by the Honduran government with overseeing local and international adoptions. The IHNFA will provide you, your lawyer, or your agency representative an Adoption Request Form, that must be presented together with the required translated, certified and authenticated documents. Once your application is approved you will be placed on a waiting list until a child is assigned (this can take up to a year). When a child is found and assigned, the applicant must then travel to Honduras to meet the child and to be evaluated psychologically and socially in preparation for a report to the family court. If approved by the court, the applicant may place the child with a foster family in Honduras until the completion of the adoption. The IHNFA will place a child in your care only if you will remain in Honduras until the adoption has been completed in the courts, which may take many months. The U.S. Embassy in Honduras and the State Department web site (**www.travel.state.gov**) maintain a list of adoption agencies and lawyers working in Honduras.

Adoption Authority
Instituto Hondureno del Nino y la Familia (IHNFA)
(a successor of the Junta Nacional de Bienestar Social)

U.S. Embassy/Visa Issuing Post
U.S. Embassy, Consular Section
Avenida La Paz
Apartado Postal No. 3453
Tegucigalpa, Honduras

Tel: [504] 236-9320
Fax: [504] 236-9107

JAMAICA

Geography: A Caribbean island 480 miles south of Florida

Capital: Kingston

Demography: About 90 percent of Jamaica's population of 2,500,000 are descendants of Africans who were brought to Jamaica as slaves.

Languages: English and Creole (an English/African patois)

Currency: Jamaican Dollar

Major Religions: Protestant, Roman Catholic

Orphans Admitted into the United States
Fiscal year 1998: 36   Fiscal year 2000: 33
Fiscal year 1999: 48   Fiscal year 2001: 51

Adoption Information: Applications have to be made to the Jamaican Adoption Board. An application form, a personal interview and a medical examination are required in addition to supporting documents. When a prospective child has been found, pre-adoption placement will be done three months before an application for an Adoption Order can be made to the Family Court.

Adoption Authority
Jamaican Adoption Board
2 King Street
Kingston, Jamaica

Tel: [876] 967-1100
Fax: [876] 924-9401

U.S. Embassy/Visa Issuing Post
U.S. Embassy, Jamaica
16 Oxford Road
Kingston 5, Jamaica

Tel: [876] 929-4850
Fax: [876] 935-6019

MEXICO

Geography: Mexico is the northernmost country of Latin America. High mountains and rolling plateaus cover more than two-thirds of the country. Mexico also has tropical forests, barren deserts, and fertile valleys.

Capital: Mexico City

Demography: More than 70 percent of Mexico's 88.6 million people are mestizos; about 20 percent are Amerindians, and less than 10 percent are people of European ancestry. Maya Indians live mainly in the Mexican states of Campeche, Quintana Roo, and Yucatán.

Languages: Although Spanish is the official language, more than ninety Amerindian languages are still in use. About one million Indians speak only their native language.

Currency: Peso

Major Religion: Roman Catholic

Orphans Admitted into the United States
Fiscal year 1998: 168   Fiscal year 2000: 106
Fiscal year 1999: 137   Fiscal year 2001: 73

Adoption Information: The adopting parents may be married or single, and male or female. All adopters must be at least 25 years of age and at least 17 years older than the child. In the case of a married couple, only one of the adoptive parents must meet the 17-year seniority requirement. If the child is over 14 years old, he or she must agree to the adoption.

Adoption in Mexico is governed by the civil codes of the 31 Mexican states. These are generally similar, but actual practice may vary from state to state or even from municipality to municipality. The Mexican State System for the Full Development of the Family (Delarrollo Integral de la Famila or the DIF) in each state is assigned responsibility for determining a child's eligibility for adoption. There is no central office for adoption. Every state has its own Procuraduria de la Defensa del Minor, which is a branch of the DIF. Contact the U.S. Embassy for a list of DIF offices in each state.

A child is considered legally abandoned six months after a determination by the public ministry of the municipality in which the child lives. The DIF is assigned responsibility to study each child's eligibility for adoption and arrange adoptions. The DIF determines whether a family would be suitable for a particular child by ensuring that a home study has been done. The DIF makes every effort to place children with relatives or Mexican citizens. The Mexican Foreign Ministry (SRE) requires that a Mexican passport be issued to the child in the child's new name after the adoption process is completed.

Adoption Authority

There is no central office for adoption. The Mexican State System for the Full Development of the Family (Delarrollo Integral de la Famila or the DIF) in each of Mexico's 31 states oversees adoptions for its locality. Contact the U.S. Embassy in Mexcio for a list of DIF offices.

U.S. Embassy

Paseo de la Reforma 305
Col. Cuauhtémoc
06500 Mexico D.F.

Tel: [52] (5) 209-9100

Visa Issuing Post

U.S. Consulate General
Avenida Lopez Mateos 924 N.
Ciudad Juarez, Mexico

Tel: [52] (16) 113-000

NICARAGUA

Geography: Nicaragua, the largest of the Central American countries, is bordered by Honduras to the north and Costa Rica to the south.

Capital: Managua (400,000)

Demography: Mestizos make up about 75 percent of the population of 3,871,000; black and Amerindian minorities live in the coastal areas near the Caribbean Sea.

Languages: Spanish; some English is spoken in the larger cities.

Currency: Córdoba

Major Religion: Roman Catholic

Orphans Admitted into the United States

Fiscal year 1998: 16   Fiscal year 2000: 9
Fiscal year.1999: 17   Fiscal year 2001: 13

Adoption Information: The child must either be orphaned or abandoned to qualify for adoption. Parental abandonment must be unconditional and irreversible. A child is not considered abandoned if the Ministry of Family is able to place the child in the custody of a relative. Nicaraguan law allows only for the adoption of children by Nicaraguan citizens or permanent residents of Nicaragua. On rare occasions, this requirement has been waived when doing so was deemed to be in the child's best interest. The adoptive parents must work directly with the Ministry of Family until the final stage of the adoption. Once the Ministry of Family authorizes the adoption, the adopting parents may hire a lawyer to complete the adoption procedures. Lists of attorneys are available from the U.S. Embassy in Nicaragua or the Department of State.

Adoption Authority
Ministry of Family
Managua, Nicaragua

U.S. Embassy/Visa Issuing Post
U.S. Embassy
Kilometro 4 1/2
Carretera Sur
Managua, Nicaragua

Tel: [505] (2) 666-010 ext. 4779 or 4519
Fax: [505] (2) 669-943

PANAMA

Geography: The southernmost country in Central America. Panama is divided by the Panama Canal, which runs through the Canal Zone between the Atlantic and Pacific oceans.

Capital: Panama City

Demography: Most of Panama's 2,418,000 people are of mixed European, Indian, and African ancestry; 14 percent are black, nine percent are whites, and seven percent are Amerindians.

Languages: Spanish; English is widely understood.

Currency: Balboa (which is really the U.S. dollar)

Major Religion: Roman Catholic

Orphans Admitted into the United States

Fiscal year 1998: 16	Fiscal year 2000: 13
Fiscal year. 1999: 24	Fiscal year 2001: 10

Adoption Information: The government offices responsible for adoptions in Panama are the two major courts, the "Juzgado de la Ninez y Adolescencia (Children's and Minor's Court)" and "Juzgados Seccionales de Familia (Family Courts)." The Children's and Minor's Court has jurisdiction over the adoption of abandoned children and orphans who are wards of the court. The Family Court has jurisdiction over adoption cases where the child has been placed under adoption by written consent of a child's birth parent(s).

To begin the adoption process, an attorney must present the necessary paperwork in the form of a "demanda" or petition for the courts to review. Usually, the adoptive parent(s) and their attorney will communicate with the judge's staff until the petition is ready for review. If the judge approves the petition, the judge will forward the documents to the "Registro Civil de Panama" (Civil Register). The adoption is not official until it is published in the Civil Register and the judge has signed a final decree. Both courts have similar processes for international adoption: The U.S. Embassy in Panama can provide a list of adoption agencies working in Panama as well as local attorneys.

Adoption Authority
Ministerio de la Juventud, la Mujer, La Niñez y la Familia
Ministry of Youth, Women, Children and Families
Apartado 680-50
El Dorado, Panama

Tel: [507] 279-0712
Fax: [507] 279-0716
E-mail: cdaven@bellsouth.net.pa

U.S. Embassy/Visa Issuing Post
U.S. Embassy, Consular Section
Balboa Ave.
Panama City 5, Panama

Tel: [507] 207-4213

PARAGUAY

Geography: Paraguay is a landlocked country in the heart of South America, bordered by Brazil, Argentina, and Bolivia.

Capital: Asuncion

Demography: Most of the population of 2,804,000 are mestizos; the rest are Guarani Indians.

Languages: Although Spanish is the official language, Guarani, the language of the Guarani Indians, is spoken almost as widely as Spanish.

Currency: Guarani

Major Religion: Roman Catholic

Orphans Admitted into the United States

Fiscal year 1998: 7	Fiscal year 2000: 1
Fiscal year 1999: 6	Fiscal year 2001: 1

Adoption Information: Paraguay suspended new international adoption cases effective September 1995 and has informed the U.S. State Department that no new adoptions will take place until the new government Center for Adoptions has been established. (Most of the orphan visas issued in recent years are related to the completion of old adoption cases initiated before the change in law.) In addition, in connection with the ratification of the Hague Convention, Paraguay has indicated that once the new Center for Adoptions is established, the country will work only with citizens of countries that have also ratified the Hague Convention and have established a central authority.

U.S. Embassy/Visa Issuing Post
U.S. Embassy, Paraguay
1776 Mariscal Lopez Ave.
Asuncion, Paraguay

PERU

Geography: Located on the northern half of South America's west coast, Peru has three main regions: the arid coastal area, the highlands of the Andes Mountains, and the thick rainforests and jungles to the east of the Andes.

Capital: Lima

Demography: About 46 percent of Peru's 21.5 million people are Amerindians; about 43 percent are mestizos, and about 10 percent are whites of European ancestry.

Languages: Spanish and Quechua, the language of the Incas, are the official languages; some highland Indians speak Aymara.

Currency: Neuvo Sol

Major Religion: Roman Catholic

Orphans Admitted into the United States

Fiscal year 1998: 26	Fiscal year 2000: 38
Fiscal year 1999: 27	Fiscal year 2001: 23

Adoption Information: All international adoptions in Peru must be processed through a U.S. adoption agency approved by PROMUDEH (the central adoption authority in Peru). A list of approved agencies can be obtained from the U.S. Embassy in Peru or the State Department web state (**www.travel.state.gov**). PROMUDEH is responsible for identifying possible orphans for assignment with prospective adoptive parents, assisting the court's investigation of the child's background, contracting and coordinating with approved U.S. adoption agencies and certifying the court adoption decrees. At least one parent must remain in Peru during the entire adoption process, which usually takes 45-60 days. There is a different process for "local" adoptions, which may be requested by Peruvian nationals, some blood relatives, or non-Peruvians who have lived in Peru for two years or more. Unfortunately, these procedures do NOT always comply with U.S. immigration requirements.

Adoption Authority

Ministerio de Promocion de la Mujer y el Desarollo Humano (PROMUDEH)
(Ministry for the Promotion of Women and Human Development)

U.S. Embassy/Visa Issuing Post

U.S. Embassy
Avenida La Encalada Cuadra 17 s/n
Monterrico, Surco
Lima 33 Peru

Tel: [51] (1) 434-3000
Fax: [51] (1) 434-3037

TRINIDAD AND TOBAGO

Geography: Two islands in the West Indies, located 10 miles from the coast of Venezuela

Capital: Port-of-Spain (250,000)

Demography: More than one-third of the population of 1,281,000 is made up of people of African ancestry and about a third are descendants of people from India. Other groups are Creoles, whites of European ancestry, and people of Chinese heritage.

Languages: English, French, Spanish, Hindi

Currency: West Indian Dollar

Major Religions: Roman Catholic, Protestant

Orphans Admitted into the United States

Fiscal year 1998: not available

Fiscal year 1999: 6

Fiscal year 2000: 3

Fiscal year 2001: 0

Adoption Information: According to the Adoption of Children Ordinance, residents of several years and citizens of Trinidad and Tobago may apply for adoption. Information concerning adoption and residency requirements is available from the Adoption Board at the address below.

Adoption Authority

Ministry of Social Development and Family Services

c/o Mrs. Hyacinth Whiteman, Secretary

Adoption Board, Fourth Floor

Salvation Building, Frederick Street

Port-of-Spain, Trinidad

Tel: [809] 625-1926

U.S. Embassy/Visa Issuing Post

U.S. Embassy, Consular Section

15 Queen's Park West

Port-of-Spain, Trinidad

Tel: [809] 622-6372 or 6376

Fax: [809] 628-5462

VENEZUELA

Geography: Located on the north coast of South America, Venezuela is bordered by Colombia, Brazil, and Guyana.

Capital: Caracas

Demography: About two-thirds of Venezuela's 19,700,000 people are of mixed Spanish, African, and Indian ancestry; the rest of the people are whites, blacks, and Amerindians of unmixed ancestry.

Languages: Spanish; English is spoken in the major cities.

Currency: Bol'var

Major Religion: Roman Catholic

Orphans Admitted into the United States

Fiscal year 1998: 6	Fiscal year 2000: 2
Fiscal year 1999: 0	Fiscal year 2001: 4

Adoption Information: There are two ways to adopt a child in Venezuela — through the Instituto Nacional de Menores (INAM), which is the Venezuelan child protection service, or through an "entrega directa." INAM is the Venezuelan child protection service. They deal with adoptions of children over the age of two who have been abandoned by their parents. "Entrega directa" is an adoption in which the mother gives up her child, through the court, directly to the prospective parents.

Venezuelan law does not specifically address completion of an adoption outside of Venezuela but it can be done, although the process may be difficult and time-consuming. Parents may be granted provisional custody of a child by a Venezuelan judge and permission to take the child out of Venezuela. Parents should be sure that the court has made it clear, in writing, that the child may travel to the United States for the purpose of emigration. Venezuelan law mandates a three-month probationary period after custody has been granted. During this time, a home study may be conducted by a social worker in Venezuela. However, home studies that have been completed in the United States and approved by an international service agency may be acceptable to the court. In such cases, the three-month waiting period may take place outside Venezuela.

Central Adoption Authority

Instituto Nacional del Menor (INAM)
Servicio de Colocaciónes Familiares y Adopciónes
Avda. San Martin
Edif. Jta. Beneficencia Pub.
San Martin, Caracas 1020
Venezuela

U.S. Embassy/Visa Issuing Post

Calle F con Calle Suapure
Colinas De Valle Arriba
Caracas, 1060, Venezuela

Tel: [58] (212) 975-6411
Fax: [58] (212) 975-8991

OCEANIA

The geographic designation of Oceania includes Australia and the Pacific Islands. With the exception of the Marshall Islands, international adoption activity is almost nonexistent in this part of the world. The total number of orphans admitted into the United States from all of Oceania in recent years is detailed below. Visa information for individual countries in Oceania is not available.

Important Note: As discussed in the introduction to the Compendium, the political and legal situations regarding international adoption for individual countries are subject to rapid change. In addition, contact information such as addresses and phone numbers may change. Be sure to consult the State Department web site (**www.travel.state.gov**) or the U.S. Embassy located in the country in which you are interested for the latest information on adoption policies and procedures.

Fiscal year 1998: 4   Fiscal year 2000: not available
Fiscal year 1999: 6   Fiscal year 2001: 19

MARSHALL ISLANDS

Geography: A group of islands in the South Pacific, about halfway between the Continental United States and China. The Marshall Islands are located just across the international dateline.

Capital: Majuro

Demography: Population is mainly Caucasoid related to Polynesians

Languages: English, Marshallese, Japanese

Currency: U.S. Dollar

Major religion: Christianity

Adoption Information: Adopters must be at least 18 years of age, married or single (for U.S. adopters, singles have to be at least 25 years of age to qualify for an Orphan Petition). Both parents (in the case of couples) must be present to complete the adoption. There are no adoption agencies in the Marshall Islands. Prospective adoptive parents must file a petition for adoption with a Republic of Marshall Islands court through a local attorney. (Lists of local attorneys are available from the U.S. Embassy in Majuro).

Under the terms of the "Compact of Free Association" between the United States and the Marshall Islands, Marshallese citizens have the right to enter the United States without a visa to live and to work; however, they are not lawful permanent residents. In the past, an uncounted number of Marshallese children have been brought to the United States under this compact. Since the adoptive parents did not comply with U.S. Immigration and Naturalization procedures, the children will have problems later on when they try to obtain proof of U.S. citizenship. The U.S. State Department warns potential parents to observe all of the rules and regulations pertaining to the adoption and immigration of these children. Prospective adoptive parents contemplating this course of action should consult with their INS office before they adopt the child. The adopters should be careful to preserve all documents pertaining to the adoption of the child: the certified Adoption Order from the Marshallese court authenticated by the U.S. Embassy in Majuro; authenticated copies of the child's birth certificate; and proof of termination of parental rights of the birth parents.

The U.S. Embassy in Majuro is not a visa issuing post. All immigration matters are referred to the U.S. Embassy in Manila, Philippines. It will be necessary for the adoptive parent(s) and the child to travel to the Philippines for the visa interview. This adds approximately six months to the time and additional travel costs.

Current information on regulations developed in regard to adoption and immigration of a child from the Marshall Islands or Oceania can be obtained from the U.S. Department of State Office of Children's Issues in Washington D.C. The telephone number is (202)-736-7000. You can also contact the U.S. Embassy in The Marshall Islands.

U.S. Embassy

> U.S. Embassy, Majuro
> P.O. Box 1379
> Majuro, MH 96960

> Tel: [692] 247-4011
> Fax: [692] 247-4012
> URL: **http://usembassy.state.gov/majuro/**
> E-mail: publicmajuro@state.gov

* Visas are issued through the U.S. embassy in Manila, Philippines. Consult the section on the Phillipines for contact information.

APPENDIX

NATIONAL ADOPTIVE PARENT SUPPORT GROUPS

Countless organizations exist throughout the United States. Those listed support foreign as well as domestic adoptions. They also provide information and literature on adoption-related issues.

Child Welfare League of America

The league is the largest publisher of child welfare materials in the country. It is also extensively involved in consulting with governmental and voluntary child welfare organizations to promote the well being of children and their families.

> 440 First St. N.W., Third Floor
> Washington, D.C. 20001-2085
> Tel: (202) 638-2952
> Fax: (202) 638-4004
> E-mail: **global@cwla.org**
> Web Site: **http://www.cwla.org**

International Association of Voluntary Adoption Agencies

This organization promotes intercountry and domestic adoptions, has a "presence" at Capitol Hill, and helps children who have AIDS or are HIV positive. IAVAAN is approved by the Hague Convention to sit in on convention meetings.

> 2001 S Street N.W.
> Washington, D.C. 20009
> Tel: (202) 299-0052
> E-mail: **iavaan@aol.com**
> URL: **www.iavaan.org**

Joint Council on International Children's Services

Oldest and largest affiliation of licensed, nonprofit international adoption agencies. JCICS membership also includes parent groups, advocacy organizations, and individuals who have an interest in intercountry adoption.

> 1320 19th Street N.W., Suite 200
> Washington, D.C. 20036
> Tel: (202) 429-0400
> Fax: (202) 429-0410
> Fax: (301) 322-3425
> E-mail: jcics@jcics.org
> URL: www.jcics.org

National Adoption Information Clearinghouse

In addition to providing a wealth of information and resources regarding domestic and international adoption, the NAIC also maintains a database of adoption-related organizations, including parent support groups.

> 330 C Street, SW
> Washington, DC 20447
> Tel: (703) 352-3488 or (888) 251-0075
> Fax: (703) 385-3206
> E-mail: naic@calib.com
> URL: www.calib.com/naic

North American Council on Adoptable Children

Founded in 1974 by adoptive parents, the North American Council on Adoptable Children is committed to meeting the needs of waiting children and the families who adopt them.

> 970 Raymond Ave., Ste. 106
> St. Paul, MN 55114
> Tel: (651) 644-3036
> Fax: (651) 644-9848
> E-mail: info@nacac.org
> URL: www.nacac.org

LOCAL ADOPTION SUPPORT GROUPS

In addition to national organizations, there are numerous local adoption support groups across the country. Contact your adoption agency or the National Adoption Information Clearinghouse's *National Adoption Directory* (www.calib.com/naic) for a list of support groups in your area.

ON-LINE ADOPTION SUPPORT GROUPS

The Internet has created a format that allows for countless adoption support groups geared to specific needs. For example, there are on-line support groups for older child adoption, older parent adoption, cross-cultural adoption, gay adoption, special needs, attachment issues, post-institution issues, etc. Visit **www.comeunity.com/adoption/listservs.html** for a more complete list of adoption support groups by topic or use your favorite search engine to locate more.

In addition, there are dozens of country-specific international adoption support groups, including

Eastern European Adoption Coalition (**www.eeadopt.org**)

Families for Russian and Ukrainian Adoption — including neighboring countries (**www.frua.org**)

Families with Children from China (**http://catalog.com/fwcfc**)

Families with Children from Vietnam (**http://fcvn.org**)

Latin America Adoptive Parents Association (**http://lapa-nnj.com**)

Visit **www.comeunity.com/adoption/listservs.html** for a more complete list of country-specific support groups or use your favorite search engine to locate more

STATE LICENSING SPECIALISTS

State licensing specialists can provide a list of adoption agencies in each state. They can also tell you if an agency is incorporated, if it has nonprofit status, and how long the agency has been licensed under its current name.

This is also where you can check up on the reliability of an adoption agency. The state licensing specialist or the licensing consultant in the county where the agency is located can tell you how many complaints they have received on the agency and if any complaints are unresolved. If you encounter a problem in dealing with an agency, this is also where you should file a complaint.

For up-to-date information on state licensing specialists, visit **http://www.calib.com/naic/databases/nadd/naddatabase.htm**.

ALABAMA

Office of Residential Licensing
Alabama Department of Human Resources
Gordon Person Bldg., Box 30400
50 N. Ripley Street
Montgomery, AL 36130-4000
Tel: (334) 242-9500
URL: **http://www.dhr.state.al.us/fsd/licresdv.asp**

ALASKA
Alaska Department of Health and Social Services
Division of Family and Youth Services
P.O. Box 110630
Juneau, AK 99811-0630
Tel: (907) 465-2817
Fax: (907) 465-3397
URL: http://www.hss.state.ak.us/dfys

ARIZONA
Arizona Department of Economic Security
Children, Youth and Families Division
Office of Licensing Certification & Regulation
1951 West Camelback Road, Suite 400
Phoenix, AZ 85005
Tel: (602) 347-6366
Fax: (502) 336-4581

ARKANSAS
Arkansas Department of Human Services
Division of Child and Family Services
Child Welfare Agency Licensing Unit,
115 Market Street
Hot Springs, AR 71901
Tel: (501) 321-2583

CALIFORNIA
California Department of Social Services
744 P Street, M/S 17-17
Sacramento, CA 95814
Tel: (916) 657-2346
Fax: (916) 657-3783
URL: http://ccld.ca.gov/default.htm

COLORADO
Colorado Department of Human Services
Division of Child Care
1575 Sherman St., 1st Floor
Denver, CO 80203-1714
Tel: (303) 866-5958 or (800) 799-5876
Fax: (303) 866-4453
URL: http://www.cdhs.state.co.us/childcare/licensing.htm

CONNECTICUT
Connecticut Department of Children & Families
505 Hudson Street
Hartford, CT 06106
Tel: (860) 550-6306
Fax: (860) 566-6726

DELAWARE

Delaware Department of Services for Children, Youth, and Families
Office of Child Care Licensing
(For the county of New Castle)
1825 Faulkland Road
Wilmington, DE 19805
Tel: (302) 892-5800
Fax: (302) 633-5112
E-mail: occl@state.de.us

(For the counties of Kent and Sussex)
Barrett Building
821 Silver Lake Blvd, Suite 103
Dover, DE 19904
Tel: (302) 739-5487 or (800) 822-2236
Fax: (302) 739-6589
E-mail: occl@state.de.us
URL: http://www.state.de.us/kids/occlhome.htm

DISTRICT OF COLUMBIA

District of Columbia Department of Human Services
Department of Health-Licensing and Regulatory Administration
825 North Capital Street, N.E.
Washington, DC 20002
Tel: (202) 442-5929
Fax: (202) 442-9430

FLORIDA

Florida Department of Children and Family
1317 Winewood Boulevard, Building 7
Tallahassee, FL 32399-0700
Tel: (850) 921-2594
Fax: (850) 488-0751

GEORGIA

Georgia Department of Human Resources
2 Peachtree Street N.W., Ste. 32-452
Atlanta, GA 30303-3142
Tel: (404) 657-5560
Fax: (404) 657-5708
URL: http://www.ors.dhr.state.ga.us/

HAWAII

Hawaii Department of Human Services
810 Richards Street, Ste. 400
Honolulu, HI 96813
Tel: (808) 586-5698
Fax: (808) 586-4806
URL: http://www.state.hi.us/dhs/

IDAHO

Idaho Department of Health and Welfare
Division of Family and Children's Services
P.O. Box 83720
450 West State Street
Boise, ID 83720-0036
Tel: (208) 334-0662
Fax: (208) 334-6699

ILLINOIS

Illinois Department of Children and Family Services
406 East Monroe
Springfield, IL 62701-1498
Tel: (217) 785-2688
URL: http://www.state.il.us/dcfs

INDIANA

Division of Family and Children
402 W. Washington Street
Indianapolis, IN 46201
Tel: (317) 232-3476

IOWA

Iowa Department of Human Services
Adult, Children, and Family Services
Hoover State Office Building, 5th Floor
Des Moines, IA 50319
Tel: (515) 281-6802
Fax: (515) 281-4597
URL: http://www.dhs.state.ia.us/ACFS/ACFS.asp

KANSAS

Department of Health and Environment
Child Care Licensing and Registration
Landon State Office Building
900 SW Jackson, Suite 620
Topeka, KS 66612-1218
Tel: (785) 296-1274
Fax: (785) 296-7025

KENTUCKY

Cabinet for Health Services
Office of Inspector General
Division of Licensing and Regulation
275 East Main Street, 4th Floor
Frankfort, KY 40601
Tel: (502) 564-2800
URL: http://chs.state.ky.us/oig/

LOUISIANA
Louisiana Department of Social Services
P.O. Box 3078
Baton Rouge, LA 70821-3078
Tel: (225) 922-0015
Fax: (225) 922-0014
URL: http://www.dss.state.la.us/offos/html/licensing.html

MAINE
Maine Department of Human Services
Bureau of Child and Family Services
221 State Street
Augusta, ME 04333-0011
Tel: (207) 287-5060
Fax: (207) 287-5282

MARYLAND
Maryland Department of Human Resources
Social Services Administration
311 W. Saratoga Street
Baltimore, MD 21201
Tel: (410) 767-7903

MASSACHUSETTS
Massachusetts Office of Child Care Services
Central Office
1 Ashburton Place, Room 1105
Boston, MA 02218
Tel: (617) 626-2000
Fax: (617) 626-2028
URL: http://www.qualitychildcare.org/

MICHIGAN
Department of Consumer and Industry Services
Division of Child Welfare Licensing
7109 West Saginaw, 2nd Floor, Box 30650
Lansing, MI 48909-8150
Tel: (517) 373-8383
Fax: (517) 335-6121

MINNESOTA
Minnesota Department of Human Services
Division of Licensing
444 Lafayette Road
St. Paul, MN 55155
Tel: (651) 296-3971
Fax: (651) 297-1490
URL: www.mnadopt.org/privateagencies.htm

MISSISSIPPI

Mississippi Department of Human Services
Division of Family and Children Services
750 N. State Street
Jackson, MS 39202
Tel: (601) 359-4994
Fax: (601) 359-4978

MISSOURI

Missouri Department of Social Services
Residential Programs Unit
1500 Vandiver Drive, Suite 103
Columbia, MO 65203
Tel: (573) 884-4394
Fax: (573) 526-3971

MONTANA

Montana Department of Public Health and Human Services
Child and Family Services Division
P.O. Box 8005
Helena, MT 59604-8005
Tel: (406) 444-5900
Fax: (406) 444-5956
URL: **www.dphhs.state.mt.us**

NEBRASKA

Nebraska Department of Health and Human Services
P.O. Box 95044
Lincoln, NE 68509
Tel: (402) 471-9331
Fax: (402) 471-0180

NEVADA

Nevada Department of Human Resources
Division of Child and Family Services
6171 West Charleston Boulevard, Building 15
Las Vegas, NV 89102
Tel: (702) 486-7650
Fax: (702) 486-7626
URL: **http://dcfs.state.nv.us/page53.html**

NEW HAMPSHIRE

New Hampshire Department of Health and Human Services
Division of Children, Youth and Families
129 Pleasant Street
Concord, NH 03301
Tel: (603) 271-4953
Fax: (603) 271-4729

NEW JERSEY

New Jersey Department of Human Services
Division of Youth and Family Services
PO Box 717
Trenton, NJ 08625-0717
Tel: (609) 292-8255
URL: **www.state.nj.us/humanservices/adoption/adopt.html**

NEW MEXICO

New Mexico Children, Youth and Families Department
Drawer 5160
Santa Fe, NM 87502- 5160
Tel: (505) 827-8428
Fax: (505) 827-8480

NEW YORK

New York Department of Family Assistance
Office of Children and Family Services
52 Washington Street, Riverview Center, 6th Floor
Rensselaer, NY 12144
Tel: (518) 474-9447 or (800) 345-5437
Fax: (518) 486-6326

NORTH CAROLINA

North Carolina Department of Health and Human Services
Division of Social Services, Children's Services Section
325 North Salisbury Street
2409 Mail Service Center
Raleigh, NC 27699-2401
Tel: (919) 733-9464

NORTH DAKOTA

North Dakota Department of Human Services
600 East Boulevard Avenue
State Capitol Building
Bismarck, ND 58505
Tel: (701) 328-3538
Fax: (701) 328-2359
URL: **www.state.nd.us/humanservices**

OHIO

Ohio Department of Job and Family Services
Office for Children and Families
255 E Main St, 3rd Fl
Columbus, OH 43215-5222
Tel: (614) 466-9274
Fax: (614) 466-0164
URL: **www.state.oh.us/odjfs/oapl**

OKLAHOMA

Oklahoma Department of Human Services
Division of Child Care/Residential and Agency Licensing
P.O. Box 25352, 2400 North Lincoln Blvd
Oklahoma City, OK 73125
Tel: (405) 521-3561 or (800) 347-2276

OREGON

Oregon Department of Human Services
State Office for Services to Children and Families
500 Summer Street NE, E.73
Salem, OR 97310-1017
Tel: (503) 947-5208

PENNSYLVANIA

Pennsylvania Department of Public Welfare
Office of Children, Youth and Families
Health and Welfare Building, Room 131, PO Box 2675
Harrisburg, PA 17105-2675
Tel: (717) 787-6292
Fax: (717) 787-4756
URL: **www.dpw.state.pa.us/adoptpakids/paeagencylist2.asp**

RHODE ISLAND

Rhode Island Department for Children, Youth and Families
101 Friendship Street
Providence, RI 02903
Tel: (401) 528-3605
Fax: (401) 528-3950
URL: **www.dcyf.state.ri.us**

SOUTH CAROLINA

South Carolina Department of Social Services
PO Box 1520
Columbia, SC 29202-1520
Tel: (803) 898-7707
Fax: (803) 898-7792

SOUTH DAKOTA

South Dakota Department of Social Services
Child Protection Services
700 Governor's Drive
Kneip Building
Pierre, SD 57501-2291
Tel: (605) 773-3227
Fax: (605) 773-6834
URL: **www.state.sd.us/social/cps/services/licensing.htm**

TENNESSEE

Tennessee Department of Children's Services
436 Sixth Avenue North,
Cordell Hull Building, 7th Floor
Nashville, TN 37243-1290
Tel: (615) 532-5598
URL: **www.state.tn.us/youth/adoption/agencies/index.htm**

TEXAS

Texas Department of Protective and Regulatory Services
PO Box 149030, E-557
Austin, TX 78714-9030
Tel: (512) 438-3269
Fax: (512) 438-3782
URL: **www.tdprs.state.tx.us**

UTAH

Utah Department of Human Services
Office of Licensing
120 North, 200 West, #303
Salt Lake City, UT 84103
Tel: (801) 538-4242
Fax: (801) 538-4553
URL: **www.hslic.state.ut.us**

VERMONT

Vermont Department of Social and Rehabilitation Services
103 South Main Street
Waterbury, VT 05671
Tel: (802) 241-2159
URL: **www.state.vt.us/srs/adoption/agencies.html**

VIRGINIA

Virginia Department of Social Services
Division of Family Services
730 East Broad Street
Richmond, VA 23219-1849
Tel: (804) 692-1773
Fax: (804) 692-2370
URL: **www.dss.state.va.us/facility/childplace.html**

WASHINGTON

Washington Department of Social and Health Services
Division of Licensed Resources
PO Box 45700
Olympia, WA 98504
Tel: (360) 902-8009

WEST VIRGINIA
West Virginia Department of Health and Human Resources
Ohio District
P.O. Box 6165
Wheeling, WV 26003
Tel: (304) 232-4411
Fax: (304) 232-4773

WISONSIN
Wisconsin Department of Health and Family Services
Bureau of Regulation and Licensing
PO Box 8916
Madison, WI 53708-8916
Tel: (608) 266-0415
Fax: (608) 267-7252
URL: **www.dhfs.state.wi.us/licensing.htm**

WYOMING
Wyoming Department of Family Services
2300 Capitol Avenue
Hathaway Building, 3rd Floor
Cheyenne, WY 82002
Tel: (307) 777-6479
URL: **http://dfsweb.state.wy.us/childsvc/certlist.htm**

PUERTO RICO
Puerto Rico Department of the Families
P.O. Box 11398
Santurce, PR 00910
Tel: (787) 722-7450
Fax: (787) 723-1223

VIRGIN ISLANDS
Department of Human Services
1303 Hospital Building A
Knud Hansen Complex
Charlotte Amalie, St. Thomas, VI 00802
Tel: (340) 774-0930 X 4181
Fax: (340) 774-3466

BIBLIOGRAPHY

Recommended Books

Adoption Agency Listings and Other Resources

Klatzkin, Amy (ed.) *2002-2003 Adoption Guide: Practical Information for a Successful Adoption*. Adoptive Families Magazine, 2002.

International Concerns for Children, Inc.. *Report on Foreign Adoption*. A comprehensive and up-to-date compilation of information on international adoption that includes 10 monthly updates. The book includes approximate costs, waiting periods, and types of children available from dozens of agencies. Other adoption-related organizations and services are included. For more information, visit the web site at **www.iccadopt.org**, call 303-494-8333 or write 911 Cyprus Drive, Boulder, CO 80303-2821.

National Adoption Information Clearinghouse. *National Adoption Directory*. This searchable, on-line directory of adoption agencies and other adoption-related services is updated daily. The *National Adoption Directory* can also be downloaded as a PDF file to your own computer (**www.calib.com/naic**). Or you can order a printed copy of the PDF file ($25.00) by contacting the NAIC by phone (888-251-0075), email (**naic@calib.com**) or mail at 330 C Street, S.W., Washington, DC 20447.

Adoption – General Information

Adamec, Christine. *There ARE Babies to Adopt: A Resource Guide for Prospective Parents*. Kensington Publishing Corporation, 2002.

Adamec, Christine. Is *Adoption for You? The Information You Need to Make the Right Choice*. John Wiley & Sons, 1998.

Adamec, Christine and William Pierce. *The Encyclopedia of Adoption.* Facts on File, 2000.

Adamec, Christine and William Pierce. *The Complete Idiot's Guide to Adoption.* Macmillan, 1998.

Gilman, Lois. *The Adoption Resource Book.* Bongo Press, 1998.

Joint Council on International Children's Services. *The Adoptive Parent Preparation Manual.* Order by calling 202-429-0400 or emailing jcics@jcics.org.

National Council for Adoption. *Adoption Factbook III.* Data, issues, regulations and resources. National Council for Adoption, 1999. For information visit **www.ncfa-usa.org** or call 703-299-6633.

Pertman, Adam. *Adoption Nation: How Adoption is Transforming America.* Basic Books, 2001.

Schooler, Jayne. *The Whole Life Adoption Book: Realistic Advice for Building a Healthy Adoptive Family.* Pinon Press, 1993.

Adoption of Older Children and Children with Special Needs

Hopkins-Best, Marjory. *Toddler Adoption: The Weaver's Craft.* Perspectives Press, 1998.

Jarratt, Claudia Jewett. *Helping Children Cope With Separation and Loss.* Harvard Common Press, 1994.

Keck Ph.D., Gregory and Regina M. Kupecky L.S.W. *Adopting the Hurt Child: Hope for Families with Special-Needs Kids.* Pinon Press, 1999.

Maskew, Trish. *Our Own: Adopting and Parenting the Older Child.* Snowcap Press, 1999.

McCreight, Brenda. *Parenting Your Adopted Older Child: How to Overcome the Unique Challenges and Raise a Happy Healthy Child.* New Harbinger, 2002.

Miller, Margi and Nancy Ward. *With Eyes Wide Open: A Workbook for Parents Adopting International Children Over Age One.* Order through Tapestry Books at **www.tapestrybooks.com**.

Tepper, Thais, Lois Hannon and Dorothy Sandstrom. *International Adoption: Challenges and Opportunities, Second Edition.* Self-published. Available through the Parent Network for the Post-institutionalized Child (**www.pnpic.org**) or by email at PNPIC@aol.com.

Adoption Support and Awareness (for Family and Friends)

Irwin Johnston, Patricia. *Adoption is a Family Affair: What Relatives and Friends Must Know.* Perspectives Press, 2001.

Meese, Ruth Lyn. *Children of Intercountry Adoptions in School: A Primer for Parents and Professionals.* Bergin & Garvey, 2002.

Wood, Lansing and Nancy Ng. *Adoption and the Schools: A Resource Guide for Parents and Teachers.* Families Adopting in Response, 2001.

Children's Books

Bartlett, Therese and William Bartlett. *When You Were Born in Vietnam: A Memory Book for Children Adopted from Vietnam.* Yeong and Yeong, 2001.

Boyd, Brain E. *When You Were Born in Korea*. Yeong & Yeong, 1993.

Brodzinsky, Anne and Diana L. Stanley. *The Mulberry Bird: An Adoption Story*. Perspectives Press, 1996.

Dorow, Sara and Stephen Wunrow. *When You Were Born In China: A Memory Book for Children Adopted from China*. Yeong & Yeong, 1997.

Katz, Karen. *Over the Moon: An Adoption* Tale. Henry Holt & Co., 1997.

Kindersley, Anabel and Barnabas Kindersley. *Children Just Like Me: Celebrations*! DK Publishing, 1997.

Lewis, Rose A. and Jane Dyer. I *Love You Like Crazy Cakes*. Little Brown & Co., 2000.

Livingston, Carole and Arthur Robinson. *Why Was I Adopted?* Carol Publishing Group, 1997.

McCutcheon, John and Julie Paschkis. *Happy Adoption Day*. Little Brown & Co., 1996.

Peacock, Carol Antoinette and Shawn Costello Brownell. *Mommy Far, Mommy Near*. Albert Whitman & Co., 2000.

Petertyl, Mary Ebejer and Jill Chambers. *Seeds of Love: For Brothers and Sisters of International Adoption*. Folio One Publishing, 1997.

Rogers, Fred and Jim Judkins. *Let's Talk About It: Adoption*. Paper Star, 1998.

Schwartz, Perry. *Carolyn's Story: A Book About an Adopted Girl*. Lerner Publications, 1996.

Schnitter, Jane T. and Gerald Kruck. *William Is My Brother*. Perspectives Press, 1991.

Turner, Ann Warren and James Graham Hale. *Through Moon and Stars and Night Skies*. Harper Trophy, 1992.

Wasson, Valentina and Glo Coalson. *The Chosen Baby*. Lippincott and Williams Publications, 1977.

Walvoord-Girard, Linda and Linda Shute. *We Adopted You, Benjamin Koo*. Albert Whiteman and Company, 1989.

Waybill, Majorie Ann and Pauline Cutrell. *Chinese Eyes*. Herald Press, 1974.

Zisk, Mary. *The Best Single Mom in the World: How I Was Adopted*. Albert Whitman and Co., 2001.

Infertility and Adoption

Johnston, Patricia Irwin. *Adopting After Infertility*. Perspectives Press, 1996.

Johnston, Patricia Irwin. *Taking Charge of Infertility*. Perspectives Press, 1995.

Aronson, Diane, Diane N. Clapp and Margaret R. Hollister. *Resolving Infertility: Understanding the Options and Choosing Solutions When You Want to Have a Baby*. Harper Resource, 2001.

International Adoption

Birdsey, Barbara. *Moving Heaven and Earth: A Personal Journey into International Adoption*. The Francis Press, 2000.

Dey, Carol and LeAnn Theiman. *This Must Be My Brother*. Victor Brooks, 1995.

MacLean, John H. *The Russian Adoption Handbook: How to Adopt a Child from Russia, Ukraine or Kazakhstan.* iUniverse.com, 2000.

Miller, Margi and Nancy Ward. *With Eyes Wide Open: A Workbook for Parents Adopting International Children Over Age One.* Order through Tapestry Books at **www.tapestrybooks.com.**

Register, Cheri. *Are Those Kids Yours? American Families with Children Adopted from Other Countries.* New York: The Free Press, 1991.

Tepper, Thais, Lois Hannon and Dorothy Sandstrom. *International Adoption: Challenges and Opportunities, Second Edition.* Self-published. Available through the Parent Network for the Post-institutionalized Child (**www.pnpic.org**) or by email at PNPIC@aol.com.

Interracial Adoption

Alperson, Myra. *Dim Sum, Bagels and Grits: A Sourcebook for Multicultural Families.* Farrar Straus & Giroux, 2001.

Fogg-Davis, Hawley. *The Ethics of Transracial Adoption.* Cornell Unversity Press, 2002.

John, Jaiya. *Black Baby, White Hands: A View from the Crib.* Soul Water Publishing, 2002.

Rush, Sharon. *Loving Across the Color Line: A White Adoptive Mother Learns About Race.* Rowman & Littlefield, 2000

Simon, Rita J. and Rhonda M. Roorda. *In Their Own Voices: Transracial Adoptees Tell Their Own Stories.* Columbia University Press, 2000.

Simon, Rita J., Howard Alstein and Marygold S. Melli. *The Case for Transracial Adoption.* American University Press, 1994.

Steinberg, Gail and Beth Hall. *Inside Transracial Adoption.* Perspectives Press, 2000.

Wright, Marguerite. *I'm Chocolate, You're Vanilla: Raising Healthy Black and Biracial Children in a Race Conscious World.* Jossey-Bass, 2000.

Learning Disabilities, Attachment Problems, ADHD and Other Challenges

Alexander-Roberts, Colleen. *The ADHD Parenting Handbook.* Taylor Publishing, 1994.

Gray, Deborah. *Attaching in Adoption: Practical Tools for Today's Parents.* Perspectives Press, 2002.

Hughes, Daniel A. *Building the Bonds of Attachment: Awakening Love in Deeply Troubled Children.* Jason Aronson, 1999.

Keck Ph.D., Gregory and Regina M. Kupecky L.S.W. *Adopting the Hurt Child: Hope for Families with Special-Needs Kids.* Pinon Press, 1999.

Kranowitz, Carol Stock. *The Out-of-Sync Child: Recognizing and Coping with Sensory Integration Dysfunction.* Perigee, 1998.

Thomas, Nancy L. *When Love is Not Enough: A Guide to Parenting Children with Reactive Attachment Disorder.* Families by Design, 1997.

Parenting Adopted Children

Brazelton, M.D. T. Barry. *Touchpoints: Your Child's Emotional and Behavioral Development*. Perseus, 1994.

Carey, M.D. William B. with Martha M. Jablow. *Understanding Your Child's Temperament*. Hungry Minds, 1999.

Dawson, Connie and Jean Illsley Clark. *Growing Up Again: Parenting Ourselves, Parenting Our Children, Second Edition*. Hazelden Information Education, 1998.

Eldridge, Sherrie. *Twenty Things Adopted Kids Wished Their Parents Knew*. Dell Books, 1999.

Greenspan, MD, Stanley and Nancy Thorndike Greenspan. *First Feelings: Milestones of the Emotional Development of Your Baby and Child*. Penguin USA, 1994.

Hopkins-Best, Mary. *Toddler Adoption: The Weaver's Craft*. Perspectives Press, 1997.

Jarratt, Claudia Jewett. *Helping Children Cope with Separation and Loss, Revised Edition*. Harvard Common Press, 1994.

Keck, Gregory and Regina Kupecky. *Parenting the Hurt Child: Helping Adoptive Families Heal and Grow*. Pinon Press, 2002.

Leach, Penelope. *Your Baby and Child from Birth to Age Five*. Alfred A. Knopf. 1997.

Maskew, Trish. *Our Own: Adopting and Parenting the Older Child*. Snowcap Press, 1999.

Melina, Lois R. *Raising Adopted Children: Practical Reassuring Advice for Every Adoptive Parent*. Harper Perennial, 1998.

McCreight, Brenda. *Parenting Your Older Adopted Child: How to Overcome the Unique Challenges and Raise a Happy and Healthy Child*. New Harbinger, 2002.

O'Malley, Beth. Lifebooks: *Creating a Treasure for the Adopted Child*. Adoption-Works, 2000.

Schooler, Jayne E. and Betsy E. Keefer. *Telling the Truth to our Adopted and Foster Child: Making Sense of the Past*. Bergin & Garvey, 2000.

Van Gulden, Holly and Lisa Bartles-Rabb. *Real Parents, Real Children: Parenting the Adopted Child*. Crossroad Publishing, 1995.

Watkins, Mary and Susan Fisher. *Talking with Young Children About Adoption*. Yale University Press, 1995.

Personal Adoption Experiences (Parents)

Bialosky, Jill and Helen Schulman. *Wanting a Child*. Farrar, Straus & Giroux, 1998.

Klatzkin, Amy. *A Passage to the Heart: Writings of Families with Children from China*. Yeong & Yeong, 1999.

Newman, Janis Cooke. *The Russian Word for Snow: A True Story of Adoption*. St. Martin's Press, 2002.

Silber, Kathleen and Phylis Speedlin. *Dear Birth Mother: Thank You for Our Baby*. Corona, 1998.

Wolff, Jana. *Secret Thoughts of an Adoptive Mother*. Vista Communications, 1999.

Psychological Issues

Brodzinsky, David M., Ph.D., Marshall D. Schecter, M.D., and Robin Marantz Henig. *Being Adopted: The Lifelong Search for Self.* Anchor, 1993.

Fahlberg, M.D., Vera. *A Child's Journey Through Placement.* Perspectives Press, 1996.

Lifton, Betty Jean. *Lost and Found: The Adoption Experience.* HarperCollins, 1998.

Schooler, Jane E. and Betsie L. Norris. *Journeys After Adoption: Understanding Lifelong Issues.* Bergin & Garvey, 2002.

Single Adoptive Parents

Engber, Andrea and Leah Klungness. *The Complete Single Mother.* Adams Business Media, 2000.

Karst, Patrice. *The Single Mother's Survival Guide.* Crossing Press, 2000.

Mattes, Jane. *Single Mothers by Choice: A Guidebook for Single Women Who are Considering or Have Chosen Motherhood.* Times Books, 1997.

Noel, Brook, Arthur C. Klein and Art Kein. *The Single Parent Resource.* Champion Press, 1998.

Magazines and Other Publications

Adoptive Families. Bi-monthly color magazine published by Adoptive Families Magazine.com. Order by visiting **www.adoptivefamilies.com** or by calling 800-371-3300.

Adoption Medical News. Published 10 times per year. Edited by Jeri Jennista, M.D., International Pediatric Specialist, and published by Pierce Group International. Order online at **www.adoptionmedicalnews.com** or by phone at (814) 364-2449.

Adoption Today. Bi-monthly magazine previously known as Chosen Child International. Order online at **www.adoptinfo.net**

Buenas Noticias. Order from Latin American Parents Association (LAPA) at 301-431-3407. PO Box 4403, Silver Springs, MD 20914-4403.

FCC National News. Published three times a year by Families with Children from China. For more information visit **www.fwcc.org**.

Korean Quarterly. A new non-profit quarterly that focuses on Korean-American life in the Twin Cities and upper Midwest. For more information, visit the web site at **www.koreanquarterly.org** or call 651-771-8164.

News of Los Ninos. On-line educational resources and listservs for adoptive parents. Visit **www.losninos.org** for more information.

The African Connection. Free newsletter published by Americans for African Adoptions. For more information, visit the web site at **www.africanadoptions.org** or call 317-271-4567.

Red Thread Magazine. Quarterly publication connecting families with children adopted from China. Available through the Red Thread web site at **www.redthread-mag.com** or by calling 877-837-1992.

Russian Life Magazine. Focuses on Russian culture, life and travel. Available through the web site of Families for Russian and Ukrainian Adoptions (**www.frua.org**).

INDEX